ALSO BY RICHARD NIXON:

SIX CRISES (1962)
RN: THE MEMOIRS OF RICHARD NIXON (1978)
THE REAL WAR (1980)
LEADERS (1982)
REAL PEACE (1984)
NO MORE VIETNAMS (1985)

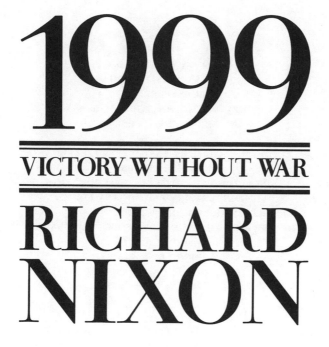

1999

VICTORY WITHOUT WAR

RICHARD NIXON

SIMON AND SCHUSTER

NEW YORK   LONDON
TORONTO   SYDNEY   TOKYO

SIMON AND SCHUSTER
SIMON & SCHUSTER BUILDING
ROCKEFELLER CENTER
1230 AVENUE OF THE AMERICAS
NEW YORK, NEW YORK 10020

1   3   5   7   9   10   8   6   4   2

LIBRARY OF CONGRESS CATALOGING IN PUBLICATION DATA
NIXON, RICHARD M. (RICHARD MILHOUS), 1913–
1999: VICTORY WITHOUT WAR.

INCLUDES INDEX.
1. UNITED STATES—FOREIGN RELATIONS—1981–
2. WORLD POLITICS—1985–1995.   I. TITLE.
E876.N59   1988   327.73   88-4547
ISBN 0-671-62712-0

FOR
LON L. FULLER

CONTENTS

1999

VICTORY WITHOUT WAR

1

THE BLOODIEST
AND THE BEST

In twelve years we will celebrate a day that comes once in a thousand years: the beginning of a new year, a new century, and a new millennium. For the first time on such a historic day, the choice before mankind will be not just whether we make the future better than the past, but whether we will survive to enjoy the future.

A thousand years ago the civilized world faced the millennium with an almost frantic sense of foreboding. Religious leaders, having consulted Biblical prophecy, had predicted that the end of the world was imminent. In the year 1000, they feared, God's power would destroy the world. In the year 2000 the danger is that man's power will destroy the world—unless we take decisive action to prevent it.

In 1999, we will remember the twentieth century as the bloodiest and the best in the history of man. One hundred twenty million people have been killed in 130 wars in this century—more than all those killed in war before 1900. But at the same time more technological and material progress has been made over the last hundred years than ever before. The twentieth century will be remembered as a century of war and wonder. We must make the twenty-first a century of peace.

———

While the twentieth century was the worst in history in terms of people killed in war, it was the best in terms of progress during peace. Two wars have swept across whole continents, but medical science has swept great diseases off the face of the earth. While more people have died in war in the twentieth century than have died in all wars in previous history, more lives have been spared as a result of agricultural advances which averted famine than died from starvation in all previous history.

In the late 1800s, some thought that progress had peaked, that mankind would have to retrench, and we would have to learn to live in a world with no growth.

- In 1876, in editorial remarks about the telephone a Boston newspaper asserted, "Well-informed people know it is impossible to transmit the voice over wires and that were it possible to do so, the thing would be of no practical value."
- In 1878, after viewing the electric light at a world science exposition, a British professor remarked, "When the Paris Exhibition closes, electric light will close with it and no more will be heard of it."
- In 1897 a British physicist declared, "Radio has no future."
- On the eve of the twentieth century, Charles H. Duell, the commissioner of the U.S. Office of Patents, urged President McKinley to abolish his office, arguing, "Everything that can be invented has been invented."

Over four million patents have been approved in the United States alone since that statement was made in 1899.

All the talk of an era of limits was shortsighted folly. Instead of sinking into stagnation, the world was on the verge of unprecedented advances in every field. The explosion of human innovation has been the central trait of the twentieth century. Hundreds of inventions not even imagined at the close of the last century have had a decisive influence on the present one.

Despite the great human casualties of war and natural disasters, the population of the world will have increased from 1.2 billion in

1900 to an estimated 6.2 billion in 1999. It was only three centuries ago that world population actually decreased over the course of a century. The population explosion of the twentieth century has resulted from unprecedented advances on two fronts: medicine and agriculture.

More progress has been made in health care than in all previous centuries combined. Diseases such as tuberculosis and smallpox that once decimated entire countries have been virtually eradicated. In 1900, the number of infant deaths for every 1,000 live births in the United States was 162. It is estimated that in 1999 the figure will be 14. It was only 250 years ago that Queen Anne of England left no heirs after having given birth to thirteen children, all of whom died before they were ten.

In the twentieth century, economist Thomas Malthus' dire prediction that population increases would outrun food production has been disproved. At the beginning of this century, 40 percent of the working population in the United States was engaged in agriculture. Now less than 2 percent produces enough to feed 230 million Americans and to export millions of tons abroad. India and China, which have suffered from famines for centuries and which experts wrote off as hopeless as recently as a generation ago, now produce more than enough to feed their own populations of almost two billion—one third of all the people in the world.

The revolutions in medicine and agriculture have led to a phenomenal increase in man's life expectancy. In 1900 life expectancy in the United States was forty-seven years. In 1984 it was seventy-two. In 1999 it will be seventy-five. If the rate of increase continues at its present pace, those born in the last year of the next century will have a life expectancy of 101 years.

The twentieth century will also be remembered as the one in which the automobile replaced the horse and buggy, when airplanes began to fly above the trains, when the telephone superseded the telegraph, when radio, motion pictures, and television revolutionized communications. It will be remembered as the century when man inaugurated the computer age and walked on the moon.

In 1900, it took over two months to travel around the world by steamboat and railroad. In 1950, the same trip could be made in four days in a propeller-driven airplane. In 1980, it took only twenty-four hours in a supersonic jet. By 1999, when an aircraft capable of exiting and reentering the atmosphere could well be in operation, the time needed to circle the globe will be measured in minutes.

This century has witnessed the primary news medium move from the printed page to the broadcast word to the televised image. It was possible in the past for a dictator to isolate a country from the outside world and control all the information its people received. That era is over. Foreign radio broadcasts already transcend borders today, and direct satellite television transmissions could do so by 1999.

In terms of material progress, the twentieth century has been the best in history, but in terms of political progress the record has been disappointing.

The greatest lesson of the technological revolution is a simple one: Only people can solve the problems people create. Technology can solve material problems but not political ones. One of the greatest challenges of the next century will be to stop marveling over and luxuriating in our technological prowess and start putting it to work in our efforts to manage the profound differences that remain—and always will remain—between peoples who believe in diametrically opposed ideologies.

Throughout history, and never more so than in the twentieth century, man has misunderstood why wars happen and what they achieve. At the end of World War II, H. G. Wells wrote, "Human history becomes more and more a race between education and catastrophe." Wells expected knowledge alone to create a more peaceful world. He mistook knowledge for wisdom. Before they became the aggressors in World War II the Germans were the best educated and the Japanese the most literate people on earth.

Woodrow Wilson proclaimed that the goal in World War I was to banish absolutist government and make the world safe for democracy. The dictatorships of Hitler, Mussolini, and Stalin were the legacies of that war. World War II replaced dictatorship with democracy in Germany, Italy, and Japan. But it enormously strengthened a fourth dictatorship: the Soviet Union. As a nuclear superpower, Moscow is now militarily stronger than the former dictators of Berlin, Rome, and Tokyo combined and represents an even greater threat to freedom and peace.

The two world wars ended absolute monarchies and colonialism, but they have not spread representative democracy throughout the world. At the beginning of the twentieth century, 11 percent of the world's population lived in democracies, 20 percent under monarchies, and 69 percent in colonies with no rights of self-government. Today, only 16 percent of the people in the world live in stable democracies. Totalitarian communism, which was only a cellar conspiracy at the beginning of the century, now rules over 35 percent of the world's population. The remaining 49 percent live under noncommunist dictatorships or in unstable democracies. While some nations have made progress, more have actually regressed.

World War II marked the beginning of the end of European colonialism as the former British, French, Dutch, Belgian, and American colonies were given their independence. This development was warmly celebrated among the West's enlightened intelligentsia. But the cold facts are that millions are now far worse off than they were under European rule and even before the colonialists came in the first place. In many nations a new, much worse colonialism has taken the place of the old. Nineteen countries in Eastern Europe, Southeast Asia, Africa, and Latin America are formally independent but totally dominated economically, militarily, and politically by the Soviet Union. On the whole the political balance sheet is negative. The most significant development of the twentieth century was not the end of colonialism or the march of democracy but the growth of totalitarian communism.

On the plus side, the twentieth century has seen the triumph of the idea, if not yet the universal fact, of government based on consent of the governed. It is a near-universal aspiration. There are demands for free elections in countries that have never had a tradition of democracy. This democratic impulse has profoundly affected even the nature of dictatorship itself. Dictators in the past claimed that it was their right to rule. Today, most dictators claim to rule in the name of the people. Ironically, most communist dictatorships describe themselves as democratic republics.

In 1999, when we look back over the twentieth century, we will have to face the fact that mankind's advances in military power and material progress have dwarfed his progress in developing the political skills and institutions to preserve peace and capitalize on our technological advances. It will be our task in the twenty-first century to end the mismatch between our technological skill and our woefully lagging political skill.

Unleashing the power of the atom is the most awesome legacy of the twentieth century. At the end of World War II, the United States had just three atom bombs, and no other nation had any. Today, the United States, the Soviet Union, Great Britain, France, and China have over fifty thousand nuclear weapons, most of them far more powerful than the bombs that destroyed the cities of Hiroshima and Nagasaki.

In spite of the enormous advances man has made in this century, it is fashionable to be negative about his prospects for the future— a result, say some of the experts, of the horrible specter of nuclear war, which is warping our children, distorting our cultural values, and turning modern man into an emotional and psychological zombie. Our impending annihilation, they assert, has made everybody a paranoid.

But the same human genius that created nuclear weapons created penicillin and the space shuttle. Some people wax philosophical about the "good" that technology can accomplish but bemoan the "evil" of which it is also capable. But in fact the contrast is imaginary. Our obsession with the evils of nuclear weapons is an example of self-flagellating irrationality. The real evil is war. Nuclear weapons ended World War II and have been the major force in preventing millions from dying in a World War III waged with conventional weapons. We must come to terms with the stark realities that nuclear weapons are not going to be abolished, that there is never going to be a perfect defense against them in our lifetimes, and that we must learn to live with the bomb or we will end up dying from it.

Nuclear weapons are not likely to kill us. Becoming obsessed with the existence of nuclear weapons, however, will certainly do so if it prevents us from dealing with the political differences between East and West that would lead to war whether the bomb existed or not.

The twentieth century has witnessed the bloodiest wars and the greatest progress in the history of man. In these hundred years man realized his greatest destructive and his greatest creative power. Winston Churchill noted the paradox forty-two years ago when he spoke in Fulton, Missouri. He said, "The Stone Age may return on the gleaming wings of science, and what might now shower immeasurable material blessings on mankind may lead to his total destruction." Which of these legacies will dominate man's destiny in the next century? Because it is the strongest nation in the free world, the major responsibility for determining which legacy endures rests upon the United States.

Regrettably, this responsibility is one that many Americans do not want. By every objective measure, the average American has never had it so good. He is healthier, better fed, better housed than ever. He has more leisure time and makes more money. But he has less sense of purpose. A century ago the Industrial Revolution was under way, the nation was expanding, and Americans spoke in terms of Manifest Destiny. The average American's potential was constricted by disease and want, but his spirit was unbounded. Today, most Americans are free from want, and yet too often we waste our creative potential in second-guessing ourselves and our values.

Peace and freedom cannot survive in the world unless the United States plays a central international role. That is a simple fact, but a fact that makes many Americans profoundly uncomfortable. As André Malraux once told me, "The United States is the first nation in history to become a world power without trying to do so." But if we fail to lead the free world, there will be no free world to lead.

Whether we like it or not, the task of leadership has devolved upon the United States. Ours is not a perfect country. Some claim that its imperfections mean it has no right to play a world role. But if the United States withdraws, the only superpower left on the field will be the one with far less benevolent intentions and far more dubious moral credentials.

The tragedy of Vietnam—not that we were there, but that we lost—has hurt America. The fact that the war was lost two years after our combat role ended did not lessen the pain. It hurt us in the eyes of our friends abroad, and it diminished us in the eyes of our adversaries. But it did the most damage at home. Our loss in Vietnam confused a nation that was not used to losing, that had always equated victory in battle with the triumph of what was right. It encouraged and strengthened the isolationist strain that has always been present in the American character. And it divided us against ourselves, and left some of us convinced, wrongly, that their government had been engaged in a shameful exercise rather than a noble one.

It is often said today that Americans' pride in their nation has been restored. It would be more accurate to say that after several years of steady economic growth, and because most of the bad news from abroad—at least insofar as Americans are involved—has been of relatively isolated terrorist incidents or an occasional minor clash in the Persian Gulf, many Americans have the sense that things are better than they were eight years ago.

But national pride not tempered by adversity is sterile. National pride that lacks awareness of our international responsibilities is empty. National pride without the impulse to share that of which we are so proud is selfish. Too often what we have called a restoration of national pride has been no more than complacent, comfortable smugness. Real pride comes not from avoiding the fray but from being in the middle of it, fighting for our principles, our interests, and our friends.

It will take more than a few successful but relatively minor military missions like the invasion of Grenada and the raid on Libya to build lasting new confidence in the United States among Americans and our friends and allies abroad. Almost nowhere else on earth are people as secure and as prosperous as in the United States. Both our great power and our great blessings challenge us to adopt policies in both foreign and domestic affairs whose ultimate goal is to make the world safer and better. The stakes in this struggle for peace with freedom are far higher than they were in any of history's struggles of arms. If the United States fails to step up to its global responsibilities, the West will lose, and the world will be infinitely more dangerous and cruel in the next century than it was in this century.

If we are to meet this challenge we must begin by shedding our illusions about how the world works.

Americans tend to believe that conflict is unnatural, that people from all nations are basically alike, that differences are products of misunderstanding, and that permanent and perfect peace is a reachable goal. History disproves each of those propositions. International conflict has been a constant through the centuries. Nations differ from one another in basic ways—political traditions, historical experience, motivating ideology—that often breed conflict. Clashing interests—the fact that we *do* understand one another—lead to disputes and ultimately to wars. Only when countries have accepted the existence of conflict and sought to manage it through a balance of power have enduring periods of general peace resulted.

Many of those who march through the streets hoisting placards calling for "peace" and "global disarmament" believe that the only solution to the danger of war is a world order preserved by an international organization. The twentieth century has demolished many myths but none more devastatingly than the wishful notion that world organizations could bring about perfect peace.

There have been two great experiments in world order in this century, the League of Nations and the United Nations. Both were tragic failures. In a speech urging U.S. membership in the League of Nations, Woodrow Wilson proclaimed, "It is a definite guarantee of peace. It is a definite guarantee by word against aggression." Less than two decades after the League was established, the world plunged into the most destructive war in history.

Franklin D. Roosevelt was no less optimistic about the United Nations. He argued, "We must not this time lose the hope of establishing an international order which will be capable of maintaining peace and realizing through the years more perfect justice

21

between nations.'' One hundred twenty wars have been fought since the end of World War II and the founding of the United Nations. Eighteen million people have been killed in those wars—more than the total number killed in World War I.

Some of the world's most able diplomats represent their countries in the UN. They could not have a more frustrating assignment. They can talk about everything and do something about nothing. They deserve our respect and our sympathy. But the United States cannot submit issues affecting its interests to a body so heavily prejudiced against us.

In the real world one tiny nation with six tanks, or six grubby terrorists with one tiny bomb, have more real power than the United Nations General Assembly gathered in all its magnificent splendor on the East River. What moves the world for good or ill is power, and no sovereign nation will give up any of its power to the UN or any other body—not now and not ever. This is an immutable aspect of national character. The sooner we face this fact—and the sooner the people of great nations, especially those in the West, stop feeling guilty about being powerful—the sooner a real international order, based on a stable balance of national power, will be achieved.

World peace is inseparable from national power. No foreign-policy goals, whether strategic, geopolitical, or related to human rights, can be achieved without the application of national power. If the American leadership class does not come to grips with that reality, the United States will lose its chance to act as a force for good in the world, for it will not be a force at all.

Of all the leaders I have met in traveling to ninety countries in the past forty years, none impressed me more than the Prime Minister of Singapore, Lee Kwan Yew. His understanding of the great forces that move the world is encyclopedic and also profoundly perceptive. I vividly recall my first meeting with him twenty years ago. He paced back and forth in his modest office, punctuating his staccato statements with expressive gestures and colorful analogies. He likened the world to a great forest with giant trees, saplings, and creepers. He said the giant trees were Russia, China,

Western Europe, the United States, and Japan. All the rest are saplings, some of which may grow into giants, and creepers, which because of shortages of people or resources cannot hope to become giants.

I am sure he would agree that two giants tower above the others: the United States and the Soviet Union. Our foreign-policy agenda in the remaining years of the twentieth century necessarily must focus on American–Soviet issues. But it cannot be limited to them. We must undertake new initiatives on four fronts:

- We must develop a new live-and-let-live relationship with the Soviet Union, one that recognizes that while the two countries have irreconcilable differences and will continue to compete with each other across the board, they also have a common interest in avoiding going to war over their differences.
- We and our allies must take on greater global responsibilities, with the West Europeans and the Japanese contributing a more equitable share of their resources to the defense of the overall interests of the West.
- We must continue to cultivate the relationship between the United States and China, focusing primarily on economic and political cooperation and following up with military and strategic cooperation where possible.
- We must have a more creative policy for promoting peace, freedom, and prosperity in the Third World. Ironically, it is among the nations of the world with the least political and military power that the most dynamic and dramatic change will occur in generations to come.

The challenges we will face if we do not shirk the responsibilities of world leadership are breathtaking in scope and complexity. But the stakes could not be higher. In 1999, man's capacity to destroy will be unlimited. But his capacity for progress will also be unlimited. One hundred years ago many thought we had reached the end as far as invention and progress were concerned. Now we know we are only at the beginning.

We stand on the shoulders of giants. The enormous scientific breakthroughs of the twentieth century are only a prologue to what we can accomplish in the twenty-first century. We can lighten the burden of labor, find cures for dread diseases, and eliminate the pangs of hunger for all the world's people. But we can do this only if we achieve our primary goal—to make the twenty-first century a century of peace.

I had my last private meeting with Leonid Brezhnev in the Crimea in 1974. While the interpreter was translating one of my remarks into Russian, I jotted down this note on a piece of paper: "Peace is like a delicate plant. It has to be constantly tended and nurtured if it is to survive; if we neglect it, it will wither and die." We failed to meet this challenge in this century. But we cannot afford to fail in the next.

In the twelve years until the end of the twentieth century we will shape the world of the twenty-first century. It is imperative that we seize this moment so that when we look back from the historical high ground in 1999 we will see that we have lost no opportunities to make the next century the best and not the bloodiest in the history of civilization.

General Douglas MacArthur received a standing ovation when he told a joint session of Congress thirty-six years ago, "There is no substitute for victory." He was referring to victory in a conventional war. In a nuclear war there will be no victors, only losers. But there still can be no substitute for victory.

The Soviets seek victory without war. Our answer cannot simply be peace without victory. We too must seek victory without war. But we seek a different kind of victory. We seek not victory over any other nation or people but the victory of the idea of freedom over the idea of totalitarian dictatorship, which would deny freedom. We seek victory for the right of all people to be free from political repression. We seek victory over poverty and misery and disease wherever they exist in the world.

The Soviets are committed to the goal of a communist world. We are committed to the goal of a free world where all people have the right to choose who will govern them and how they should be governed. The Soviets believe that history is on their side. We must make sure that when the history of the next century is written, it will have been on our side.

2

THE
SUPERPOWERS

Nearly one hundred fifty years ago, Alexis de Tocqueville observed with incredible foresight that the future of the world was in the hands of two profoundly different nations: the United States and Russia. "The principal instrument of the former is freedom, of the latter servitude," he wrote, adding that their size alone meant they were bound to play decisive roles. "Their starting point is different and their courses are not the same; yet each of them seems to be marked out by the will of heaven to sway the destinies of half the globe."

Tocqueville could not have contemplated at that time the cataclysmic events of the twentieth century—the two world wars, the invention of the atomic bomb, or the Russian Revolution of 1917, in which an absolute monarchy was replaced by a far more repressive communist dictatorship. But what he predicted about the destinies of the United States and Russia in 1840 is true now and will continue to be true into the twenty-first century. The gulf between the United States and the dictatorship in the Soviet Union today is far greater than that between the United States and absolutist Russia in the nineteenth century.

The United States and the Soviet Union have never been enemies in war. We were allies in World War II. But as World War II drew to a close, Tocqueville's prophecy became reality. Stalin set the Soviet Union on a collision course with the rest of the world. The Third World War began before the Second World War ended. While the United States demobilized its armies and the other major allies began to rebuild their countries, the Soviet Union embarked on a drive for brazen imperial conquest. In less than five years, Moscow annexed Latvia, Lithuania, Estonia, and parts of Finland and Japan, imposed communist puppet governments on the peoples of Poland, Czechoslovakia, Hungary, Romania, Bulgaria, and northern Korea, and made unsuccessful attempts to grab Greece, Turkey, and parts of Iran. Over the next thirty years, the Kremlin created satellite states in East Germany, Cuba, Vietnam, Cambodia, Laos, Angola, Mozambique, Ethiopia, Yemen, Afghanistan, and Nicaragua. Without ever issuing a formal declaration, the Kremlin has been at war against the free world for over forty years.

We are in a war called peace. It is a conflict that has not ended and that will probably continue for generations. The Soviets do not use armies or nuclear weapons to wage this war. Their principal weapons in the struggle with the West are propaganda, diplomacy, negotiations, foreign aid, political maneuver, subversion, covert actions, and proxy war. In this conflict, not only our own freedom but that of the rest of the world are at stake. Whether freedom survives depends on the actions of the United States.

Since Mikhail Gorbachev came to power three years ago as General Secretary of the Communist Party of the Soviet Union, there have been no signs that the Soviet Union has altered its international goals. His personal style, so refreshingly different from that of his predecessors, has captured the imagination of many in the West. If we underestimate him by continuing to mistake style for substance, he may capture the rest of the West as well.

Under Gorbachev the Soviet Union's foreign policy has been more skillful and subtle than ever before. But it has been more aggressive, not less. If his dramatic domestic reforms are as successful, in the twenty-first century we will confront a more prosperous, productive Soviet Union. It will then be a more formidable opponent, not less, than it is today.

That some observers believe the emergence of Gorbachev is a hopeful sign for the United States is an indication of how thoroughly they misunderstand the true nature of the U.S.–Soviet relationship. The beginning of the Gorbachev era does not represent the end of the U.S.–Soviet rivalry. Rather it represents the beginning of a dangerous, challenging new stage of the struggle between the superpowers. He has already earned our respect as the keenest, ablest adversary the United States has faced since World War II. Contrary to the wishful pronouncements of some political-science professors and editorial writers, Gorbachev does not seek peace in the way we do.

In the past forty years, I have had the opportunity to meet a number of great leaders—Churchill, de Gaulle, Adenauer, de Gasperi, Yoshida, Mao Tse-tung, and Chou En-lai. Gorbachev is in that league. Only a heavyweight should get into the ring with him. America is the only country capable of countering Gorbachev's Soviet Union. Whether peace and freedom are secure as we enter the twenty-first century will turn on whether we set the right strategy and adopt the right foreign and defense policies today.

Nuclear weapons have made war obsolete as a means of resolving conflicts between great powers. In the nuclear age, our goal must be peace. But perfect peace—a world without conflict—is an illusion. It has never existed and will never exist.

Real peace is not an end to conflict but a means to living with conflict. Once established, it requires constant attention to survive. Americans are idealists, and idealists long for a world without conflict, a world in which all differences between nations have been overcome, all ambitions forsworn, all aggressive or selfish impulses transformed into acts of individual and national beneficence. But conflict is intrinsic to mankind. History, ideas, and material aspirations have always divided the peoples of the world, and these divisions have continually led to conflict and war. That will not change. We must accept the permanence of conflict and devise policies that take this immutable fact of international life into account.

We must not vainly search for perfect peace but turn our efforts to creating real peace. Perfect peace assumes the end of conflict. Real peace is a means of living with unending conflict. Real peace is a process—a continuing process for managing and containing conflict between competing nations, competing systems, and competing international ambitions. It is the only kind of peace that has ever existed and the only kind we can realistically hope to achieve.

Americans have often confused real peace and perfect peace. For most of its history, the United States was invulnerable to threats from external foes. Its great size and its location between two vast oceans allowed the United States to opt out of international affairs. For 150 years, it stood back in blissful isolation while the nations of Europe jousted in dozens of crises and wars. Americans felt so secure that in the early 1930s their army was the sixteenth largest in the world, ranking just below that of Romania.

America's unique history taught Americans the wrong lessons. Many came to believe that the only obstacles to world peace were either selfish and cynical leaders who were unwilling to put aside parochial national interests in the interest of peace or the regrettable lack of international understanding among leaders and nations. For them, idealism and determined effort were all that was needed to produce peace.

Those characteristics have not been lacking in American diplomacy. U.S. statesmen have almost always led the efforts to create an idealistic perfect peace. It started with Woodrow Wilson's campaign to make World War I "a war to end all wars" through the creation of the League of Nations. It continued in the late 1920s when U.S. diplomats drafted the Kellogg-Briand Pact to outlaw war. It persisted with Franklin Roosevelt's trust in the ability of the United Nations to restrain aggressors. Even today many Americans cling to the belief that the conflict between the United States and the Soviet Union would evaporate if the leaders of the two countries would just sit down at the negotiating table, "get to know each other," and hammer out their differences.

We will never have real peace unless Americans shed their idealistic delusions. Conflict is the natural state of affairs in the world. Nations are bound to come into conflict over a variety of issues and through a variety of means, and the danger will always exist that those conflicts will lead to violence. Our task is not to try to eliminate all conflict—which is impossible—but to manage conflict so that it does not break out into war.

We are not helpless in a chaotic world. We have the necessary tools to build real peace. Those who might initiate aggression will do so only if they believe they will profit from it. No state will go to war unless its leaders believe they can achieve their goals at an acceptable cost. We can affect that calculus of costs and benefits by ensuring that no potential aggressor can conclude that aggression pays. Our goal must be to take the profit out of war.

There is a double lock on the door to peace. The Soviet Union and the United States both hold a key. We cannot achieve real peace without at least the tacit cooperation of Mikhail Gorbachev.

I have met with three of the principal postwar leaders of the Soviet Union—Nikita Khrushchev in 1959 and 1960, Leonid Brezhnev in 1972, 1973, and 1974, and Gorbachev in 1986. Gorbachev is by far the ablest of the three. In just two years, he has become an international superstar. At age fifty-five, much younger than his immediate predecessors, he can expect to rule the Soviet Union for over a generation, facing as many as five U.S. Presidents. That makes him a far more formidable adversary. But it also opens up greater possibilities for real peace.

Many Western reporters and diplomats have tripped over themselves in gushing over Gorbachev. But, like self-proclaimed Soviet experts in the past, they have generally been totally obsessed with style. After meeting Joseph Stalin, an American diplomat commented, "His brown eyes are exceedingly wise and gentle. A child would like to sit on his lap, and a dog would sidle up to him." When Khrushchev rose to power, some pundits wrote him off as a buffoon because he wore ill-fitting clothes, was poorly educated, spoke bad Russian, drank too much, and had crude manners. Brezhnev received higher marks—he wore silk shirts with French cuffs—but was ridiculed for his earthiness and his awkward public manner. Newspapers across the ideological spectrum from the *Washington Post* to the *Wall Street Journal* had feature stories on the fact that Yuri Andropov played tennis and liked American jazz, Scotch whisky, and abstract art.

Gorbachev's neatly tailored suits, refined manners, beautiful wife, and smooth touch with reporters have made him a star with the press and the diplomatic corps. An American official who met him was impressed by the startling fact that he had "good eye contact, a firm handshake and a deep, melodious voice." A British politician even remarked that Gorbachev was the man he most admired in the world. A disarmament activist took this a step further, saying, "Gorbachev is like Jesus. He just keeps giving out good things like arms control proposals and getting nothing but rejections."

All of that is fatuous nonsense. Stalin's "gentle" eyes belied his brutal mind. Khrushchev's peasant manners did not stop him from building the Berlin Wall, and Brezhnev's clumsy speech did not prevent him from undertaking the greatest military buildup in world history. Andropov's "with it" style could not conceal the fact that he had been the ruthless head of the world's most repressive police force. Whoever reaches the pinnacle of power in the Kremlin has learned his politics in the toughest school in the world. If we accept the views of Gorbachev propounded by the antinuclear left, we would be leaving ourselves psychologically disarmed before the man who controls the most powerful armed forces in the world.

I have met fifteen leaders of communist countries over the past forty years; I have never met a weak one. While we must note the weaknesses of communist governments in terms of their popular appeal, we must not overlook their strengths. Only the strong claw their way to the top in the brutal struggle for power in communist countries. Like other communist leaders, Gorbachev will be determined, ruthless, and skilled at exploiting not only his own strengths but also his adversary's weaknesses.

We have and always will have profound differences with Gorbachev and other Soviet leaders. One reason is that we believe in our system and the Soviets reject it. That is easy for most Americans to grasp. But some Americans have more difficulty with the other side of the coin, which is that the Soviets believe in *their* system and believe it is superior to *ours*. No matter how critical we are of the Soviets and their actions in the world, we should never be contemptuous of them. We must respect the Soviet Union as a strong and worthy adversary. Respect is important between friends; it is indispensable between potential enemies in the nuclear age.

Soviet leaders are particularly sensitive about their right to be treated as equals. As Russians, Gorbachev and his colleagues are proud of their history and their culture—their literature, their music, their theater. The homes of Tolstoy and Tchaikovsky are national shrines. They are proud of the strength of the Russian people. They often refer to the fact that the Russians defeated Napoleon in the nineteenth century and Hitler in the twentieth and that Russian casualties in World War II were greater than those suffered by the United States, Britain, and France combined.

As Harold Macmillan told me before I went to Moscow in 1959, the Soviets have an overwhelming desire to be treated as "members of the club." They may still feel psychologically inferior, but there is no arguing that in the three decades since then the Soviets have earned the right to be called a superpower. Gorbachev pointedly observed in his press conference after meeting with President Reagan in Geneva, "We are not simpletons." We cannot quarrel with that statement. Our technology is more advanced than theirs, but what we do they can do. The first man in space was a Russian, not an American. Whether it was the atom bomb, the H-bomb, or the MIRVing of missiles, they caught up with us and not just because their spies stole our secrets.

Gorbachev himself, more than his predecessors, is a powerful reminder that we underestimate the Soviets at our peril. He is the antithesis of the common perception of a bearded Bolshevik who wants to blow up the world. He is a highly intelligent, sophisticated man of the world. He exudes charisma, a quality everyone recognizes but no one can describe. He is a great communicator. He earned a bachelor's degree in law; he was born with a master's degree in public relations. If he had been born in the United States, he would be a surefire winner as a candidate for public office.

Gorbachev has supreme self-confidence, iron self-control, and a healthy degree of self-esteem. He is not as quick as Khrushchev, but he is therefore not as prone to mistakes. He thinks before he speaks. He is an *homme sérieux,* in both the literal and broader senses. He is good at small talk but prefers to get on with the

31

business at hand. Like most extremists on the right as well as the left, he seldom indulges in humor. He prefers to concentrate on the serious issues he has prepared so well to discuss. Some say he has a quick temper. I disagree. He uses his temper; he does not lose it. On the rare occasions he does lose it, he quickly snatches it back and puts it in the service of his relentless drive for domination of the dialogue. He may digress from time to time, but only for the purpose of making his point. He never loses his train of thought. He has an exquisitely disciplined mind.

When he applied his public-relations talents at the superpower summit in December 1987, the city of Washington lost its collective senses. He had conservative senators eating out of his hand. He dazzled and charmed the Washington social set. The usually aggressive star reporters of American adversary journalism became pussycats in his presence. Business leaders and media moguls, when they met him in a private audience, did not question some of his obviously outlandish statements. He completely captivated a group of self-styled intellectuals. According to one observer, they served up softball questions that allowed him to hit a home run with each of his answers. No democratic leader—not Churchill, not de Gaulle, not Adenauer—ever enjoyed the kind of fawning, sycophantic treatment Gorbachev did.

Within establishment circles in Washington, the style of a leader means more than the substance of the policies. But what is important is that more than style distinguishes Gorbachev from his predecessors.

He is the first top Soviet leader I have met who is a hands-on leader in foreign affairs. He understands the intricate details of East–West issues. Khrushchev fulminated about the rightness of Soviet policies but never stepped beyond the most recent Soviet propaganda line. Brezhnev read prepared statements and then deferred all discussion to his subordinates. When I saw him Gorbachev alone spoke for the Soviet side, without notes, and he exhibited a thorough understanding of all the intricacies of arms control and other issues. He understands power and knows how to use it. He is tenacious but not inflexible. He is the kind of leader who can exercise judgment independent of his advisers and who can strike a deal.

Gorbachev is a new kind of Soviet leader. Khrushchev tried to cover up Soviet weaknesses by bragging outrageously about Soviet superiority. Brezhnev knew that his nuclear forces were equal to ours, but he still talked defensively by constantly insisting that the Soviet Union and the United States were equals as world powers. Gorbachev is so confident of his strengths that he is not afraid to talk about his weaknesses.

His recognition of Soviet weaknesses does not mean he has lost faith in the Soviet system. It is as useless to try to convert the Soviets to our way of thinking as it is for them to try to convert us to theirs. Whenever we try to debate ideology with them it is like two ships passing in the night. Human rights are a case in point. The Soviets consider the major human rights to be free health care, free housing, free education, and full employment. We consider the major human rights to be freedom of speech, freedom of the press, freedom of religion, and free elections.

We believe we are on the right side of history. They believe they are. Therefore, as a start in developing a new live-and-let-live relationship, both superpowers should accept how and why they are different, learn to respect each other's strength and abilities, and avoid rhetoric which gratuitously puts the other down, while recognizing that we will both remain forceful advocates of our own beliefs.

Like his predecessors, Gorbachev seeks to expand the influence and power of the Soviet Union. Regardless of the refinements he has introduced into Moscow's public-relations techniques, he has preserved the long-term objective of pushing for global predominance. But he is the first Soviet leader who has faced up to the fact that the Soviet Union suffers from fundamental internal problems that threaten its status as a superpower. He is a dedicated communist. But when he looks at the Soviet position in the world, he wears no ideological blinkers.

As he looks back over the twentieth century, he sees an impressive historical record for communism. Lenin was the leader of only a small band of conspirators at the turn of the century. Until World War II, only one country with only 7 percent of the world's population had a communist government. Now two of the greatest powers in history, the Soviet Union and China, and over a third of the world's population live under communist rule.

Gorbachev knows that the country he rules has tremendous potential. While the United States—including Hawaii—covers six time zones, the Soviet Union covers eleven. Its vast natural resources match its expanse. It has a highly literate, well-educated population. Its peoples have produced great literature and art. Its scientists have made great contributions to man's knowledge. It has more graduate engineers today than the United States. While its standard of living lags behind that of the West, we should never assume that the Soviet Union is simply a Third World state with nuclear-tipped rockets.

He also knows that in the last fifteen years the Soviet Union has made significant gains. Moscow has increased its great superiority in conventional military power. It has expanded its coastal navies into a blue-water navy—the largest in the world in terms of tonnage. Most disturbing, it has acquired decisive superiority in the most powerful and accurate nuclear weapons, land-based intercontinental ballistic missiles. It has projected its power into Southwest Asia, and its proxies have tallied up victories in Southeast Asia, southern Africa, and Central America. Its sustained political and propaganda offensive in Western Europe has prompted major political parties to adopt essentially neutralist platforms, which, if implemented, would lead to the dissolution of the North Atlantic Treaty Organization alliance.

In his lifetime Gorbachev has seen the Soviet Union rise from the status of one of many major powers to that of one of two superpowers. Whatever its other weaknesses, communism has proven to be an effective means for winning and keeping power. That experience serves to confirm Gorbachev's ideological beliefs. While he knows that the Soviet Union must address great problems, he still believes it represents the wave of the future.

Gorbachev wants to keep what he has inherited from his predecessors. He also wants to add to the gains if possible. But as he surveys the international scene, he cannot be encouraged. Formidable external and internal obstacles lie in his path.

As he looks to the west, he sees signs of political unrest in virtually every country of the Soviet bloc, from Poland through Bulgaria. With these uncertain allies at its side, the Soviet Union confronts an alliance that has lasted longer than any other in history. NATO, after a decade of increased defense spending, has significantly strengthened its forces in the field. While the Soviet Union has undermined the international resolve of the Labour Party in Britain and the Social Democratic Party in West Germany, their drift toward neutralism has in turn undercut their electoral appeal. Chancellor Helmut Kohl has been reelected to another five-year term. Prime Minister Margaret Thatcher routed her divided opposition at the polls. Under President François Mitterrand and Prime Minister Jacques Chirac, France has bolstered its military forces and increased its cooperation with NATO.

As Gorbachev looks to the east, he sees the enormous long-term challenge posed by China and Japan. China, still a potential enemy, does not represent a military threat to the Soviet Union today, but its huge population and enormous natural resources create an awesome danger for the future. Beijing's economic reforms compound the threat. If the Soviet Union's growth rate continues to lag behind China's as much as it has over the last five years, China will surpass the Soviet Union in terms of gross national product by the middle of the next century.

Japan, with no energy resources and with less than one-half the population and one-sixtieth the territory of the Soviet Union, has a per-capita income more than twice as high. With its growth far outpacing Moscow's, Japan will leave the Soviet Union hopelessly behind in the next century. More ominous from the Kremlin's point of view, the Japanese government has recently rescinded the formal limitation keeping defense spending under one percent of GNP and has undertaken a significant, though still modest, program to upgrade its defenses.

Like all Soviet leaders, Gorbachev approaches foreign policy with the long term in mind. Americans think in terms of decades. The Soviets think in terms of centuries. He knows the Soviet Union cannot ignore these ominous trends in the Far East. For Moscow, threats in the future are problems in the present.

As he looks to the south, the threat is already at hand: The Soviet Union is mired in a war in Afghanistan with no prospect for a quick victory. Eight years after the invasion, the Kremlin still cannot pull out its 120,000 troops without precipitating a collapse of the communist government in Kabul. More than 25,000 Soviet troops have been killed in action. Over $40 billion has been spent on the war, and expenses are running at over $10 billion annually. Its forces have ravaged the countryside, yet Moscow controls little more than the country's major cities and the main roads. What's worse, the war carries the risk for ominous political repercussions among the Soviet Union's Muslim peoples.

No one should doubt that Moscow has the potential power to prevail. But at the current rate victory will not come for at least twenty years, and it may never come. For the Kremlin leaders, there is no light at the end of the tunnel.

When Gorbachev looks beyond the regions on his immediate frontiers, he finds all his communist clients in the Third World queuing up for handouts. They are not allies but dependencies. Not one of Moscow's friends in the Third World could survive without massive economic subsidies or military assistance. Lenin wrote that capitalist countries turned to imperialism as a profit-making venture. If that was true, the communist revolution in Russia certainly did usher in a new era, since Moscow's empire impoverishes rather than enriches the Kremlin. Vietnam costs the Soviet Union over $3.5 billion a year, Cuba over $4.9 billion, Angola, Mozambique, and Ethiopia a total of over $3 billion, and Nicaragua over $1 billion. Moscow's imperial domain costs the Kremlin over $35 million a day.

When Gorbachev looks at the battle of ideas, he sees that the communist ideology has lost its appeal. After a visit to the Soviet Union seventy years ago, a liberal newspaper reporter, Lincoln Steffens, wrote: "I have seen the future and it works." Now we have all seen that future and it does not work. This is true not only in Eastern Europe and the Soviet Union itself, where the people have lived under communism in practice, but also in the rest of the world. In the 1950s, many noncommunists in the Third World admired the Soviet model of economic development. Today, no Third World government aspires to become a bureaucratic nightmare like the Soviet Union, with its jungles of red tape and its stagnant swamp of an economy. In the 1930s, Americans who spied for Moscow acted out of ideological conviction. Today, Americans who have been convicted of spying for the Soviets did it for cold, hard cash.

Moscow's military power is its only asset. Great as that may be, military power cannot be sustained over the long term without matching economic power. Moscow's dilemma is that its assets are ill-suited to solving its problems, and its problems are undermining its assets.

Gorbachev does not underestimate the Soviet quandary. Nor do his communist neighbors to the east. A Chinese leader, after explaining why China's current economic reforms were essential if it intended to step into the front rank of nations, once commented to me that if the Soviet Union did not adopt similar changes Moscow would "disappear" as a great power in the next century. That is true, and Gorbachev knows it.

Economically, it has abysmally failed to capitalize on its great human and material resources. It has not surpassed any other major country in GNP since the end of World War II; meanwhile it has been surpassed by Japan and Italy. Moscow's economy is a basket case. The growth rate is virtually zero. Productivity is dropping. Absenteeism, corruption, malingering, and drunkenness are rife. The standard of living is sinking, so much so that the life expectancy of Russian men is actually going down. A Soviet worker must spend more than seven times as many hours as a West European to earn enough money to buy a car. The Soviet Union has fifteen times fewer industrial computers than advanced West European countries and forty-five times fewer than the United States. What few positive blips have been detected in the vital signs of the Soviet economy in recent years have resulted from the Kremlin's manipulation of its own economic statistics.

Western economists used to undertake esoteric extrapolations to gauge the depths of Moscow's economic crisis. Today, they only have to read Mikhail Gorbachev's speeches. Khrushchev claimed the Soviet Union would catch up and surpass the United States economically in a decade. Brezhnev swept economic problems under the rug. Andropov thought more discipline among the workers was the solution. In Gorbachev the Soviet Union finally has a leader who grasps that without a growing economy its international position will steadily erode and its military power will gradually atrophy. He has formally repealed the Communist Party's goal of Khrushchev's era which called for the Soviet Union to surpass the United States in gross national product in the 1980s. He has labeled Khrushchev's boastful predictions of Soviet economic growth as "groundless fantasies." Gorbachev knows that more than wishful thinking and pep rallies is needed to get the Soviet system back on its feet.

He also understands that his major priority must be to revitalize the Soviet economy. Without economic growth, he cannot afford the current level of Soviet military spending, provide even a marginal improvement in the standard of living of the Soviet peoples, or hold the Soviet system out as a paragon for developing nations.

Gorbachev faces the classic dilemma of communist totalitarian systems. In order to have progress he must allow more freedom. But allowing more freedom threatens his power. Excessive centralization is the principal problem of the Soviet economy. But decentralizing economic decision-making carries the risk of prompting demands for political decentralization. And political decentralization would mean the dissolution of the communist system.

When Gorbachev totals up the balance sheet of Soviet strengths and weaknesses, the bottom line is not encouraging. Moscow has put itself into a unique historical position: It does not have a single ally among the major powers of the world. The Kremlin faces potential adversaries in Western Europe, China, Japan, Canada, and the United States, whose combined gross national products account for over 60 percent of the world economy. Moreover, never in history has an aggressive power been more successful in extending its domination over other nations and less successful in winning the approval of the people of those nations. In not one of the nineteen nations of the world in which they rule did the communists gain power by winning a free democratic election, and none of them dares to have one. If the Soviet Union's strength wanes, its satellites will certainly try to break out of the Kremlin's orbit.

Gorbachev feels the pressure of these problems and has responded with a far-reaching reform campaign. As he tackles the difficult tasks before him, we need to analyze the consequences of his reforms for the world. We need to answer these questions: What kinds of reforms has he proposed? What do these reforms tell us about Gorbachev's intentions? What is the likelihood that these reforms will succeed? What does Gorbachev's reform drive portend for Soviet behavior in the world? How should the West respond?

Gorbachev has pressed forward with a three-pronged reform program. But while he has departed from the policies of his immediate predecessors, we must view the scope of these changes with historical perspective.

Glasnost. This is the catchword for the new openness about problems in the Soviet Union and the greater tolerance of dissent. Gorbachev has allowed the Soviet press to publish exposés about the failures of and corruption in the Soviet system. He has brought Andrei Sakharov back from internal exile and has released a few other prominent dissidents. He has increased the number of Jews allowed to emigrate and has given exit visas to Soviet citizens divided from their spouses in the West. All these steps have been widely hailed in the West.

These developments are significant and represent a welcome change from the past. But we should always remember that the literal translation of the word *glasnost* is "transparency." Repression remains the keystone of the Soviet system. While fewer than 100 political dissidents have been released, another 40,000 still languish in prison camps. While 8,000 Jews were allowed to emigrate in 1987, another 400,000 are still waiting to do so. While more criticism of the system is permitted, it is still all officially sanctioned criticism. It is no accident that those who are criticized under Glasnost never argue back.

Gorbachev's purpose is threefold. He wants to create a more favorable attitude toward the Soviet Union in the West in order to facilitate his pursuit of more important goals, agreements on trade and arms control. He wants to use Glasnost to weed out his political opponents. He wants to create a new spirit among intellectuals and particularly young people in the Soviet Union. Glasnost is a small price to pay.

Democratization. Gorbachev's speeches overflow with paeans to democracy. But what he means by democracy is very different from what we mean by it. He wants to open up the system; he wants to encourage people to step forth with new ideas; but he has no intention of relinquishing any of the power and prerogatives of the Communist Party. His democratization stays strictly *within* the party. There is no real democratization *outside* the party. He wants to shake up the system to get it moving again. But it will not lead to anything remotely resembling a Western democracy.

Perestroika. This slogan for economic reform literally means restructuring. Gorbachev has spoken in sweeping terms about this program. He has called for the dismantling of much of the central planning apparatus. He has endorsed the idea of joint ventures with private Western firms. He has proposed giving greater decision-making power to factory managers. He has pushed for allowing some opportunities for very small enterprises to make private profit. But he has so far achieved little. Few of Gorbachev's proposals have been enacted, and they in no way compare to the revolutionary initiatives that Deng Xiaoping has undertaken in China. The day-to-day workings in the Soviet Union still run by the dictates of the old regime.

That Gorbachev seeks to take a new approach to Soviet problems does not mean that he rejects the basic premises of his system. He believes that the system is fundamentally sound but needs to be made more effective. We must always remind ourselves that the reforms themselves tell us nothing about Gorbachev's intentions. Their purpose is not to move the Soviet Union toward more freedom at home or a less aggressive policy abroad, but rather to make the communist system work better. He wants the system to be more efficient, not less communist.

Gorbachev's success is far from guaranteed. He faces monumental political and cultural obstacles. Some people have even argued that he has only a fifty-fifty chance of lasting five years in power. They point out that in every speech he makes he refers to the opposition against his reforms. They recall that when the last great Soviet reformer, Nikita Khrushchev, tried to revitalize the system his colleagues in the Politburo promptly gave him the boot. They conclude that the same could happen to Gorbachev.

Those who hold this view rightly point out that there is opposition to Gorbachev's reforms but underestimate his ability to handle it. A shake-up of the Soviet system will always be opposed by those who have been shaking it down through perks and corruption. He is trying to impose new changes on those who benefit from the old ways. They do not want to lose their dachas, their limousines, their ballet tickets, their Black Sea vacations, and their rights to expert medical care and preferential education for their children. But the analogy to Khrushchev does not fit. Like Khrushchev, Gorbachev is bold and unpredictable; but unlike Khrushchev, he will not be rash.

Gorbachev has also shown great skill in consolidating his power. Unlike Stalin, he does not have his rivals killed. Unlike Khrushchev, he does not leave them in positions where they can threaten his power. (Brezhnev, for example, was standing next to Khrushchev during our Kitchen Debate in 1959.) Instead, Gorbachev ferrets them out of their key positions and replaces them with supporters. In just two years, he has replaced all but one of the members of the party Secretariat, the key body which runs the party apparatus. Of the thirteen members of the all-powerful Politburo, the body which runs the country's day-to-day affairs, only three are holdovers from the Brezhnev era. He has also replaced two thirds of the provincial party secretaries and more than 60 percent of the government ministers. His ruthless sacking of Boris Yeltsin, who was one of the strongest supporters of reform, was a shot across the bow to anyone—friend or foe—who is tempted to challenge his authority. Gorbachev is firmly in charge, and he will remain so as long as he keeps playing his cards with such masterful skill.

But even if Gorbachev stays in power his economic reforms face three profound difficulties. The first is his communist ideology. He is a deeply believing communist. Communism is his faith. His occasional references to God in private conversations do not make him a closet Christian. A communist cannot become a Christian without ceasing to be a communist. Communism and Christianity have irreconcilable differences. He has been hailed as a pragmatist

41

and has spoken of the need to create incentives to guide the decisions of workers and managers. But that runs contrary to one of the fundamental premises of the Stalinist command economy. Our economic system works because the market guides virtually all economic actions. If Gorbachev's reforms are enacted, there will be a basic tension built into the system. How will Gorbachev determine which decisions should be made by the market and which by the state? It will be difficult for him to move away from the beliefs of a lifetime about the superiority of state control over what he believes to be the heartless exploitation of the masses by selfish capitalists. As problems arise, there will be a powerful motivation for the Soviet state to step in and hand out orders to solve them.

The second obstacle is the hidebound Soviet bureaucracy. Gorbachev must implement his reforms through millions of lower-level Soviet functionaries and managers. It is not easy to teach old bureaucrats new tricks. They simply do not know how to act like entrepreneurs. They are used to taking orders, not initiating ideas. Like bureaucrats everywhere, they know that the best way to win promotions is to play it safe and not take chances. They do not have the slightest idea of how to judge which economic risks are worth taking. It will take nothing less than a cultural revolution, one in which individual initiative is promoted over party discipline, to overcome the habits of seventy years of centralized Stalinist planning.

The third problem involves the Russian people. Unlike the peoples of Eastern Europe and unlike many in China, the Russians have never known anything but government-controlled enterprise, whether under the old czars of the nineteenth century or the new czars of the twentieth century. The Chinese generally, as demonstrated by their success in any country to which they emigrate, are born entrepreneurs. Most Russians are not. We tend to believe that people will always respond to the challenge of opportunity. That is not true. Many even in this country who have become used to the security of the welfare state value it above all else.

Ironically, while Marx attacked religion as the opiate of the people, the secular religion of Marxism-Leninism has proved to be an even more insidious addictive. When people become accustomed to a system that provides total security and that makes playing it safe rather than taking a chance the best way to get ahead, it is difficult to change them. For them, change means instability and represents a threat. Even those who benefit little from the system fear they will lose what little they get.

Gorbachev is aware of these problems. He has a deep faith in his ideology, but he knows that his economy is not working. He wants to reform the system, but he cannot do so without the participation of the people who make up the system. He can act only through his bureaucracy. But his bureaucrats and managers are unaccustomed to making their decisions without guidance from above. He must also enlist the cooperation of people who must change the habits of a lifetime, who must respond to the challenge of opportunity, with all its risks, rather than huddle in the comfort and security of a totally planned society. His task is almost as difficult as making drones into productive bees.

So far there is no reason to believe that Gorbachev's reforms will make the world a better or a safer place. First of all, he has not broken with the horrors of the Soviet past. In his secret speech in 1956, Khrushchev said that "Stalin was a man of capricious and despotic character whose persecution mania reached unbelievable dimensions" and that Stalin had personally ordered the mass executions of his opponents and the mass deportations of whole nations away from their native lands in the Soviet Union. Gorbachev, on the other hand, endorsed the brutal policy of collectivizing agriculture, praised "the tremendous political will, purposefulness and persistence, ability to organize and discipline the people displayed in the war years by Joseph Stalin," and criticized only the "excesses" of the Stalin years. To a man who killed tens of millions of Soviet citizens Gorbachev gave a pat on the back and a slap on the wrist.

Moreover, for the Soviet Union, reform at home does not automatically lead to restraint abroad. We should not bet the ranch on the expectation that these reforms will bring about a softer Soviet foreign policy. In czarist Russia as well as in communist Russia, reformers traditionally couple new domestic policies with a strong foreign policy. Peter the Great was a prime example. So was Nikita Khrushchev. He sought to reform the economy, but he also put missiles in Cuba, built the Berlin Wall, and ordered Soviet tanks to shoot down Hungarian freedom fighters in the streets of Budapest just nine months after he delivered the famous secret speech condemning the crimes of Stalin.

Gorbachev cannot afford to appear weak. He must convey the impression of a strong, successful, formidable leader. If he retreats abroad, he will quickly lose support within the Soviet power elite, and his enemies within the Communist Party will tear him apart. He will be cautious in taking on new initiatives around the world, but he will be tough in fighting to preserve what he inherited from his predecessors. He wants to consolidate the gains of the 1970s before seeking new gains in the 1990s.

It is a mistake to buy the idea that Gorbachev is a foreign-policy "moderate" beset by conservative rivals. While he may have his internal foes, the entire leadership forms a united front to confront the external world. Creating the impression of a battle between "hawks" and "doves" within the Kremlin is a common Soviet ploy. Some of Roosevelt's advisers were conned into believing that Stalin was fending off hard-liners. In meetings with Henry Kissinger and me, Brezhnev made a great show of stepping out to consult with his "hawks," in the hope that we would later make more concessions to help him out with his domestic opposition. We must not be fooled by this shopworn tactic. Gorbachev's rivals oppose him not because he is a moderate, but because they want his power.

Finally, there is no evidence that under Gorbachev the Soviet Union has pulled back from its aggressive policies. Nowhere in the world is Gorbachev doing less than his predecessors to further Soviet global ambitions. While Soviet sources have spread rumors that Soviet strategic doctrine has shifted to a purely defensive posture and that Gorbachev has announced a new military approach based on "strategic sufficiency" rather than a quest for superiority, he has not reduced the Soviet defense budget or scaled back Soviet deployments. He has endorsed the Brezhnev Doctrine, which justifies Soviet intervention to suppress popular uprisings in the communist countries in Eastern Europe and the Third World. He has increased Soviet military aid to and the Soviet military presence in Nicaragua, Afghanistan, Angola, and the Persian Gulf.

Under Gorbachev, Soviet rhetoric against the United States has taken a dark turn. It makes President Reagan's talk about the "evil empire" sound like a Sunday-school lesson. Gorbachev's government-controlled Soviet press has charged the United States with conspiring in the assassination of Indira Gandhi and Olof Palme. It claims that while the Soviet Union has been giving aid to Africans, the United States has been giving them AIDS. As Dimitri Simes has observed, "The Soviet leopard has changed its spots but it is still a leopard."

We must not heed the counsel of the so-called experts on the Soviet Union who are forever reading signs of a softening in Soviet foreign policy in the Kremlin tea leaves. When Gorbachev recalls that in the Khrushchev era "a wind of change swept over the country," they jump to the conclusion that Gorbachev intends to bring about a Moscow spring. We must always remind ourselves that the purpose of the Gorbachev reforms is not to move toward more freedom at home or toward a less threatening foreign policy abroad, but rather to make the communist system work better. If his reforms succeed and his foreign policy remains the same, Gorbachev will have more resources with which to strengthen and expand the Soviet empire.

Under no circumstances should we allow our foreign policy to be affected by changes in Soviet domestic policy. It would be utter folly to follow the advice of those who believe we should make concessions in arms-control negotiations in order to "help" Gorbachev succeed at home. His reforms will rise and fall on their own merits. Nothing we do can affect what happens in the internal politics of the Kremlin. If we offer concessions every time the Soviet press publishes exposés of problems in the Soviet Union, Moscow will collect strategic gains while we collect newspaper clippings.

At the same time, we should keep our minds open to the possibility of far-reaching reform in the Soviet system. Though far from certain, it is possible that Gorbachev's reforms will take on a life of their own and lead to real change within the system. We must remember, however, that economic reform does not necessarily lead to political reform. As Charles Krauthammer has pointed out, "Economic liberty can engender an appetite for political liberty but modern dictators have the necessary repressive apparatus to deal with appetites. Some degree of economic freedom can coexist with an extraordinary degree of political repression."

In the long run, until the Soviet Union changes internally, we can expect no fundamental change externally. This requires us to apply a stiff standard in measuring the meaningfulness of Soviet reforms. Do they decentralize political as well as economic power? Do they give greater autonomy to the non-Russian peoples of the Soviet Union? Do they protect freedom of thought and religion? Do they release the countries of Eastern Europe from their status as satellites? If reforms do not break ground in these areas, they will not affect Soviet foreign policy and will be of little solace to the West.

A fresh breeze is blowing in the Soviet Union. We do not yet know its strength or its direction. Yet even a tiny whiff of freedom can give relief from the oppressive heat of Soviet repression. We should therefore welcome the change, while remaining wary of its purpose.

Our quest for real peace must begin with the recognition of the fundamental fact that profound differences exist between the United States and the Soviet Union.

The stark truth is that the ideologies and the foreign policies of the two countries are diametrically opposed. The struggle between the Soviet Union and the United States is between an avowedly and manifestly aggressive power and an avowedly and manifestly defensive one, between a totalitarian civilization and a free one, between a state that is frightened by the idea of freedom and one that is founded on it.

Our aspirations are in direct conflict. America wants peace; the Soviet Union wants the world. Our foreign policy respects the freedom of other countries; theirs tries to destroy it. We seek peace as an end in itself; they seek peace only if it serves their ends. The Soviets pursue those ends unscrupulously, by all means short of all-out war. For the Soviets, peace is a continuation of war by other means.

There are those who believe that the United States and the Soviet Union are morally equivalent, that they pose equal threats to peace and freedom. But the United States threatens neither peace nor freedom, while the Soviet Union takes aim at both. While we need to have the power to deter the Soviets from attacking or intimidating the West, Moscow knows very well that it has no need to deter us. We must keep in mind Churchill's admonition to Parliament in 1945: "Except so far as force is concerned, there is no equality between right and wrong."

One of Gorbachev's principal goals, as Abe Rosenthal has observed, has been to create an image of moral equality between the United States and the Soviet Union in the eyes of the world—but "without paying the price of changing the essential elements of the communist system upon which the dictatorship of the communist party rests." He has gone far toward achieving that goal. He is a pop hero throughout Europe, and in Britain and West Germany his approval rating in opinion polls stands higher than President Reagan's. At high-society cocktail parties in New York and Washington, the established wisdom is that the Russians are just like us after all. What the glitterati ignore is that "people just like us" do not maintain armies to occupy eight satellite states and do not operate concentration camps to jail tens of thousands of political prisoners.

During his visit to Washington in December 1987, Gorbachev's stock reply when questioned about Soviet restrictions on the right to emigrate was to ask why the United States had immigration agents along the border with Mexico. We should respond by saying, "It is true that we have to place limits on immigration because so many people want to come to our country, including thousands from behind the Iron Curtain. How many are applying to go live in the Soviet Union? What's more, anyone who wants to leave the United States may do so at any time. Very few do. How many people do you allow to leave the Soviet Union? How many would leave if they could?"

Whenever we fail to answer the Soviet Union's absurd charges about our human-rights policies, we encourage the notion that our system is not any better than theirs. A democracy and a dictatorship are not moral equals. Gorbachev's reforms have not touched the police power of the state. Whatever improvement Glasnost might bring, it is not freedom. As long as there is no freedom in the Soviet empire, there is no moral equivalence between the Soviet Union and the United States. If we pretend that no moral gulf separates the superpowers, it will erode our own values and our resistance to Soviet expansionism.

The greatest disservice to the cause of real peace is to propagate the myth that the problem between the United States and the Soviet Union is simply a giant misunderstanding. If we would only sit down and *get to know* each other our differences would evaporate—or so teaches the touchy-feely school of superpower politics. In fact the opposite is true. The problem is not that we do not understand each other, but that we *do* understand each other and that we have irrevocable differences. We must recognize that all that we can hope to achieve by negotiation is to prevent those differences from escalating into armed conflict.

Soviet foreign policy is a deadly mix of traditional Russian expansionism and the revolutionary drive of ideological communism. It is imperialism multiplied by a factor of two. Even without communism, Russia would still be an expansionist power. Communism, however, adds impetus to the quest for global predominance. For the Soviets, expansionism is the status quo. As Khrushchev told President Kennedy at Vienna in 1961, "The continuing revolutionary process in various countries *is* the status quo, and anyone who tries to halt this process not only is altering the status quo but is an aggressor."

Anyone who wants to understand the intentions of the Kremlin leaders should go to Afghanistan. In 1979, when Soviet forces invaded the country to prevent the Afghan people from overthrowing a universally despised communist government, I was writing *The Real War,* and I cited Moscow's invasion as the most recent step in a long-term strategy to win control over the oil resources in the Persian Gulf. Moscow knew that the invasion would carry great political and military costs, but it took the decision to intervene as coolly as a master chess player makes a bold but well-studied gambit.

For over eight years the Soviet Union has been waging one of the most vicious wars ever waged against a defenseless people. No brutality has been beyond the imagination of Moscow's forces.

Soviet troops once came into a village, bound the hands and feet of the civilians, stacked their bodies like cordwood, and burned them alive. That was not an accident or the result of overzealous troops. It was part of a systematic policy to terrorize the population and to depopulate the countryside so that the Afghan resistance would be deprived of its base of support. Of the prewar Afghan population of fifteen million people, five million have fled into Pakistan and Iran and one million have been killed. Comparing Moscow's genocide against the Afghan people with Hitler's against the Jews is not overblown Cold War rhetoric but cold, hard fact.

In 1985, I traveled through the areas in Pakistan that border on Afghanistan and saw the squalor in which millions of proud Afghans now live. The final chapter of the Afghan story has yet to be written, for the Afghan resistance will not soon die. But so far the principal lesson of the Soviet–Afghan war is that the Kremlin leaders are willing to inflict tremendous human suffering in the pursuit of strategic gains. That lesson must not be lost on the rest of the world. Even if the Soviet Union withdraws from Afghanistan in the next few years, we should not forget what the Kremlin leaders have been doing to the Afghan people for the last eight years.

While we must have a clear-eyed understanding of the foreign policy of the Soviet Union, we must always be careful to distinguish between the leaders in the Kremlin on the one hand and the peoples of the Soviet Union on the other. The latter are every bit as much victims of the Kremlin's oppression as those countries Moscow has conquered. A peasant in the Ukraine shares the same fate as a shipyard worker in Poland.

While the government of the Soviet Union is aggressive and capable of the greatest inhumanities, anyone who wants to understand the peoples of the Soviet Union should travel through their country, meet them, and talk to them.

I have been to the Soviet Union on six occasions—once as Vice President, twice as President, and three times as a private citizen. I have chatted with shoppers in markets in Moscow, Samarkand, and Alma-Ata, coal miners in Sverdlovsk, and factory workers in Novosibirsk. I never failed to be impressed with their strength and vigor as people, their proud patriotism and their deeply felt desire for peace. I also found that despite government propaganda the average citizen had a genuine respect and even admiration for the United States. I cannot imagine that more than a small fraction support the Kremlin's war in Afghanistan.

The peoples of the Soviet Union are great peoples. A testament to their greatness is the fact that despite the suffering inflicted upon them by revolution, two world wars, and terrible repression, the Soviet Union has still emerged as a superpower. Other peoples would have collapsed under the pressure, but the peoples of the Soviet Union survived and propelled their country forward.

In 1986, Gorbachev commented to me that since the American and Russian people had so much in common—great-power status, a global rather than a parochial outlook, similar interests in sports and entertainment—the two nations should be able to overcome their mutual hostility and mistrust. I am sure he believes that. But while the parallels he drew were correct, the conclusion he reached was wrong.

The American people and the peoples of the Soviet Union can be friends. But because we have irreconcilable differences the governments of the United States and the Soviet Union can never be friends. We must always remember, however, that our differences are with the Kremlin, not with the peoples ruled by the Kremlin. This is true for the Russian people, but particularly for the non-Russian peoples who view Moscow's rule as imperial rule. Stalin's brutal collectivization campaign in the Ukraine killed over eight million people. Russian immigration into Kazakhstan in Central Asia has made the Kazakhs a minority in their own land. Byelorussians, Georgians, Tadzhiks, Turkomens, and scores of other non-Russian nations share similar legacies. Lenin's characterization of Russia as the "jailhouse of nations" fits as well today as it did in the times of the czars. The fast-growing populations of the non-Russian nations—which will eventually make the Russian people a shrinking minority within the Soviet Union—are a time bomb ticking in the walls of the Kremlin.

Our policies must always take into account this distinction between the central government of the Soviet Union and its highly diverse peoples. We must not allow our differences with the Soviet government to prevent us from expressing our friendship with the Soviet people. We must seek to increase contacts between the

West and the peoples of the Soviet Union. It must be done in ways that do not aid the Soviet Union's aggressive ambitions. But contact with the free peoples of the West is bound in the long run to foster internal pressures on the Soviet government to grant its peoples more control over their own lives.

Our political differences with the Soviet Union are real, not the product of misunderstanding or paranoid imaginations. Anyone who has doubts about it should ask the Afghans or the other peoples whose nations have been forcibly incorporated into the Soviet empire. Soviet–American friendship societies or vodka toasts at summit meetings will not produce real peace. Real peace between the governments of the United States and the Soviet Union cannot be based on mutual friendship because the values and goals of the two superpowers are totally at odds with one another. It can only be grounded on mutual respect for each other's strength and legitimate interests.

While our differences are profound and unbridgeable, the United States and the Soviet Union have one overriding common interest: to avoid nuclear war over our differences. While the United States and the Soviet Union can never be friends, they cannot afford to be enemies. Our irreconcilable differences prevent us from making peace. Nuclear weapons prevent us from settling our differences by war. This common interest in survival makes real peace possible despite the political differences that make continued conflict inevitable.

We must not pursue the unachievable—perfect peace—at the expense of the attainable, real peace. Neither the United States nor the Soviet Union will cast aside its values or compromise its interests. But if we are to live with our differences instead of dying over them, we must devise a process for settling them short of war. We should seek to create peaceful rules of engagement for our a conflict that will last until 1999 and well into the next century. This will never satisfy those in the West who march in the streets for perfect peace and instant brotherhood. It will not satisfy them —but at least it will keep them alive and healthy, and also free to march some more.

In the eleven years before 1999, we should adopt foreign and defense policies aimed at accomplishing the three requisites for real peace.

First, we must avoid nuclear war. Each superpower now has over ten thousand nuclear warheads on its strategic weapons and thousands more on its intermediate-range and tactical nuclear weapons. A war at the nuclear level would lead to the destruction of civilization.

Radiation released from the Chernobyl nuclear-reactor disaster contaminated food over a thousand miles away. Western experts have calculated from official Soviet estimates of the amount of released radiation that as many as 45,000 more people will die from cancer in the Soviet Union. Yet detonating just one nuclear warhead would release a hundred times more fallout than Chernobyl. In addition to killing hundreds of millions of people instantly, a full-scale nuclear war would not only poison the earth but also create an epidemic of cancer that would make the Black Death of the sixteenth century look like a bout with the flu.

Second, we must avoid defeat without war. No one in the Kremlin underestimates the danger of a nuclear war. But neither do the Soviet leaders adhere to the trite belief that the invention of nuclear weapons has rendered military power irrelevant. For the Kremlin, all that nuclear weapons have changed is the means through which it pursues its traditional ends.

The pages of history are littered with the ruins of countries that were indifferent to an erosion of the balance of power. Losses on the periphery, where a country's interests appear marginal, never seem to merit a response or warrant a confrontation with the enemy. But small losses add up. Expansionist powers thrive on picking up loose geopolitical change. If their aggression goes unchecked, a clash becomes unavoidable. When it comes, it usually takes place under the worst possible circumstances for those on the defensive. The greatest conflict in history, World War II, was an unnecessary war. If Britain and France had blocked Hitler's remilitarization of the Rhineland in 1936, when Nazi Germany was still weak, they would never have had to face the decision of whether to go to war in 1939, when Hitler commanded the most powerful armed forces in the world.

The United States must recognize that it cannot remain indifferent to conflicts in the distant corners of the world. America's loss in Vietnam in 1975 led to the Soviet acquisition of naval bases at Cam Rahn Bay and Danang from which its naval forces can today threaten Japan's oil lifeline to the Persian Gulf. The consolidation of Sandinista communist power in Nicaragua could force the United States to commit troops to defend the rest of Central America and thereby undercut U.S. capabilities to act in crises in Europe, Korea, or the Middle East. We cannot afford to sit idly by while the Soviet Union tallies up a string of small victories. If we do, we will wake up one day to find that the global balance of power has tilted fatally against us.

That does not mean the United States should be cavalier about military interventions or commit itself to the defense of every square inch of the whole world. As Frederick the Great warned, "He who tries to defend everywhere defends nothing." But it does mean that the United States must place equal emphasis on avoiding a nuclear war and on preventing defeat without war. Since both superpowers know the dangers of a nuclear war, defeat without war becomes the greater threat.

Third, we must actively engage in peaceful competition with the Soviet Union, not only on our side of the Iron Curtain but also on theirs. Whether we like it or not, we are rivals with the Soviet Union. If we do not actively compete with Moscow, the Kremlin will rack up gains on its own. As Trotsky once said, "You might not be interested in strategy, but strategy is interested in you."

We must recognize that foreign policy is not directed simply toward short-term interests. It is about shaping the future of the world we live in. We oppose Soviet expansionism not out of a lust for power but because Moscow would destroy our values if it were to prevail. We must therefore adopt a long-term strategy for competing with Moscow.

Our rivalry will focus primarily on the countries of the Third World. In the next century, when it will be ever more costly to engage in overt aggression, economic power and ideological appeal will become decisive. We must prepare ourselves to compete on those terms. But in our rivalry it makes no sense to restrict the competition to the free world. Soviet leaders take the position that what's theirs is theirs and what's ours is negotiable. We should never acquiesce in that unbalanced and dangerous approach.

Whenever the Soviet empire expands, human rights are denied to millions of other people. We should be just as concerned about these people as about those living within the Soviet Union. We can be more effective in preventing the extension of Soviet repression abroad than in reducing its repression at home. But we must also recognize that its external aggression is only an extension of its internal repression. While Soviet foreign policies are more important to our survival than their internal ones, we must not make the mistake of ignoring the latter.

In the short term, our first concern must be Soviet aggression abroad. But we must never forget that until the Soviet Union reduces its repression at home it will continue to export that repression around the world. The Soviet Union is an inherently aggressive power because its totalitarian system cannot survive without expanding. The Soviet system of internal repression is the root cause of its aggressive foreign policy.

We must find ways to compete with the Soviets within their own orbit and within the Soviet Union itself. If we put ourselves on the perpetual defensive and cede the initiative to our adversary, we will lose. No team can win if its defensive players never leave the field. We must adopt an offensive tactic as well.

Those who ask whether Gorbachev is "sincere" in his desire for peace beg the question. He sincerely does not want war. But he just as sincerely wants victory. The Soviets seek victory without war. If we seek peace without victory we are doomed to defeat. Only if we encourage peaceful change within the Soviet bloc can we bring about a genuine reduction in tensions in the American–Soviet conflict. Only then is real peace possible.

Gorbachev wants change in the Soviet Union. We should not, however, conclude from his statements about the Soviet economic plight and the need for reform that he wants to overturn the Soviet system. What he intends to do is make his system run more efficiently. He wants to gain a respite from his external problems to gain breathing space to deal with his internal ones, as his overtures to Western Europe and China show. Our goal is an enduring peace; their goal is a temporary peace—a respite to gain strength for a new offensive toward achieving their goal of victory without war.

In light of Gorbachev's need for some kind of accommodation, how should we react?

The bottom line is simple. We should give Gorbachev what he wants only if he gives us what we want—the elimination of Soviet superiority in first-strike land-based nuclear missiles which confronts the West with an unacceptable threat of war or nuclear blackmail; a reduction in Soviet repression at home as called for by the Helsinki Accords; and a halt to Soviet aggression abroad.

Unfortunately, American policy toward the Soviet Union has swung back and forth between hopes for perfect peace between Washington and Moscow and fears of total war between the nuclear superpowers.

From the start of the Cold War until 1969, the United States policy was containment. It sought to encircle the Soviet Union with a string of alliances and thereby block Soviet expansionism. It was based on the assumption that in time internal forces would prompt Moscow to reform its political system and mend its aggressive ways. It was totally defensive, avoiding any American actions that might provoke the Soviet Union.

That policy succeeded in the short run but failed in the long run. Its hopeful prediction has not come about. Except for NATO, all of the great alliances sponsored by the United States have long since crumbled. As early as the 1950s, Moscow broke out of containment, leapfrogging our alliances to set up a relationship first with Gamal Abdel Nasser in Egypt, then with several nationalist leaders in Africa, and finally with Fidel Castro in Cuba. The Kremlin now has a string of clients and satellites throughout the world, running from Libya on the Mediterranean Sea to Cuba on the Caribbean Sea, to Vietnam on the South China Sea, to South Yemen on the Arabian Sea, and to Ethiopia on the Red Sea. Containment doomed America to constantly responding to Soviet probes at Western weak points. In the 1950s and 1960s, the United States was trapped in a policy of running around the globe putting out brushfire wars as fast as the Soviet Union started them. Since the arsonist always has the strategic initiative, he also has the advantage over the fireman. In the long run, containment was a prescription for defeat.

Starting in 1969, the United States pursued a policy of hard-headed détente. As distinguished from an entente, which is an agreement between powers with common interests, détente is an agreement between powers with different interests. It did not mean that the United States and the Soviet Union agreed on all issues. Instead, it meant that while we disagreed on most issues, we wanted to work out agreements on some and did not want to go to war over any.

Hardheaded détente sought to combine détente with deterrence. A reduction in tensions did not mean a reduction in vigilance. America maintained a strength of arms and a strength of will sufficient to blunt the threat of Soviet expansion and blackmail. The United States was prepared to stop Soviet aggression, direct and indirect, not only with diplomatic pressures but also with military ones. It did not reassure those who were threatening its interests that it would not use force unless attacked. Instead, it stated that the United States would do whatever was necessary to defend its interests and those of its allies.

What was more important, America had the will to back up its words with actions. In 1970, as a result of U.S. pressure, the Soviet Union retreated from its attempt to establish a nuclear-submarine base at Cienfuegos in Cuba and from its effort, through Syria, to topple King Hussein of Jordan. In 1971, during the Indo–Pakistani war, it pulled in the reins on India when New Delhi sought to gobble up Pakistan. In 1972, after the United States bombed and mined Haiphong in response to a massive North Vietnamese offensive against South Vietnam, Moscow still went forward three weeks later with a planned U.S.–Soviet summit meeting. In 1973, after the United States put its forces on worldwide alert during the Arab–Israeli war, Moscow abandoned its threat to send its forces into the Middle East.

For the Soviet leaders, the sharp deterrent edge of hardheaded détente did not make superpower talks worthless, but rather made the Americans worth talking to.

Deterrence was combined with a mixture of prospective rewards for good behavior and penalties for bad behavior that gave the

Soviet Union a positive incentive to keep the peace rather than break it. The United States undertook negotiations with the Soviet Union on a broad range of issues. Some, like arms control, the settlement of World War II debts, and the conclusion of the Berlin accords, were of mutual interest. Others, like the granting of most-favored-nation trading status and the purchase of American grain, were of particular interest to the Soviets.

These negotiations gave the United States a measure of leverage over the Soviet Union. When Moscow threatened U.S. interests, the United States slowed or suspended the talks. Kremlin leaders never failed to get the message. When they relented, the United States proceeded with the talks.

Hardheaded détente was founded on a determination to resist Soviet expansionism while at the same time searching for areas of potential agreement. Détente with deterrence, as practiced from 1969 through 1974, maintained the needed balance that led the Soviet leaders to conclude that limited cooperation was in their interest. The Soviet Union made no territorial gains during the period when the policy of détente with deterrence was vigorously implemented.

After 1975, détente lost the hard edge of military deterrence. When Saigon fell to communist aggression, American will to protect its interests waned, and détente too often degenerated into a naive pursuit of whatever U.S.–Soviet agreements the Kremlin would accept. The positive and negative incentives for Moscow to reach a genuine accommodation with the United States were destroyed. That led the Soviet leaders to believe that they could have their détente and swallow other nations too.

The demise of détente began in the halls of Congress. Hardheaded détente requires the use of both the carrot and the stick. Congress undercut both halves of the policy.

In 1973, Congress passed the Jackson-Vanik amendment that blocked the granting of most-favored-nation trading status to the Soviet Union until its citizens were allowed to emigrate freely. As a result, the most important positive incentive for Soviet restraint was revoked.

Between 1968 and 1975, Congress cut a total of $40 billion from the defense budgets submitted by the White House. In addition,

Congress cut the administration's request for military assistance to South Vietnam by half in 1974 and another third in 1975, and reduced aid to Cambodia even more. Furthermore, by passing the War Powers Act over my veto and resolutions banning the use of American airpower in Vietnam, Congress denied my administration and that of President Ford the power to enforce the Paris peace accords. Meanwhile, the Soviet Union was increasing its military aid to North Vietnam. The communists won in Indochina in 1975 because Congress would not allow the United States to do as much for its allies as the Soviets did for theirs. This pattern was repeated in Angola in 1975.

When Congress refused to grant the Soviet Union most-favored-nation status, it took away the carrot. When it cut the defense budget and hamstrung the President's ability to react to Soviet aggression, it left the United States with a weak stick.

Those actions sent the wrong message to the Kremlin. They in effect telegraphed Moscow that it could pursue its aggressive policies at little or no cost. It was an offer the Soviet Union could not refuse. Kremlin leaders soon embarked on a campaign of foreign adventurism throughout the world.

American leaders failed to learn the right lessons from the U.S. reversals in Southeast Asia and southern Africa. In the late 1970s and early 1980s, American policy toward the Soviet Union swung from one extreme to the other.

At one extreme were the superdoves. In the early years of the Carter administration, they were the dominant influence, even though some of his advisers, like national-security adviser Zbigniew Brzezinski, were definitely not superdoves. The central argument of the superdoves was that the United States should recognize that the only reason for Soviet aggression was their fear of us and their insecurity. This meant that the fault for East–West tensions was ours, not theirs. Superdoves found excuses for every instance of Soviet aggression, from its domination of Eastern Europe to its invasion of Afghanistan, by conjuring up some threat to which each Soviet action was merely a defensive response. The United States, in their view, should seek to reassure the Soviets that America wanted peace, with unilateral steps if necessary. If we set a peaceful example, the superdoves believed, the Soviets would respond in kind.

That view was naive. It did not recognize the Soviets for what they were. We did not have to convince the Soviet leaders that we wanted peace. They knew that. We had pulled out our forces from Europe after World War II. We had not exploited our nuclear monopoly in the immediate postwar years. We never became involved in distant regions except as a response to communist expansion or subversion. Our military deployments and contingency plans in Europe and elsewhere were totally defensive.

President Carter adopted the policy of the superdoves when he came into office. It led to disaster. When he unilaterally cut back on U.S. defense programs, Moscow accelerated its arms buildup, moving from a position of strategic parity in the mid-1970s to one of decisive superiority in land-based ballistic missiles in the late 1970s. When he broke the linkage between progress on arms control and progress on other East–West issues, Moscow stalled talks except on those issues in which it was most interested. When he exercised unilateral restraint in regional crises, Moscow went on the offensive. It expanded its domination in the Arabian Peninsula, in Southwest Asia, in Africa, and in Latin America. That string of reversals culminating in the invasion of Afghanistan led President Carter to move away from the policy advice of the superdoves. He proclaimed the Carter Doctrine of opposing Soviet probes in the Persian Gulf and asked for an increase in the defense budget.

When the superdoves controlled policy, war became more likely, not less. Unilateral U.S. restraint lowers the costs of Soviet adventurism and raises the chances that Kremlin leaders will embark on an aggressive course.

When President Reagan came into office, American policy swung to the opposite extreme. Some of his most influential advisers were superhawks. They called for the total isolation of the Soviet Union. They argued that the Soviets were in deep trouble economically and that the Kremlin was out to do us in by any and all means. They urged the United States to respond in kind. America, in their view, should not only strive for military superiority but also cut Moscow off from all Western loans, credits, and trade.

If we squeezed them enough, the superhawks argued, the faltering Soviet economy would eventually collapse, taking the communist system with it.

That was an appealing view, but an unrealistic one. While it was based on an accurate appraisal of the nature of the Soviet Union, its assumptions about international and domestic American and Soviet political realities were as naive as the superdoves' lack of understanding of the Kremlin's motivations.

The superhawks failed to see that a total financial and trade embargo could not work. The United States could never induce Western Europe and Japan to cooperate in such an action. That lesson was finally learned after the fiasco of the Soviet gas pipeline crisis in 1982, which did more damage to the Western alliance than to the Soviet economy. The fact was that without allied participation, an American embargo was meaningless and counterproductive.

The superhawks overestimated the influence of external pressure on the Soviet system. A totalitarian government does not pack up and go home if external powers press it economically. When squeezed, the Soviet Union can clamp down on domestic consumption. The Soviet Union is not going to collapse despite its enormous weaknesses and problems. As they demonstrated in World War I and World War II, the people of the Soviet Union have a great capacity for sacrifice and suffering. A leader as skillful as Gorbachev will be even more successful than Stalin in mobilizing the people against any effort to bring the Soviet empire to its knees.

The superhawks did not understand how to use economic power in the U.S.–Soviet relationship. While economic incentives do not determine Soviet foreign policy, they can influence it. By attempting to isolate the Soviet Union, the administration minimized its own leverage. On the one hand, it did not reduce the Soviet access to Western goods. Moscow simply turned to other suppliers. On the other hand, it did reduce the American proportion of East–West trade. That meant the superhawks had achieved none of their goals but had minimized whatever leverage America could gain from its economic power.

The superhawks failed to understand basic American and allied

political realities. American policy too often amounted to belligerent rhetoric without strategy. Unless deeds match words, words
become meaningless. American public opinion *hopes* for a quick
resolution of the U.S.–Soviet conflict but does not *expect* one. It
does, however, expect American leaders to try to reduce the risk
of war with the only other nuclear superpower. Without hope for
peace, free people will not make the sacrifice necessary to deter
those who would wage war. Most Americans would categorically
reject the theoretical proposition "Better red than dead." But if
they were ever faced with the stark fact of imminent death, it
becomes a closer question. We must make sure that they do not
have to make that choice. A strategy based on that approach was
both practically and politically unsustainable.

A major problem with the Reagan administration has been that
some of its policies have appeared to be dictated by politics, not
strategy. It repealed President Carter's grain embargo because of
pressure from American farmers. When polls showed that after the
Carter years a majority wanted a strong anti-Soviet policy, it took
the position that both SALT I and SALT II were bad agreements
and that the United States should find ways to derail any serious
efforts to reach new arms-control accords. As the 1984 campaign
drew near, President Reagan dropped the approach of the superhawks and indicated more willingness to negotiate with the Soviets. Some say he did so because the polls showed that his principal
weakness was the peace issue. This may have been true of some
of his political advisers, but I doubt if it was true of the President.
I am confident that the man who said no to a bad deal at Reykjavik
will say no to a bad deal in Moscow.

We should not, however, underestimate the consequences of an
obsession with opinion polls. If Moscow concludes that an administration policy will be affected by the polls it will concentrate on
affecting the polls rather than negotiating seriously. In dealing with
the Soviets, the worst mistake a President can make is to follow
the polls rather than lead them. In the future, Moscow is sure to
use public opinion as a lever against the United States. As negotiations near a conclusion and as crises call for a strong American
response, Moscow will test the willingness of each U.S. administration to buck the polls in protecting American interests.

Since 1976, our policy toward the Soviet Union has been deeply flawed. It has been inconsistent, ambivalent, defensive, and plagued with starts and stops. Whatever else we say about the Soviets' foreign policy, we must concede that it is consistently hard-line. We might not like their policy, but we cannot claim we do not know what it is.

As we look to the future, none of the failed policies of the past is adequate for the eleven remaining years of this century. Containment is outdated. Détente has lost its meaning. For the super-hawks, it is institutionalized surrender. For the superdoves, it is institutionalized brotherhood. The policy of the superdoves fails to understand the nature of Soviet foreign policy. The superhawks do not make this mistake, but their doctrinaire policies are unrealistic and politically unsustainable.

We need a new policy that recognizes the Soviets for what they are but which is designed to deal with them in an effective way. In developing a strategy for dealing with the Soviet Union, we must first take the steps necessary to assure a sound American economy. A strong, productive, growing economy is the indispensable foundation for the role the United States must play in the world. Without a strong economy we cannot have a strong foreign policy. Without a strong economy we will not be able to afford the defense expenditures necessary to deter Soviet aggression. Without a strong economy we will not be able to finance our foreign-assistance program for our friends and allies threatened by aggression. Most important, a strong, free economy can be a powerful example for newly developing countries that are searching for the road to progress with freedom. A protectionist, isolationist, fiscally irresponsible America weakens our ability to lead through the power of our ideas as well as through our military power.

In U.S.–Soviet relations, what America needs is a comprehensive policy that combines deterrence, competition, and negotiation.

We must start by recognizing that we must undertake whatever actions are necessary to ensure the security of the United States and its allies. That must involve keeping up our nuclear deterrent. We will not be able to agree with Moscow on total disarmament. We will not be able to build a perfect defense against nuclear weapons. We should decide today what kinds of strategic forces we need to best deter the Soviet Union in the future. We must also maintain forces sufficient to deter a Soviet attack on our key allies in Europe and the Far East and on our vital interests in the Persian Gulf.

Our task is to deter the Soviet Union not only at the nuclear level but also on the conventional level in Europe and elsewhere. Great as the task may be, we can succeed. As B. H. Liddell Hart wrote of the Soviets, "Their very belief in force makes them more susceptible to the deterrent effect of a formidable opposing force."

Beyond deterrence, the United States must adopt the policies necessary to compete effectively with the Soviet Union across the board on those issues and in those areas in which mutual agreements are not possible. There will eventually be a winner and a loser in the American–Soviet rivalry—and we cannot win if we fail to compete.

Our negotiating strategy must also be founded on an understanding of what the two superpowers can agree about and what we cannot agree about.

We can agree on measures to reduce the likelihood of accidental nuclear war. We can agree on ways to reduce and stabilize the strategic nuclear balance. We can agree on means to prevent the proliferation of nuclear weapons. We can agree on ways to resolve some—but not all—conflicts in contentious regions of the world. We can agree on ways to structure mutually beneficial relations, such as trade and cultural exchange. We should work with the Soviet Union to prevent conflicts in the Third World from erupting into a major war, while not expecting to settle all the differences that divide the two superpowers in those conflicts. All of those issues belong in the negotiating process.

We should make it clear that we are prepared for a genuinely peaceful and cooperative relationship whenever they are. But we should also make it clear that the burden of overcoming Western suspicion rests with the Kremlin, because it arose not from paranoia on our part but from a long history of aggression on their part. We should reward positive change but must keep the reward proportionate to their actions, not to our hopes.

We have never had an adequate comprehensive strategy for deterring Moscow, for competing with Moscow, and for negotiating with Moscow. We must develop one today or risk repeating the failures of the recent past. If we ignore any one of these three key tasks—deterrence, competition, and negotiation—we will do irreparable damage to the chances of forging real peace between the superpowers.

Finally, in our election campaigns and in the halls of Congress we should debate our differences about policy toward the Soviet Union fairly and freely. Let us agree that those who are anti-Soviet are not prowar and that those who are antiwar are not pro-Soviet. The issue is not whether a policy is anticommunist. Anticommunism is not a policy. It is a faith—faith in freedom. Most Americans support the faith, but they disagree about the policy that will best defend or extend the faith. We should debate the policy without questioning the faith of those who disagree with us.

If Tocqueville were alive today, what would he predict for the future of the American–Soviet struggle?

No doubt he would shake his head over the sorry state of American policy vis-à-vis the Soviet Union. He would conclude he was correct in writing that in "foreign affairs democractic governments do appear decidedly inferior to others" and that "a democracy finds it difficult to coordinate the details of a great undertaking and to fix on some plan and carry it through with determination in spite of obstacles." Consequently, he would be forced to acknowledge that Moscow holds a natural advantage in the American–Soviet conflict.

We should not despair at Tocqueville's hypothetical conclusion. We should take it as constructive criticism and turn it to our advantage. His pessimism about the capabilities of a democracy in foreign policy does not tell the whole story. America's inherent economic and political strength is so great that it overcomes our weakness in executing foreign policy. Moscow's inherent economic and political weakness is so great that its strength in executing policy cannot compensate. If the United States sharpens its skills in strategy and foreign policy, it will have overcome the key weakness about which Tocqueville warned.

If we adopt a strategy combining deterrence, competition, and negotiation, we can succeed in building a structure for real peace beyond 1999.

The change we would like to see in the Soviet Union will not come soon, but we should never lose patience in trying to bring it about. Most important, we must put it into historical perspective. Before I went to Moscow in 1959 Harold Macmillan pointed out to me that one hundred years had elapsed between Queen Elizabeth I, who sent her advisers who fell out of favor to the scaffold, and Queen Anne, who sent those she did not like into exile. Only five years elapsed between Stalin, who had his adversaries executed, and Khrushchev, who sent Malenkov out to run a power plant in Siberia.

Gorbachev is in an enviable position. He can become not just the man of the year but the man of the century. He comes on the center stage of history at a time when his decisions as to which way he leads his country will affect the lives of not only his own people but all of the people in the world. Change in the Soviet Union can lead to a safer world or to a more dangerous world. How much, what kind, and how fast change will take place under Gorbachev depends on him *and* on us.

3

HOW TO
DETER MOSCOW

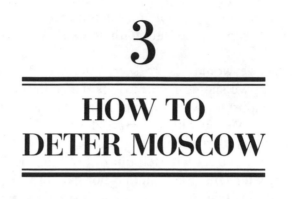

We live in a world with nuclear weapons. Since that fact is not going to change, we must learn to live with the bomb. We must also recognize that achieving our two most important goals, avoiding nuclear war and avoiding defeat without war, depends on the existence of the bomb. We cannot begin to build real peace unless we can deter the Kremlin leaders from engaging in nuclear war or nuclear blackmail. A structure of real peace can only be founded on the bedrock of nuclear deterrence.

Nuclear weapons revolutionized the way the world works. In the age of balance-of-power politics, war was an accepted tactic of statecraft. Armed conflict took place between armies and left civilian populations largely untouched. Not so today. A direct clash between the superpowers would almost certainly escalate to nuclear weapons. Over 400 million people in the United States and the Soviet Union alone would be killed in an all-out exchange. In the nuclear age, war can no longer be used as an instrument of policy by one superpower against the other. It is no longer an exaggeration to say that the next war would be a "war to end all wars," because it would also end civilization as we know it.

Some analysts contend that since firing nuclear weapons risks catastrophic retaliation, no rational leader could ever contemplate their use and that therefore they are useless. That view is wrong.

While the great nuclear arsenals of the superpowers would have no *military* utility in a total war, they continue to have *political* utility in the American–Soviet rivalry: nuclear weapons can still be used to intimidate. What has been termed the unusability of nuclear weapons makes them more usable to the Soviet Union than to the West. As Stalin once said, "Nuclear weapons are things that can be used to frighten people with weak nerves."

Soviet nuclear blackmail, not nuclear war, is the principal danger facing the United States and our allies in the remainder of the twentieth century and into the twenty-first. If we hope to make progress toward real peace in the years before 1999, we must understand the meaning of superiority in the nuclear age and adopt the arms-control and defense policies needed to keep Moscow from acquiring it.

Ironically, the enormous destructive power of nuclear weapons has spawned three contradictory ideas about how to avoid war. Some argue that total disarmament is the only answer to the nuclear dilemma. Others hold that the sole remedy lies in total military superiority. Still others contend that a perfect defense will make nuclear weapons obsolete. All three of these views are deceptive myths. Looking directly at a nuclear explosion would leave a person blind. Contemplating the horrors of an irradiated planet or a world ruled from the Kremlin has apparently left many people intellectually blind.

Those who believe in the myth of peace through disarmament argue that the source of all evil in the world is the arms race and that therefore absolute priority in superpower negotiations should go to arms-control talks. They contend that the United States should not link progress in arms control to progress on other issues. These talks should seek to eliminate nuclear weapons from the face of the earth or at least to reduce massively the current nuclear stockpiles of the superpowers. Total disarmament, in their view, would guarantee peace.

Arms controllers fail to understand the basic fact that since arms are not the cause of war, arms control cannot produce peace. War results not from the existence of arms but from the political differences among nations that lead to the use of arms. An arms race has never caused a war, but aggressive powers with territorial ambitions often have. War becomes most likely not when a defensive power and an offensive power both engage in an arms race, but when a defensive power falls behind and loses the race. A buildup of arms is a symptom, not a cause, of political conflicts. While we should seek to alleviate the symptom, we must not ignore the disease.

A great reduction in the nuclear arsenals will not solve the nuclear dilemma. Since the 1950s, we have reduced the actual explosive power of the U.S. nuclear arsenal by a factor of twenty, but we still have enormous destructive power. Even if the two superpowers were to agree to destroy half of their current nuclear weapons, each side would still have over five thousand strategic warheads, each many times more powerful than the atomic bombs that wiped out Hiroshima and Nagasaki. A war between the superpowers would still bring the end of civilization. As Deng Xiaoping commented to me in 1985, "The United States and the Soviet Union now have the power to destroy the world ten times over. Would the world be any safer if they could destroy it only five times over?"

Those who call for the elimination of nuclear weapons are living in a dream world. People understandably long for the day when the threat of nuclear war will be lifted. Talking as if we could bring this about by an arms-control agreement to get rid of all nuclear weapons may be good politics, but it is bad statesmanship. If men were angels, we could ban the bomb. But they are not. We should not advocate arms-control policies that pretend that they are.

To sign an agreement with the Soviet Union to eliminate nuclear weapons would be a catastrophe. Our defense policy is decided in public; theirs is formed in total secrecy. Moscow could be sure that the United States would keep the agreement, but we would never know whether the Kremlin was breaking it. That would risk disaster. Cheating would give the Kremlin a nuclear monopoly and would imperil our national survival. Even if the Soviet Union did not cheat, banning the bomb is not in our interest. Moscow has overwhelming superiority in conventional forces. The West counters that edge with the threat of nuclear escalation. A world without nuclear weapons would be a world under Soviet domination.

Even if we succeeded in eliminating the bomb, no agreement between the superpowers could abolish the knowledge of how to make the bomb. Nuclear weapons are based on simple principles of physics, and nuclear technology is within the reach of a dozen countries. Both the United States and the Soviet Union could assemble a new nuclear arsenal in a matter of days. A world without the bomb would be a world far more perilous than today's. A crisis between the superpowers would be like a showdown between two gunslingers at high noon: A quicker hand to the draw in assembling new nuclear weapons would lead to total victory. But while a showdown in the Old West might kill one person, a shootout in the nuclear age could kill one hundred million.

Calling for the "elimination of nuclear weapons from the face of the earth" is nothing more than a political applause line. When elevated to the level of a presidential policy, as occurred during both the Carter and Reagan administrations, it has clouded the public debate and diverted our efforts toward unrealistic goals. We must recognize that the "ban the bomb" syndrome has no place in a serious discussion of how to create real peace in the nuclear age.

Regaining total military superiority is another myth of peace in the nuclear age. Those who advocate this view contend that if the United States spends enough money and builds enough missiles it can regain the superiority it enjoyed from 1945 until the late 1960s. To achieve total offensive nuclear superiority, the United States would need to build strategic forces capable of destroying all of the Soviet Union's retaliatory weapons in a first strike. That would require construction of over a thousand new highly accurate land-based missiles. This idea fails the test of basic common sense. Since Congress has in the last eight years cut the MX-missile deployment from 200 to 100 to 50, and finally to 40, no one can seriously argue that it would provide the funds for building 1,000. Also, there is no way that the Soviet Union would acquiesce as the United States moved to gain total superiority. Whatever its economic problems, Moscow would spend the money needed to prevent the United States from attaining that decisive lead. Neither superpower can accept nuclear superiority by the other. The security of one superpower cannot be based on the insecurity of the other.

A call for a perfect defense against ballistic missiles is just an updated version of the myth of perfect peace through total military superiority. A defense to protect the American people from nuclear attack by ballistic missiles would have to be perfect. Even if a defense were to stop 99 percent of enemy warheads, in an all-out war the remaining one percent would represent 100 nuclear bombs, which would inflict cataclysmic casualties on the American people. What is worse, the likelihood that we could build a 99-percent-effective defense is remote. Advocates of a total population defense call for us to create a "space shield." But for now all we can realistically build is a space sieve. Research on a population defense should continue, but we cannot assume that it is the answer to our problem until we know what it will be able to do.

Even a perfect shield against ballistic missiles would not make nuclear weapons obsolete. It could not defend against nuclear bombs carried on long-range bombers. It could not defend against nuclear warheads carried on cruise missiles, which can be launched from any Soviet aircraft, ship, or submarine and which can fly so low that radar cannot detect them. It certainly could not defend against small nuclear devices smuggled into the United States. No one who understands the issue can seriously argue that the United States—whose borders are so porous that thousands of drug smugglers and millions of illegal immigrants cross them with little risk—could deploy a perfect defense against the bomb in the foreseeable future.

While we cannot make nuclear weapons obsolete by a perfect defense, a limited defense of U.S. strategic forces is possible now. It is also desirable. As we think about the role of strategic defense in deterrence, we must always make the distinction between a population defense, which is a dream in the next century, and a defense of U.S. strategic forces, which could be a reality in this century. We should pursue the Strategic Defense Initiative to enhance deterrence, not to substitute for it.

At the Reykjavik summit in 1986, the United States made the mistake of combining the myth of total disarmament and the myth of a perfect defense and calling it a strategy. President Reagan agreed to Gorbachev's proposal that the United States and the Soviet Union eliminate *all* nuclear weapons in ten years. The President also insisted that after ten years each superpower be allowed to deploy a nationwide defense of its population as an insurance against Soviet cheating. What happened at Reykjavik was a classic example of an administration becoming a captive of its own rhetoric.

Our subsequent progress in arms-control negotiations has been in spite of, not because of, the Reykjavik summit. No genuine progress on the central issue of arms control—the strategic balance between the superpowers—will be possible until the mythologists of Reykjavik abandon the twin fantasies of eliminating all nuclear weapons and of making nuclear weapons obsolete.

There are those who contend that, since the United States cannot resurrect its nuclear superiority of the 1950s and 1960s, superiority does not matter in the nuclear age. That view is wrong. While the United States no longer seeks superiority, we must deny superiority to the Soviet Union. The Soviet Union clearly will do whatever is necessary to prevent the United States from acquiring total superiority. It is an open question whether the opposite is true. If there is an arms race between the superpowers, the United States can certainly keep up. The problem is that for the last two decades the Soviet Union has been racing and the United States has not left the starting line.

Those who make the argument that superiority does not matter overlook the fact that the United States and the Soviet Union have foreign policy objectives that are diametrically opposed. Whether a leader in Washington or Moscow wields nuclear superiority would have decisively different consequences for the world.

The United States is a defensive power. It has never been an offensive power. Circumstances, not a conscious plan, made the United States a superpower. If the Soviet Union had not threatened to subordinate Western Europe after World War II, the United States would have retreated into its prewar isolation. If it were possible, most Americans would still like to return to the simpler days when the United States was on the periphery of world events.

The Soviet Union is an offensive power. Its stated goal today is a communist world ruled from Moscow. No one in the nineteen countries dominated by Moscow would deny this. Not even the communists in Beijing—who were close allies with their comrades in Moscow for a decade—dispute this. The Sino–Soviet split occurred because the Kremlin leaders insisted that the Chinese submit to Soviet leadership. This does not imply that Kremlin leaders have the global equivalent of the Schlieffen plan secreted away in a Kremlin vault. Gorbachev does not want war. A world of charred cities and dead bodies is a dubious prize. But he does want to expand Soviet control by means short of war. The threat of nuclear war, implicit and explicit, is an indispensable instrument in this effort.

Whether a defensive or an offensive power has nuclear superiority makes a profound difference. Superiority in the hands of a defensive power is a guarantee of peace; superiority in the hands of an offensive power is a threat to peace. Aggressors embark on war when they believe they hold a significant military edge. To preserve peace, a defensive power must be strong enough to convince potential aggressors that they cannot prevail by resort to arms.

For a quarter century, from the end of World War II to the early 1970s, the United States had nuclear superiority. Western Europe remains free today because American nuclear superiority offset the Kremlin's massive conventional superiority. At its peak in the mid-1950s American superiority served as a powerful deterrent to Soviet adventurism and aggression in other regions. No one in the Kremlin took it lightly when John Foster Dulles explained that the American doctrine of massive retaliation meant the United States would respond to communist expansionism "at a time and place of its own choosing." Kremlin leaders knew that the time would be the twelve hours a B-52 needed to cross the Arctic and that the place would be Moscow.

Nothing could have prevented the gradual erosion of American superiority. But the tendency among nuclear revisionists to downgrade the decisive role of nuclear diplomacy since 1945 contradicts history. American nuclear superiority was the key to the our success in the Korean War in the early 1950s, in the Suez crisis in 1956, in the Berlin crisis in 1959, and in the Cuban missile crisis in 1962.

In the Korean War, America was fighting not only to repel communist aggression on the Korean peninsula but also to protect an unarmed Japan and to discourage Soviet and Chinese expansionism elsewhere in Asia. By 1953, after the Chinese intervention, the war in Korea had bogged down into a stalemate near the 38th parallel. With South Korea rescued, the American people soon tired of the continuing bloodshed and certainly would not consider an escalation in conventional U.S. forces. President Eisenhower also opposed a prolonged ground war in Asia. He therefore instructed John Foster Dulles to inform India's ambassador to the United Nations, Krishna Menon, who had good relations with both Communist China and the Soviet Union, that the President's patience was wearing thin and that he was considering the use of nuclear weapons in Korea. As a result, after a half year with Eisenhower in office, an armistice was signed in July 1953.

In the Suez crisis, Eisenhower faced the threat of a Soviet intervention in the Middle East. After the British and the French intervened militarily to wrest control of the Suez Canal from President Nasser of Egypt, Khrushchev tried unsuccessfully to convince Eisenhower that the two superpowers should jointly deploy forces to compel London and Paris to withdraw. The Soviet leader then threatened to send forces to help Egypt unilaterally and to shoot Soviet missiles at Britain and France as covering fire. Eisenhower instructed the American commander of NATO to deliver our response. In a press conference, General Gruenther, the NATO commander, described what would happen if Khrushchev followed through on his threats: "Moscow would be destroyed as night follows day." Khrushchev backed down.

In the Berlin crisis in 1959, the Soviet Union sought to conclude a separate peace treaty with East Germany, which would have had the effect not only of formalizing Soviet control over the government in East Berlin in violation of wartime Allied agreements, but also of obstructing Western access to West Berlin. In a press conference, Eisenhower seemed to equivocate. He said that we were "certainly not going to fight a ground war in Europe" and that "nuclear war as a general thing looks to me a self-defeating thing for all of us," but he added that we were "never going to back up on our rights and responsibilities" and that he "didn't say that nuclear war is a complete impossibility." Four days later, in congressional testimony, the chief of the U.S. Air Force removed all doubt as to what Eisenhower meant. He declared unequivocally that if we were challenged in Berlin we would use nuclear weapons. As a result, while Khrushchev continued his bluster over the Berlin issue, he did not follow through on his threat to act unilaterally.

In the Cuban missile crisis in 1962, the nuclear diplomacy of President Kennedy, while unspoken, was the key to forcing Khrushchev's hand. When Kennedy discovered that Khrushchev had secretly shipped missiles to Cuba, the President demanded their removal and backed up his words with a naval blockade. When confronted with the U.S. threat to board and search a Soviet freighter, Khrushchev countered by saying that this "would make talk useless," bring into action "the forces of war," and have "irretrievably fatal consequences." Kennedy called Khrushchev's nuclear bluff. Khrushchev backed down, though not before he extracted American promises to remove U.S. missiles from Turkey and not to support anti-Castro forces in Cuba or the United States. While some former Kennedy administration officials today contend that overwhelming American conventional, not nuclear, superiority played the decisive role, it is highly doubtful that our conventional superiority would have been persuasive enough to deter Khrushchev if it were not backed up with massive U.S. nuclear superiority.

In those four cases, the United States prevailed. In each case we had vital interests at stake, we had a margin of nuclear superiority, the President demonstrated unquestionably his will to do whatever was necessary to protect U.S. interests, and, except in Cuba, an American intervention with conventional forces either was impossible or would not have carried the day. Only American nuclear superiority made the difference. In Korea, it ended a war.

In Suez, it kept the Soviets out of the Middle East. In Berlin, it prevented a superpower clash in Central Europe. In Cuba, it prevented Moscow from stationing nuclear forces ninety miles from the United States.

Those who contend that superiority is irrelevant in the nuclear age forget how useful it was when we had it. But a tale of two crises, in Iran in 1945 and Afghanistan in 1979, demonstrates its importance conclusively. In both 1945 and 1979, Moscow had overwhelming superiority in conventional forces, not only in Southwest Asia but also worldwide. In 1945, America had a nuclear monopoly. By 1979, Moscow had attained nuclear parity with the United States and even had acquired a decisive superiority in land-based intercontinental ballistic missiles.

In 1945, at a time when wartime agreements required the withdrawal of Soviet, British, and American forces from Iran, Stalin attempted to carve off two provinces for eventual incorporation into the Soviet empire. He engineered proclamations of independence by the Kurdish People's Republic and the Autonomous Republic of Azerbaidzhan. President Truman, who had learned his lesson very early in trusting the Soviets in Europe, sent Stalin a back-channel message threatening grave consequences if Soviet forces did not leave Iran. Given the American monopoly in nuclear weapons, Stalin had little choice but to comply and did so within months. The United States had no conventional forces to compel Moscow to withdraw, for Washington had already pulled its troops out of Iran and was demobilizing most of its forces from World War II. That meant Stalin could only have been reacting to U.S. nuclear superiority.

In 1979, as the communist government of Afghanistan neared the brink of collapse in the face of an anticommunist insurrection, the Soviet Union rapidly built up its invasion forces on the Soviet–Afghan border. Though slow in recognizing the growing danger, the Carter administration finally warned Moscow that a Soviet intervention in Afghanistan would bring grave consequences. But President Carter had neither the conventional nor the nuclear forces to back up that threat. Kremlin leaders knew that the only immediate options the President could choose were a total nuclear

75

war on the one hand or a set of political and economic measures on the other. Moscow concluded that this choice was no choice and ordered 85,000 troops to invade Afghanistan.

Only one conclusion is possible: When the United States had nuclear superiority, it could deter Soviet expansionism. Once the Soviet Union erased our nuclear advantage, it was free to exploit its own massive superiority in conventional forces. Like Sherlock Holmes's dog that did not bark, the critical clue to understanding the importance of nuclear superiority in the case of Afghanistan was the threat the United States could not make.

The key lesson we must learn is that if superiority was so decisive in our hands it would be no less decisive in Moscow's. But the danger is that for the last twenty years the United States has been slipping toward nuclear inferiority.

Official views on nuclear weapons inside the Kremlin differ strikingly from those inside the Washington beltway. Americans believe that nuclear war is unthinkable. In its two-hundred-year history the United States has lost a total of 650,000 lives in war. Therefore, in the minds of Americans, no rational leader could contemplate starting a war that would kill tens of millions of people.

But the leaders of the Soviet Union, which has lost over 100 million lives in civil war, two world wars, purges, and famines in this century, have a different perspective. Kremlin leaders put an entirely different value on human life. The Soviet government, after all, killed tens of millions of its own citizens just for the sake of creating collective farms. While the Soviet Union has been a victim in war, its government has made victims of millions of its own people. Also, while those who have experienced such great wartime suffering cannot be eager to repeat it, they do know it can be survived. They also know, since it happened once, that it could happen again. That means Kremlin leaders, unlike Americans, think seriously about the unthinkable and plan for it. While the current Soviet propaganda line is that a nuclear war is unthinkable, Moscow intends to take whatever measures will help it prevail if the unthinkable ever occurs.

As a result, after the Cuban missile crisis, superpower strategies totally diverged. Washington made a conscious decision to relinquish its nuclear superiority; Moscow made a conscious decision to acquire it.

If the lesson of Cuba was the importance of nuclear superiority, the Kennedy administration failed to learn it. Secretary of Defense Robert S. McNamara decided that the United States would deploy no more than one thousand land-based missiles. He assumed the Kremlin leaders shared his belief that after a point building nuclear weapons became meaningless. He also expected Moscow to stop further deployments when it drew even with the United States.

The Kremlin leaders thought otherwise. Moscow spared no efforts in its drive for nuclear superiority. After Khrushchev backed down in the 1962 confrontation, a Soviet official, Deputy Foreign Minister Kuznetsov, told American negotiator John J. McCloy, "You Americans will never be able to do this to us again." Moscow has kept its word.

Since 1963, the Soviet Union has deployed eleven new types of long-range ballistic missiles, while the United States has fielded only three new types. Since 1975, Moscow has produced and deployed 840 new long-range missiles; we have deployed 310. The Kremlin has deployed the world's only anti–ballistic-missile defense system around Moscow and a continental antiaircraft defense around the entire perimeter of the Soviet Union. It has spent over $150 billion on strategic defense, including billions of dollars for research and testing of exotic laser and particle-beam weapons. It has constructed an elaborate system of nuclear shelters for protecting its top 175,000 military and political leaders. Meanwhile, the Congress balks at allocating just $5 billion a year for the Strategic Defense Initiative.

Statistics abound in the calculation of the superpower nuclear balance. Only one matters: the ratio of first-strike warheads to first-strike targets. A first-strike warhead is one that is accurate and powerful enough to destroy a target protected against nuclear attack. A first-strike target is a strategic nuclear weapon, like a land-based missile or a wartime communications facility. If a country's first-strike warheads far outnumbered the enemy's first-strike targets, it would have the capability in theory to launch a preemptive attack that would leave the enemy unable to retaliate except by launching inaccurate sea- or air-based weapons against cities. A successful first-strike attack does not mean simply that one side strikes first, hitting both cities and military targets, but that the attack fatallv damages the other side's strategic nuclear forces and communications systems and therefore its ability to respond with precise attacks on military targets or even to retaliate at all.

We face the problem that the Soviet Union's stockpile of first-strike warheads has been rising rapidly. Unlike the United States, the Soviet Union did not stop after reaching the level of 1,006 land-based missiles. It kept production lines rolling at full bore. Its deployments peaked at 1,620. Moscow then turned to replacing old missiles with newer and more accurate ones. As a result, the Soviet Union had 5,240 first-strike warheads in 1985 and will have at least 8,000 in 1995. The fact that the United States has only 1,500 first-strike targets casts the Soviet strategic threat into stark relief.

Moscow's favorable ratio of warheads to targets does not mean that Kremlin leaders are quietly priming their missiles for a first strike. Gorbachev knows that a first strike would be the most complicated technological operation in the history of warfare. Complex weapons never tested under wartime conditions would have to work perfectly, and any error could lead to total disaster. Clausewitz warned that "everything in war is simple but the simplest thing is difficult." Gorbachev understands that. He will be especially cautious of putting too much faith in high technology after the melt-down at Chernobyl and the explosion of Challenger. He will not casually stake the future of his country on a high-tech roll of the dice.

But technology continues to advance. When nuclear weapons were first invented, professional military men ridiculed the idea that they could be delivered by rockets to targets half a world away. Today, both sides have weapons that can reliably destroy even those targets that are specially hardened to withstand nuclear attack. In the future, missiles will become ever more accurate, and the uncertainties of a first-strike attack will diminish.

Although a Soviet first strike remains highly unlikely, Moscow's massive strategic buildup poses three real threats to the United States:

If war were to break out, the Soviet Union now has the capability to destroy 90 percent of U.S. land-based strategic forces in a first strike and have enough warheads left over to take out our cities. A President then would face a stark choice. With 90 percent of his most accurate missiles gone, he would not have enough left to take out the remaining Soviet land-based missiles. He could choose either to attack Soviet cities with less accurate sea-based or airborne weapons, which would in turn lead to an even more devastating reprisal on American cities, or to acquiesce to Soviet war demands. Putting it more bluntly, his options would be surrender or suicide.

If the Soviet Union were to launch an attack with conventional forces on American vital interests—such as the Persian Gulf—we would face a double dilemma. On the one hand, if the United States did not have conventional forces to counter Moscow, a President without nuclear superiority could not force the Soviet Union to back off with a nuclear threat. On the other hand, even if the United States did have significant conventional forces available, as was the case in the Cuban missile crisis in 1962, the Kremlin could engage in nuclear blackmail. It could threaten the United States with its superiority in nuclear weapons and thereby deter an American conventional intervention.

If the strategic imbalance leads our allies to conclude that our nuclear umbrella is riddled with holes, the West Europeans and the Japanese might decide to seek a separate accommodation with Moscow. If our allies do not believe in our nuclear-security guarantees, our alliances would soon dissolve. While we would have avoided nuclear war, we would have been defeated without war.

To achieve real peace, we must be able to deter Moscow. But our deterrent is imperiled. We face a fundamental problem: A threat to commit mutual suicide is not credible, and a threat which is not credible will not deter.

The most popular concept among foreign-policy experts is that the United States does not need to enhance deterrence and should base its strategy on the doctrine of mutual assured destruction. They begin with the premise that superiority is impossible in the nuclear age. They then argue that since both superpowers have thousands of nuclear weapons, neither could destroy all of the other's strategic forces in a first strike. That means that even after a first strike the victim could inflict unacceptable damage on the aggressor in a retaliatory attack. Even a loser in nuclear war could decimate the winner. Advocates of mutual assured destruction also argue that a strategic defense, even if possible, is undesirable because it would reduce the ability of one side to retaliate against the other.

The theory of mutual assured destruction is based on a false premise. It assumes that the United States and the Soviet Union are equal threats to peace and that *both* must be deterred from launching a nuclear attack. And while a persuasive case can be made for the theory in the abstract, a fatal flaw undercuts it: For the strategy to work, it must be *mutual*. Not only the United States but particularly the Soviet Union needs to subscribe to its tenets. If only one side adheres to the strategy, it assures not mutual destruction but unilateral superiority for the other side. The problem is that the Kremlin leaders have never signed on. If the United States had stood pat with its strategic bomber force of the 1950s, Moscow would have a total first-strike capability today. If we stand pat with our current strategic forces, the danger is that the Kremlin might be able to achieve a first-strike capability in the decades ahead.

As President, I did not subscribe to the doctrine of mutual assured destruction—and I knew Moscow did not either. I won a hard-fought struggle to get congressional approval for an ABM system to defend our strategic forces. When I signed the ABM Treaty, I was not returning to a strategy based on mutual assured destruction. I traded limitations on defensive systems for a cap on the offensive threat. Moreover, in my administration's annual reports on the state of the world, I explicitly moved American policy away from mutual assured destruction, a shift upon which all subsequent administrations built.

Moscow still believes in military superiority. Its leaders accept the *fact* of mutual assured destruction but not the theory. If our strategic forces can survive a first strike, the Kremlin leaders will accept American deterrence as a fact of life. But facts change.

Moscow will not view American deterrence as a *permanent* reality and will do everything within its power to change it. When Secretary McNamara unilaterally limited the size of American nuclear forces, Kremlin leaders pushed ahead with theirs. When President Carter canceled or slowed down American strategic programs, Kremlin leaders accelerated theirs. Moscow viewed American restraint as an opportunity to gain an advantage.

Advocates of mutual assured destruction also fail to realize that advances in the accuracy of intercontinental ballistic missiles will create the possibility of a surgical first strike, perhaps as early as the turn of the century. Strategic weapons used to be crude weapons which were so inaccurate that they could only hit a target the size of a city. That is no longer the case. Both sides today have missiles accurate enough to land a warhead on a target the size of Yankee Stadium on the other side of the world. Technological advances will soon make it possible to target the opposing team's dugout. That means it will become increasingly feasible for one side to destroy the other's retaliatory forces. A first strike that is now possible only in theory might become possible in practice.

A strategy of mutual assured destruction would leave the United States with no viable options if deterrence were to fail. If war were to break out, an American President would be left with the single option of ordering the mass destruction of enemy civilians, in the face of the certainty that it would be followed by the mass slaughter of Americans. That is unacceptable and not credible. Even worse, any policy based solely on the threat to kill millions of civilians is profoundly immoral, especially if an effective alternative exists.

Our ability to launch an all-out retaliation might deter an all-out attack. But deterrence must also cover limited attacks. If the United States cannot meet a limited challenge with a limited response, an American response becomes less likely and an American threat to retaliate less credible. That, in turn, makes the Soviet challenge more likely. It is no longer tenable to base our deterrence solely on a threat of mutual suicide.

Those who advocate mutual assured destruction fail to see that the strategy does not fit the times. Negating the U.S. nuclear deterrent still stands as a principal Soviet objective. Moscow's strategic buildup has already made American land-based missiles and bombers vulnerable to a first strike. Advances in technology could in the coming decades create the possibility of a successful surgical attack against all of our nuclear forces that would leave the United States without the ability to retaliate. That weakness would not only prompt greater Soviet aggression below the nuclear level but also reduce the American willingness to run risks needed to turn back Soviet challenges.

What does the United States need to do to maintain deterrence in the years beyond 1999? We must have strategic forces that achieve three essential purposes:

No first-strike vulnerability. At a minimum, the United States must have strategic counterforce weapons that the Soviet Union cannot destroy in a first strike. Without retaliatory forces that can survive an attack and that can be used against military targets in the Soviet Union, deterrence evaporates. This capability is doubly important for the United States because Soviet superiority in conventional weapons forces us to rely much more heavily on the threat of nuclear retaliation. We must not allow the strategic balance to deteriorate further and must take measures to reduce the current vulnerability of our land-based forces.

Equivalent capabilities. Our strategic forces must match Moscow's in terms of capabilities for conflicts other than all-out war. This is most important in a superpower crisis. If the Soviet Union were able to threaten to undertake a limited nuclear strike knowing that the United States did not have an equivalent capability, the Kremlin would have a decisive advantage. It could exploit its greater flexibility and its nuclear superiority through intimidation and nuclear blackmail.

Extended deterrence. We must have nuclear forces that will extend our deterrence to prevent Soviet aggression against key U.S. allies and friends. We have maintained our extended deterrence for forty years through the threat to attack the Soviet Union with nuclear weapons if Moscow moved against our allies. That worked when the United States had nuclear superiority. Kremlin leaders are still faced with the problem that the United States *might* escalate to the nuclear level to stop Soviet aggression. But we must recognize that, since the Soviets have achieved a margin of nuclear superiority over the United States, the threat has lost much of its credibility.

Through its continuing strategic buildup, the Kremlin threatens our ability to achieve all these goals. But we can counteract Moscow's efforts in three ways. We can build up our offensive strategic forces, especially our land-based missiles. We can deploy a strategic defense. We can negotiate an arms-control agreement with Moscow that creates a stable and enduring balance of power. Our objective must be to undercut the military value of Soviet first-strike forces. No one of these approaches would be adequate by itself. But action on all three fronts could provide the deterrence we need.

Alone, a buildup of our offensive forces in fixed silos would be counterproductive. It would put us on a hopeless treadmill. An offensive arms race favors an offensive power. Increasing the number of warheads is easier than increasing the number of missiles, because each missile can carry several warheads. The largest Soviet land-based missile has ten warheads, but could be equipped to carry as many as thirty. Even if three Soviet warheads are needed to destroy one American missile, the United States would, at best, need to deploy three times as many missiles as the Soviet Union to reduce the vulnerability of American forces.

An alternative would be to develop mobile land-based missiles, like the proposed Midgetman. I strongly endorsed this concept when it was recommended by the Scowcroft Commission. I still favor it, but it now faces two major problems. First, it is unlikely that the American public and Congress will agree to allow nuclear missiles to roam over the wide areas a mobile system needs to be invulnerable. Federal-government reserves might not be large enough to make the missiles invulnerable, and deploying these weapons on the U.S. railroad or interstate highway system would prompt great opposition. Second, if the Soviet Union continues to develop its strategic defense capabilities, the United States needs to develop multi-warhead, not single-warhead, missiles. If we commit a large proportion of our resources for strategic weapons to a fleet of single-warhead missiles, even a moderately effective

Soviet strategic defense could seriously cut down the effectiveness of an American retaliatory strike. Small, mobile missiles should be a significant part of our deterrent force, but unless these problems are solved they cannot play as big a role as we hoped when the Scowcroft Commission first made its report.

We can and should build strategic weapons capable of hitting hard targets so that we can put at risk a significant portion of the Soviet arsenal. We have done so with the deployment of the first group of MX missiles and with the future deployment of the new Trident II missiles. But that is inadequate. The United States plans to build only forty MX missiles and has deployed them in fixed silos vulnerable to a Soviet first strike. The new Trident II is invulnerable at sea, but communication with submerged submarines is difficult at best. The fact is that we still need to build a more substantial land-based force that can survive a Soviet first strike.

A push to deploy a strategic defense to protect the American population, as advocated by many of the proponents of the Strategic Defense Initiative, would not solve our strategic problems. The idea of building a defense that would render nuclear weapons obsolete is a myth. It would have to be perfect to work, and not even the most optimistic advocates of the idea believe it would be technologically feasible until well into the next century.

But it is possible to build a limited defense that makes our strategic weapons less vulnerable and that could protect the country against an accidental launch of a few weapons or against a small attack by a nonsuperpower. That kind of defense does not need to be perfect. Even if it were only 50 percent effective, it would so complicate the calculations for executing a Soviet first strike that no Soviet leader could ever be confident of success. Under the best of circumstances, a first strike would be a dicey gamble. With a limited U.S. strategic defense, Moscow's odds would become even longer. The threat of a Soviet first strike would lose its credibility, and the Kremlin therefore could not use it to blackmail the United States in a superpower crisis.

A limited strategic defense is the key to solving the critical problem of the vulnerability of U.S. land-based forces to a Soviet first strike. President Reagan's Strategic Defense Initiative not only has been useful in forcing the Soviets to negotiate seriously but also has created the possibility of deploying a limited defense. Though the call for a perfect defense is unrealistic, he deserves high praise for pressing forward with SDI. We should direct the bulk of research and development funds in the Strategic Defense Initiative toward designing a limited defense of our strategic forces, rather than toward the unrealistic hope of a nationwide population defense. An attempt to build a total defense would give us only the chimeral protection of an electronic Maginot Line. We should not pursue the unattainable at the expense of the achievable.

A limited defense would remedy the problems with both the MX and the Midgetman missiles. Putting an MX missile in a fixed silo does not improve the survivability of our forces—but with a limited defense it would greatly improve our security. Deploying Midgetman missiles on federal reserves might leave them vulnerable to a saturation attack—but with a limited defense they would improve our security and improve strategic stability. We should therefore move forward with *both* a modernization of our offensive forces and a deployment of defensive forces.

We should not bog ourselves down in a legalistic argument about what kind of research, testing, and deployment the ABM Treaty of 1972 permits. I signed the treaty because it served American security interests in the strategic setting of the early 1970s. It was an important achievement and has lasted longer than any other major arms-control pact. To engage in a debate over whether the treaty should be broadly or narrowly interpreted is neither useful nor necessary. When the United States enters into a treaty, we should abide by its terms and not try to squirm out of them by legalistic maneuvering. The treaty specifically provides that either side can opt out on six months' notice if it finds that events have "jeopardized its supreme interests." We should determine what we need to do to assure our security. If that requires a limited strategic defense, we should find out what kind of a defense is feasible and then take the steps to develop and deploy it. If that requires the renegotiation of provisions of the ABM Treaty, we should put our demands on the superpower agenda. If Moscow refuses to negotiate, we should then invoke our rights under the treaty to suspend its provisions after a six-month notice.

We should declare that we intend to deploy a limited defense as early as technological advances permit. We should indicate that we prefer to do so through a negotiated timetable but that we will go forward alone if talks fail to produce a timely agreement. The issue of early deployment should be negotiated, but negotiations should not stop us from deploying a system as soon as possible.

While a limited strategic defense would solve some of our problems, it would not solve all our problems. We need to complement it with additional offensive forces. We should not seek a first-strike capability. That would turn out to be politically impossible because the American people would not support it and technologically impossible because the Soviet Union would adopt countermeasures, like its own strategic defense, to render our effort futile. But we still need to deploy new strategic weapons which would, if war broke out, provide an American President with more options than mutual suicide and surrender.

Arms control alone cannot solve our strategic problems, but it can play a major role in doing so. Those who oversell arms control do their cause great damage. While Americans tend to view arms control as an end in itself, the Soviets consider arms control a means to an end. Moscow is right. Arms control alone cannot produce peace or ensure our security. It is only one part of our overall defense policy. It is not an end in itself but a means to maintain our security. To improve our security and mutual stability, defense and arms-control policies must go forward in a coordinated fashion. Each can reinforce the other. It is ironic that so many arms-control proponents oppose SDI, because if President Reagan had not proposed SDI the Soviets would not be negotiating arms control.

A properly negotiated arms-control agreement can be constructive in three ways. First, it can help to produce the strategic stability which could reduce the chances of a crisis escalating into a war. Strategic instability results when either side or both sides deploy weapons that create the potential for a first strike. This in turn creates an incentive to use these weapons in a crisis in order to gain a decisive advantage. The danger is greatest if these weapons themselves are vulnerable to a first strike because in a crisis a leader would be tempted to use his arsenal before he loses it. An agreement that prevents either side from attaining a first-strike

86

capability would enhance strategic stability and reduce the likelihood of war.

Second, an arms-control agreement limiting offensive weapons can increase the effectiveness of a limited strategic defense. Without such an agreement, the Soviets could try to increase their offensive forces in order to overwhelm our defense. Since our defense would seek only to achieve the limited aim of protecting our strategic forces, a Soviet buildup would almost certainly fail to restore its present advantage. But the fact remains that an arms-control agreement capping the level of offensive forces enhances the prospects for an effective strategic defense by limiting the threat.

Third, a serious effort to negotiate on arms control is a political imperative. Western leaders will not be able to mobilize public support for defense spending without a credible arms-control policy. We should not argue about whether or not to negotiate. Those who initially refuse to negotiate, like the superhawks in the Reagan administration, will sooner or later be forced to negotiate by Congress or public opinion. Our focus should be on how to negotiate in a way that serves our interests.

As the United States and the Soviet Union look toward a future strategic-arms-control treaty, we must ensure that it meets four conditions:

Equality. It must be based on equality. Equality in numbers is important, but numbers alone should not be the sole measure of equality. We should negotiate the number and size of missiles and the number of warheads so that each side has the same military capability. In this respect, the capability of each side to destroy hardened targets of the other is the most crucial measure. It is vitally important therefore that the sublimits—which are limits on specific types of weapons included under the overall limit—be designed to provide qualitative equality.

Warhead-to-target ratio. It must not allow either superpower to have a credible first-strike capability. It must reduce the ratio of Soviet first-strike warheads to American first-strike targets below the present level. If an agreement allowed an offensive power like the Soviet Union to maintain or increase its present advantage in first-strike weapons, it would actually increase the danger of war and of defeat without war.

Modernization. It must have ironclad provisions against upgrading old missiles into first-strike missiles. Both SALT I and SALT II tried to deal with modernization but failed. The Soviet Union not only violated the spirit of the agreements by exploiting ambiguities in their language to modernize their weapons but also violated the letter of the treaties in deploying more new systems than allowed. If we are to sign an enduring strategic-arms-control agreement, we must treat modernization as a central issue, not as a sideshow.

Verification. It must provide means for each side to verify the compliance of the other. We have relied in the past on satellite reconnaissance and other national technical means of verification. But advances in military technology now require that we settle for nothing less than on-site inspection. The Soviets have always rejected such provisions in the past, but have agreed in the INF Treaty to compromise on this point. This is a good start, but it is not enough for START. We must insist that the provisions for on-site inspection are more than cosmetic. We must make the Soviets understand that two thirds of the Senate will vote for ratification only if we have absolute confidence that both sides will carry out the agreement.

In addition to pursuing these goals, our arms-control policy cannot ignore Soviet violations of past arms-control agreements. These must not be swept quietly under the rug in the rush toward new accords but should be met with a measured response. Soviet arms-control violations should not lead us to throw out the old agreements and quit negotiating. Instead, we should put the issue of Soviet compliance high on the superpower agenda. If Moscow fails to address our concerns to our satisfaction, we must take the position, as the Reagan administration has, that Soviet arms-control violations will be met with proportional American responses.

Unilateral compliance is unilateral disarmament. We sign agreements for the sake of our security, and we must not abide by agreements when Soviet violations threaten our security. Unilateral compliance will win us not goodwill but contempt from the Kremlin leaders.

We need a comprehensive compromise on the strategic issues. We need such a deal, not only between the United States and the Soviet Union, but also between the administration and the Congress. For the first time in over a decade, the pieces are in place for just such a comprehensive accommodation.

A domestic compromise should be easier to achieve than a good international compromise. The Congress today has as much power to determine American defense policy as the President. The administration must recognize this basic political reality. If it does not, the House and the Senate will use their budgetary powers to wrest control away from the executive. If it does, the possibility exists for a coherent strategic policy to emerge.

This is not to say that the administration should simply follow the prevailing political winds in Congress. The President alone can provide leadership—but he cannot act alone. He must decide what we need to do to maintain our security and must seek congressional approval for his program. He will never prevail unless he takes the opinions of responsible congressional figures into account. There is a responsible majority in Congress, and the President must be responsive to its concerns.

The reason the administration has had so much difficulty in winning congressional approval for its strategic programs has been its failure to make its case in terms of strategic stability. That is what preoccupies responsible members of Congress. From this point of view, the administration's decision to deploy the MX missile in silos vulnerable to a Soviet first strike makes no sense. If the problem is the vulnerability of land-based missiles, the answer is not to stick missiles into fixed holes in the ground. These silos simply become tempting targets for a Soviet first strike.

Congress will continue to cut funding for the Strategic Defense Initiative as long as the administration remains obsessed with building a total defense of the American population. Requests for billions of dollars to develop a "space shield" will not survive because Congress knows that the goal of a leakproof defense, while politically popular, is technologically and strategically unrealistic.

Responsible members of Congress are further turned off by the administration's negotiating position on strategic defense. Those who want to trade away the entire Strategic Defense Initiative are a vocal minority. Those who argue that negotiations on limiting strategic defense should be linked with negotiations for offensive reductions represent a consensus around which a coherent strategic program can be built.

If the administration wants continued offensive modernization and initial defensive deployments, it must change its strategy in Congress. It should adopt a two-part program. First, it should ask for additional MX missiles that would be based in fixed silos but that would be deployed in tandem with a limited strategic defense. It should also ask for the deployment of some mobile, single-warhead missiles, though not as many as originally envisioned. With fewer of these mobile missiles and with a limited strategic defense, the area in which they would need to roam would shrink to a feasible size. At the same time, the number of highly accurate warheads on these missiles should be held below the level that would represent a first-strike threat to the Soviet Union, and the strategic defense would be designed to make a Soviet first-strike impossible. Since the defense need not be perfect, the combination could be deployed in the mid- to late 1990s.

Second, it should announce a new negotiating strategy with Moscow. The approach of the Reagan administration has been flawed on two counts. On the one hand, its intransigent and unrealistic pursuit of a defense of the American population united a majority in Congress against the administration. On the other hand, some administration officials have shown a willingness to negotiate with the Soviets to restrict strategic defense testing in a way which would in effect gut the chances of deploying a limited defense of our strategic forces. As a result, it has thinned the ranks of supporters who want to deploy a strategic defense and has aided and abetted its opponents who want stop the SDI dead in its tracks. If this President agrees to testing limits that strangle the

SDI, no future President will be able to refuse an extension of those limits.

A more flexible position that continues research for a population defense and retains the right to test and deploy a limited defense of increasingly vulnerable U.S. strategic forces would attract majority support.

That would create the basis for a strong negotiating position with Moscow. With Congress supporting the President, the Kremlin leaders would know that they could no longer count on the Senate and the House to undercut the administration's position. They would also know that if they do not come to terms with our negotiators, the United States has set itself on a course to solve its strategic problems on its own. We would then have the leverage needed to strike a deal.

The lines of a sound strategic-arms-control agreement are clear. What worries the leaders of the Soviet Union is the American Strategic Defense Initiative. What worries the American leaders is the growing capability of the Soviet Union to destroy our strategic forces with the largest Soviet land-based missiles. A trade-off between the two would be mutually beneficial.

We must be extremely careful about the kind of deal we accept. On the issue of strategic defense, we must take a tough but rational stance: Our research is not negotiable. Our testing is not negotiable. Our development of specific weapons systems is not negotiable. Our option to deploy is not negotiable. The only thing that should be negotiable is the *extent* of our deployment. We should make it clear to Gorbachev that the extent of our deployment will be determined by the extent of the threat posed by highly accurate missiles capable of use in a first strike. We should stake out that position and never retreat from it.

We should keep the card of strategic defense in our hand and move forward vigorously in developing a limited defense, not only to create negotiating leverage but also to deploy if negotiations fail. We should lay it out cold turkey to the Kremlin: The precondition for any deal is the link between offense and defense. We will link the number of our defensive systems we deploy to the number of highly threatening offensive systems they deploy. If they want to limit our defense, they can do so by reducing their offensive threat. If they add to their offensive arsenal, we will counter with greater defensive deployments.

In the communiqué issued after the summit in Washington in December 1987, the broad lines of the START agreement being negotiated by the Reagan administration emerged. It has sought an agreement to cut the strategic forces by 50 percent. Both sides would reduce their arsenals to 1,600 launchers, such as bombers and missile silos, and to 6,000 warheads; and only 4,900 warheads would be permitted on ballistic missiles. While such a radical reduction may be politically appealing, it requires close scrutiny. We must keep in mind that what is at stake is nothing less than the West's survival.

Before we look at the numbers, we need to understand what security problems we face on the strategic level and what makes Gorbachev seek an agreement along these lines. Our problem is the Soviet advantage in so-called counterforce warheads—the weapons that are powerful and accurate enough to destroy even the missile silos and communication systems that are hardened to survive a nuclear attack. For an arms-control agreement to serve our interests and the interests of real peace, it must address that Soviet advantage in counterforce weapons.

Gorbachev's motives are traditional Soviet motives. Soviet arms-control negotiators have consistently sought to limit developments in American weapons technology and to preserve or increase Soviet advantages in weapons deployments. In that respect, Gorbachev's proposals are old formulas in new rhetoric.

We must first ask whether the terms of the agreement kill the chances for strategic defense while preserving the Soviet advantage in highly accurate offensive weapons. While he hedged somewhat during the Washington summit, Gorbachev has consistently sought to get the Reagan administration to abandon the Strategic Defense Initiative as part of a deal to cut strategic forces by 50 percent. Gorbachev's top preference has been an explicit ban on new defensive systems. His second preference would be for a moratorium on certain kinds of SDI testing or a seven- to ten-year extension of the ABM Treaty. He might be confident that either would induce Congress to gut the SDI program, because deployment would become such a distant prospect. Moreover, he might be confident that the Soviet Union could exert decisive political pressure on any future administration to extend the testing moratorium or to remain bound by the ABM Treaty, particularly because he would assume that no future President would be as enthusiastic a supporter of the SDI as Ronald Reagan.

It would be a disaster for U.S. security if Gorbachev succeeds in undercutting the SDI—either through a direct U.S. concession or through an agreement which induces Congress to starve the program. Only if Gorbachev agrees to dismantle the threat posed by his highly accurate land-based missiles will U.S. concessions on strategic defense be justified. Without a landmark concession of this kind by Moscow, the United States must stand its ground. If the United States makes concessions on research, testing, and development or trades away the option to deploy a strategic defense at all, the START agreement will actually diminish American security.

What if Gorbachev backed off his demands on SDI? What if he delinked the talks on offensive and defensive weapons and simply agreed to cut strategic forces by 50 percent? That would not necessarily be cause for celebration. If Gorbachev were to break the linkage, we would first have to look closely at why he did so.

We know Gorbachev has an advantage in highly accurate counterforce missiles—an advantage in what he would call the correlation of forces. Gorbachev is a different kind of Soviet leader. But no Soviet leader can survive if he unilaterally gives up an advantage in the correlation of forces without getting something in return. Specifically, he cannot go back to his military leaders with a strategic-arms-control agreement that fails to stop the SDI yet also gives up Moscow's present advantage in offensive land-based weapons. Thus, we must remain highly suspicious if the Soviets accept a formula for major cuts in offensive forces without any linkage to limits on strategic defense. If Gorbachev is happy with those terms, we should be wary of them.

In order to evaluate whether a 50 percent reduction in offensive forces helps or hurts our security, we must examine what impact it will have on the Soviet offensive threat to our strategic forces. We need to answer one simple question: Will the agreement for a 50 percent cut diminish or increase the Soviet capability to launch a successful first strike against U.S. strategic forces? So far, few have paid attention to the consequences such a reduction would have on the strategic balance. Too many pundits and politicians assume that since nuclear weapons are bad, any cut is good. What matters here is the fine print, the sublimits that prescribe how many and what kinds of warheads can be deployed on land, on submarines, or on bombers. Alone, a sublimit of 4,900 warheads on ballistic missiles would increase, not decrease, the vulnerability of American strategic forces.

Under this kind of agreement, Moscow would retain a land-based force composed almost entirely of missiles accurate enough to be used in a first strike. It would be a mix of SS-18s, SS-25s, and SS-24s. At the same time, the cuts would reduce the number of targets in the United States that would have to be destroyed for a first strike to succeed. In addition, the agreement would restrict the deployment of our most capable and survivable forces, the fleet of Trident II submarines, to about ten boats. As a result, these could well become vulnerable. Half will always be in port, and the other half will be tracked by over 270 Soviet attack submarines.

If we agree to these terms for a 50 percent cut, we would see the ratio of Soviet first-strike warheads to U.S. first-strike targets become drastically worse. Thus, the bottom line is that current terms of the emerging START agreement are not in the interest of the United States or in the interest of real peace. Our national security would be hurt, not helped, if we go forward with such a fatally flawed accord.

While the 50 percent cut under negotiation is unacceptable, we should not walk away from the table. What we should do is negotiate in the areas in which our interests are threatened and negotiate for agreements that increase mutual security and strategic stability.

First, we must put conventional-arms control front and center on the agenda. We should not go forward on talks for large-scale reductions in strategic forces without making progress in negotiations on the conventional level. If we fail to establish linkage between the two negotiations, we will be accepting the Soviet agenda —and we will be playing right into Moscow's hands.

Second, we must keep open the option—and maintain a viable program—to deploy strategic defenses as soon as possible. As long as Moscow has an advantage in counterforce weapons, we must make clear to Gorbachev our determination to deploy strategic defenses—and we should immediately take the symbolic step of beginning the construction of the one ABM base permitted under the 1972 treaty, something Moscow has already done.

Third, we should redirect the START talks. We should propose a strict limit on the number of strategic warheads capable of destroying hardened military targets in a first strike. Both superpowers would be allowed to retain equal numbers of counterforce warheads. But the level of these most threatening weapons would be scaled back dramatically. This limitation should involve a 75 percent cut from the present level of such Soviet weapons as the SS-18, the SS-24 and the SS-25. It would also require reductions in planned deployments of comparable U.S. weapons, like the MX and Trident II D-5 missiles. In conjunction with such an agreement, the United States should agree to limits on the extent of the deployment of a space-based defense system against ballistic missiles. We should deploy only enough defensive weapons to counter the threat of the Soviet Union's decreased offensive force.

An agreement along these lines would create both quantitative and qualitative equality between our forces. Even more important, these terms would reduce the ratio of first-strike warheads to first-strike targets for both sides, thereby improving mutual security and bolstering strategic stability. The bottom line is that under such an agreement we would have true strategic stability. Neither side would have a first-strike capability. Both would have a retaliatory, second-strike capability against the other side's strategic forces.

In recent months, some analysts have claimed that under Gorbachev the Soviet Union has undergone a revolution in strategic thinking. Soviet strategists, in this view, have finally accepted the Western concepts of "strategic sufficiency" and "strategic stability." Since there have been no changes in Soviet military programs or arms-control strategy, a dose of skepticism is in order. But we should put this so-called new thinking to the test. We should put forward a proposal, like the one above, designed to enhance mutual security by cutting to an equal and stable level the weapons systems accurate and powerful enough for use in a first-strike attack.

We must always keep in mind that, with a total of more than twenty thousand strategic warheads in the superpower arsenals, the relative numbers of nuclear weapons on each side do not matter as much as the relative vulnerability of each to a first strike by the other. Vulnerability, not arithmetic, must guide our arms control negotiating strategy. After all, if we haphazardly subtract from the number of weapons, we could add to our vulnerability, thereby jeopardizing our security. If we wish the START talks to mark a turning point in the U.S.–Soviet competition, we must redirect them toward the objective of limiting the counterforce weapons which pose the greatest threat to security and stability.

Fourth, any cut in strategic forces also requires ironclad verification. Those who have argued that the INF agreement has solved the thorniest problems of verification are wrong. The agreement broke new ground by permitting limited on-site inspection. That was a positive development. But no one would dispute that, given the small size and the mobility of the SS-20 missile, a determined Soviet effort to cheat would evade detection. In addition, the provision for on-site inspection lasts for only thirteen years. After that, the United States is on its own. While the verfication provisions in the INF agreement are better than those in any previous arms-control accord, they will not be an adequate model for a START agreement.

Verification for a START treaty will be far more difficult—and far more important—than verification for the INF agreement. Eliminating a whole class of weapons can be verified much more easily than reducing various classes of weapons, with some based at sea or under it, others on long-range bombers, and still others in fixed silos or on mobile launchers on land. No one in the American government has yet come to grips with the complexity of this task. We must not rush into a START agreement until the problems involved have been painstakingly considered. At the same time, we must remember that verification is *a* central issue, but not *the* central issue. The fact that a bad agreement can be verified does not make it a good agreement.

We must recognize that it would be suicidal to enter a START treaty with slipshod verification provisions. Cheating on the INF accord would provide a significant but marginal edge, but cheating on a START treaty—especially after deep reductions in strategic forces—could produce a profound shift in the balance of power. This potential payoff would create a tremendous incentive to cheat. We would be certain to keep our end of the bargain, but would Moscow? Kremlin leaders have never been noted for resisting such temptations in the past—so we must not dangle such tantalizing opportunities before them in the future.

If we are to go forward with a START agreement during the Reagan administration, all of these issues must be addressed. We must link progress on START to progress in conventional-arms-control talks. We must not undermine the possibility of deploying in the near term a limited strategic defense to protect our strategic forces. We must not reduce offensive strategic forces in a way that increases our vulnerability to a first strike. We must never sign an agreement on the central issue of the U.S.–Soviet strategic balance unless we can guarantee verification. If a START agreement fails on any of these points, we are better off without it.

We must recognize that the only way we can get a good deal out of Moscow is to demonstrate to Gorbachev that the Soviet Union would be worse off without a deal. We should make it clear to his negotiators that we intend to deploy whatever defenses are necessary to negate Moscow's current advantage in first-strike weapons. He will then have the choice of accepting a comprehensive compromise that serves both our interests or pouring good money after bad in seeking to restore his offensive superiority.

If Gorbachev then signs an agreement that preserves a stable balance of forces, arms-control talks will have achieved their purpose. If not, America will still have the strategic forces needed to deter Moscow.

4

HOW TO COMPETE
WITH MOSCOW

If we succeed in deterring the Kremlin, we can avoid a nuclear war. But if we fail to compete with Moscow, we will be defeated without war. Competition is at the center of the American–Soviet relationship and will determine who wins the superpower struggle. We cannot afford a policy based on ad-hoc responses to Soviet thrusts. That is a prescription for defeat. Stopgap measures are no match for the calculated, persistent expansionism of the Kremlin. We not only must develop the capability to engage the Kremlin's tactics on their terms, but also must adopt a long-range strategy to compete with Moscow on ours.

Kremlin leaders are already expert at waging this battle by all means short of nuclear war. Americans are not. As a nation, we only reluctantly recognized the danger posed by Soviet expansionism after World War II. We put our trust in Stalin at the Yalta Conference, only to lose Eastern Europe. We pulled our forces out of Western Europe, only to reintroduce them when Moscow threatened to dominate the continent. We withdrew our troops from the Asian mainland, only to send them back when Soviet-supported North Korean armies invaded the south. Diplomatic treachery, military intimidation, and aggression by proxy are standard operating procedures for the Kremlin leaders.

We tried a strategy of containment which sought to ring the

Soviet bloc with a string of alliances. It failed when the Soviet Union broke out of containment and when the chain of alliances broke down. We tried a strategy of détente which sought to mitigate conflict where possible but which recognized the need to engage in active competition where compromise was impossible. It failed when some American leaders assumed that an end to the open hostility of the Cold War meant an end to superpower conflict in general. The Soviet Union took advantage of this naiveté to embark on a global drive for imperial conquest. We cannot afford to return to those failed policies of the past.

We must begin by recognizing two fundamental facts. First, an improvement in the atmosphere of American–Soviet relations does not mean the end of the competition between the superpowers. Cordiality is not concord. Even if compromises are worked out on issues like nuclear-arms control, we will still be in conflict on others, such as the future of Europe and regional conflicts in the Third World. If an improvement in the atmospherics of U.S.–Soviet relations leads us to lower our guard, we will be engaging in the worst kind of unilateral disarmament.

Second, a strategy which consists only of defending static positions in Europe and Asia will lead to defeat. Moscow will continue to press forward in the Third World. It is essential that the United States counter these Soviet moves, because the Third World is where territory and people will actually swing from one side to the other. At the same time, we must not grant the Soviets sanctuary in their own sphere or concede the initiative to the Kremlin in ours. If we are to compete, it must be on their side of the Iron Curtain as well as ours. If we compete only on Moscow's terms, Soviet leaders will take what we give them and come back for more. They will mass their forces for a breakthrough at our weakest point and patiently accumulate small gains at low cost and little risk. And we will eventually find that the balance of power has tipped in Moscow's favor.

No Soviet leader has ever lost sight of these two key points. Gorbachev is no exception. The eloquence of his words about peace and friendship is contradicted by his deeds in Africa, in Southeast and Southwest Asia, and in Central America. He does not want war, but he does want victory, and he believes he can get it with tactics short of war. That is the danger we must confront and the challenge we must overcome.

If we sit behind a Maginot Line of nuclear deterrence, we will lose the American–Soviet struggle. Nuclear weapons can deter a Soviet nuclear attack on the United States and can deter a Soviet attack in a central theater of conflict like Europe. But nuclear deterrence works only if the stakes involved justify the risks of nuclear war. We therefore cannot rely on nuclear weapons to deter direct or indirect Soviet aggression in peripheral regions where American interests are less than vital. That means that our nuclear arsenal will be useless in crises in the Third World. The problem is that this is where superpower confrontations are most likely to occur in the years before 1999.

Moscow understands how to compete despite the existence of nuclear weapons. Since World War II, it has geared its global strategy to exploit geopolitical opportunities that have not involved a risk of nuclear war. When the United States enjoyed nuclear superiority, the Soviet Union was cautious, taking few initiatives and withdrawing at the first sign of American resolve. That changed after Moscow acquired nuclear parity in the early 1970s. While we had used our nuclear umbrella to protect allies in Europe and the Far East, the Soviet Union employed its nuclear umbrella as a cover for aggression in the Third World. In less than five years, between 1975 and 1980, over 100 million people were either conquered by the East or lost by the West.

Nuclear parity has changed the nature of the American–Soviet conflict. We could not threaten nuclear war to stop the Soviet Union from supplying arms and ammunition to the communists in the Vietnam War. Nor can we threaten the apocalypse to block Soviet moves in Africa, the far-flung reaches of Asia or even in Latin America. That does not mean the United States must abandon its interests in those regions. It does mean that in addition to maintaining adequate nuclear deterrent forces the United States must learn to compete without direct military intervention.

We should not make the mistake of believing that simply because the Soviet Union's superpower status depends on its military power Moscow has no other assets. As William Sherr warns, "This leads to a tendency to slight the nonmilitary instruments of power and influence available to the Soviet Union, some of which are uniquely available to her and unfamiliar to ourselves." Kremlin leaders are masters at strategic deception, disinformation, subversion, and other tactics which democracies cannot employ. As a result, we must develop six key capabilities to be able to compete effectively with Moscow:

Ideological power. Our competition with the Soviet Union is military, economic and political, but the root cause of the Soviet–American rivalry is ideological. The Soviet Union wants to expand communism and destroy freedom, and the United States wants to stop communism and expand freedom. All our weapons, treaties, trade, foreign assistance, and cultural ties will amount to nothing if we lose the battle of ideas.

We hold high cards in the ideological competition with the Soviet Union. Our values of freedom and democracy have a tremendous appeal around the world. Their strength is that they do not prescribe how people should live but only that individuals and nations should be free to choose how they live. And while not all peoples are capable of governing themselves democratically, almost all wish for democratic rule.

No one who knows what life is like in the Soviet Union would want to live there. It should be no contest. But they have done a good job of selling a poor case, and we have done a poor job of selling a good case. Moscow devotes enormous resources to ideological competition. It transmits Radio Moscow in scores of languages to every corner of the world, publishes and distributes thousands of books and newspapers abroad, and provides scholarships at Soviet universities for almost 100,000 foreign students.

Too often, the United States steps onto the battlefield of ideas unarmed. One of the most effective foreign-policy programs the United States has ever undertaken has been its support for Radio Free Europe and Radio Liberty. These stations alone have prevented the complete indoctrination of the peoples of Eastern Europe and the Soviet Union. The problem is that they stand virtually alone as examples of American action on the ideological front.

We need to expand vastly our programs in this area. We must

match Radio Moscow's foreign broadcasting. That does not mean we should fill the airwaves with crass propaganda. We should never broadcast lies or disinformation. The problem is that our programs are often not worth listening to. We must stop transmitting the pap that passes for programming on the Voice of America. It is often so trivial that Gorbachev has announced that the Soviet Union will no longer bother to jam its frequencies. We must also find ways to exploit the new information technologies—microcomputers, satellites, and videocassette recorders—to fight the battle of ideas.

Our overhaul of American foreign broadcasting should redirect it to serve two purposes. Where state censorship exists, we should seek to tell the people what their own governments refuse to tell them about their own countries. Also, we must ensure that American positions on world issues and American ideas and values get a fair hearing in the world. At present, they do not.

Diplomacy. Since World War II, diplomats as much as generals have altered the balance of power between the superpowers. For Moscow, soldiers and diplomats serve the same purpose: both are instruments to achieve Soviet strategic objectives. The Soviets have mastered the art of integrating their diplomacy into overall strategy. While the United States has had some diplomatic successes, there have been far too many instances where we have failed to recognize that diplomacy is not just a means for compromise but is a tactic of competition. We must always remember that for the Soviets the purpose of negotiation is not compromise but victory.

We should steer our course between two extremes. On the one hand, too many professional diplomats tend to believe that there is no substitute for negotiation. Whenever our interests are challenged, their first—and often only—reaction is to negotiate with the adversary. They reflexively treat disputes as if they were simply great misunderstandings rather than insurmountable differences. They fail to understand that adversaries sometimes use talks as a play for time and that, in addition to negotiating, the United States often needs to take other actions to create incentives for the other side to come to terms. We sometimes even have to use force at the same time as we negotiate. If Eisenhower had not threatened in a back-channel message to use nuclear weapons in Korea, the communists would not have agreed to an armistice. If the United States had not bombed Hanoi in December 1972, the North Vietnamese would not have signed the Paris cease-fire agreements in January 1973.

At the other extreme, there are those who believe that to accept the need to negotiate is to fall into a communist trap. They argue that if the United States talks with its adversaries it will be paralyzed and fail to take needed stronger actions. In their view, talking with communists is tantamount to trafficking in communism. But they fail to recognize that we have achieved a great deal through negotiations since World War II. Our diplomatic support for and contacts with Yugoslavia enabled Tito to break with Stalin in 1948. Our role in the Austrian Peace Treaty freed the country from Soviet occupation in 1955. The Berlin agreement of 1971 ended Soviet harassment in the corridor between Berlin and West Germany, which had been a potential flashpoint for superpower conflict for twenty-five years. Our participation in the diplomacy to end the Yom Kippur War widened the split between Egypt and the Soviet Union in 1973. Our secret negotiations with the Chinese communists brought about the Sino–American rapprochement in 1972. President Carter's Camp David Accords established a peaceful relationship between Egypt and Israel and finalized the political break between Egypt and the Soviet Union. That does not mean that talking is a substitute for acting. It does mean that we must think of negotiations as a tactic to achieve our objectives.

Economic aid. Never has the United States had a greater competitive edge over the Soviet Union than in foreign economic assistance, and never has the United States failed so abysmally to capitalize on its advantage. Since the American economy is twice the size of that of the Soviet Union, we have the resources to race ahead of the Soviets in this area. In terms of dollars we have, but in terms of impact we have not.

Since World War II, the United States has loaned or given foreign governments more than $134 billion in economic aid, and the Soviet Union has provided less than $50 billion. While our overall foreign-aid program has concentrated on economic assistance, Moscow has given four times as much military aid as economic.

While our assistance has gone to over 150 developing countries, the Soviet Union has focused its aid on its communist client states. While our aid has been in most cases primarily altruistic, Moscow's assistance has been solely directed toward increasing its global influence.

Foreign-aid programs have never been politically popular in the United States. Because of the budget crunch, support for such programs today is at an all-time low. They must be radically revived if they are to survive. But in doing so we have to overcome the myth that foreign aid is just a waste of money. That is true if the money is used poorly. The $3 billion the world sent to Tanzania in the last ten years subsidized the worst economic policies in Africa. Much of the money we contribute to international agencies for distribution to Third World governments is misspent on boondoggles or diverted by corrupt officials. But foreign aid is not wasteful if spent wisely. Certainly the $14 billion we expended on the postwar reconstruction of the nations of Western Europe and Japan was not a waste. Our economic aid did more to prevent communist expansion in those countries than ten times as much military aid would have done.

We need to learn to serve our strategic purposes with our foreign aid. Our economic and political support for the Central American democracies and for Pakistan are excellent illustrations of how we can succeed. Our assistance has prevented an economic collapse and a communist victory in El Salvador. It has reduced the potential for political instability in Pakistan and has enabled Islamabad to resist Soviet military intimidation on the issue of Afghanistan. In 1986 we spent $435 million on aid for El Salvador and $628 million for Pakistan. That is far less than we would need to spend if a deteriorating situation forced us to use American troops to defend our interests in Central America and Southwest Asia—and far less than it would cost if we forfeited those interests.

We must exploit our economic superiority in the American–Soviet competition. We should therefore substantially increase the amount we invest in strategic foreign assistance and should enlist our allies to increase their aid programs as well. But we must target our aid to achieve strategic purposes. We must not simply pour

our money into global pork-barrel projects. That would disserve not only our interests but also those whom we seek to help.

Military aid. Americans instinctively cringe at the thought of shipping off tons of weapons and military equipment to countries around the world. They do not want to think of themselves as arms merchants. But military aid is often the best way to protect our interests and those of our friends and allies. It is also the principal way in which the Soviet Union will seek to challenge our interests in the coming decades.

Since the late 1940s, Moscow has used its own forces to annex a country to its empire only once—in the invasion of Afghanistan in 1979. In every other Soviet expansionist push, the Kremlin recruited a proxy force and supplied them with the arms to do the job. North Korea invaded South Korea in 1950. North Vietnam subverted and invaded South Vietnam, Laos, and Cambodia starting in the mid-1950s. Cuban proxy forces put communists into power in Angola in 1976. Soviet aid through Cuba propelled the communists into power in Nicaragua in 1979. In the early 1980s, the Soviet Union delivered twice as much military aid to its proxies in the developing world as the United States did to its allies and friends.

It is not philanthropy but expansionism that drives the Soviet Union to pump weapons into the Third World. Its goal in exporting arms is exporting communism. The Kremlin's modus operandi is far more sophisticated today than it was when North Korean armies marched across the South Korean border. Instead of going over borders, the Soviets now go under and around them. Sometimes the Soviets spark a revolution; other times they capture a revolution already taking place. In both cases, Soviet military assistance is Moscow's principal weapon to undermine American friends and allies.

In response, we must do at least as much for our allies as the Soviets do for theirs. Many argue that it is morally wrong to supply arms to peoples engaged in distant conflicts. They contend that this merely adds fuel to the fire. But it was not wrong to send military aid to Greece and Turkey to block Soviet-sponsored subversion after World War II. Nor was it wrong to aid anticommunist forces in Indochina. North Vietnam overran South Vietnam in 1975 not because the communists were more motivated or more popular. Hanoi won because after the Paris peace accords of 1973 the Soviet Union increased military aid to its allies in Hanoi while the Congress cut American aid to Saigon by 75 percent over two years. What resulted was not only a tragedy for the people of Indochina, but also a growing threat to Western interests in the region, as Soviet ships operating from Vietnamese harbors acquired the capability to threaten sea lanes vital to Japan.

People will not fight for freedom if they must stand alone while their enemies enjoy carte blanche at the near-limitless Soviet arsenal. If we fail to provide our allies and friends with adequate military assistance, Moscow's clients will advance on every front. We will then face a stark choice: we can either forfeit our interests or forfeit the lives of American troops to defend them. We must recognize the fact that if we spend a little money on military assistance now, we will avoid having to expend blood, as well as money, later.

Military power. Since the Vietnam War, many have argued that military power no longer has any utility in international politics. American military interventions or American security guarantees and military presence have prevented 707 million people from falling under Soviet domination. Without American support, Western Europe, Japan, South Korea, and the countries of Southwest Asia would all now have to defer to the demands of the Soviet Union. American military power achieved our objectives in Korea in the early 1950s, in Lebanon in 1957, in the Dominican Republic in 1965, and in Grenada in 1983.

It would be dangerous to assume that because we succeeded in those instances a military intervention can succeed anywhere. But it is more dangerous to assume that because we failed in Vietnam, we can succeed nowhere. We must not allow our failure in Vietnam to blind us to the stark reality that without military power and the will to use it surgically and selectively in crucial conflicts, we will be routed in our rivalry with the Soviet Union.

Ironically, the strongest ally of those who oppose any military interventions in Third World conflicts is the American military establishment. Since Vietnam, the only battle the Pentagon seems ready to wage is the battle to get more money from the Congress. The Defense Department has laid down five conditions which must be met before the United States intervenes militarily. First, the actions must be "vital to our national interests" or those of our allies. Second, we should commit forces only as a last resort. Third, when we commit our troops, we must do so with the sole object of winning. Fourth, we must enter conflicts only if they are winnable in the sense that we have the means to achieve quick and certain victory. Fifth, we must have assurance—ahead of time—of the support of the Congress and the public.

While no one would question many of those conditions if properly defined, taken as a whole they are unreasonably restrictive. In effect, these require that we intervene only if victory is guaranteed in advance. If these had been applied in the past, they would have ruled out the intervention not only in Vietnam but also in Korea. Even our role in the European Theater in World War II—in which victory was in doubt as late as 1944—would have been out of bounds. For the future, these ground rules would prohibit any U.S. intervention in virtually all conflicts in the Third World.

No one disputes the military's understandable reluctance to become bogged down in another Vietnam. But the lesson of Vietnam was not that we should never intervene. Rather, it was that any future U.S. intervention must be decisive, not tentative, guided by strategy, not improvisation, and carried through with force adequate to achieve our goal, not just to avoid defeat.

Since Vietnam, the American military establishment has concentrated its resources on maintaining its forces in Europe and the Far East. It has devoted a disproportionate share to preparing for the big war that will probably never be fought and has virtually ignored the need to be ready for the smaller wars that we might be forced to fight. It has woefully neglected to develop our ability to intervene in conflicts in the Third World. That would not be a problem if we knew that the Soviets were likely to challenge us in the central theaters where our nuclear power deters them. But in fact the opposite is true: Moscow is most likely to seek to outflank Europe and Japan with aggression in the Third World, where our nuclear power is useless. We should intervene militarily in such conflicts only as a last resort. But if we fail to develop the capability to parry Soviet thrusts in the Third World, we will find ourselves unable to compete with Moscow.

Another legacy of the Vietnam War is the War Powers Act. It was passed over my veto in 1973. The law stipulates that first the President must consult with Congress before intervening with our forces in an armed conflict. Then he is permitted to continue the intervention for sixty days without congressional approval and another thirty days if he certifies in writing that the safety of our fighting men requires it. If the Congress does not by that time authorize his actions by a declaration of war or other legislation, the War Powers Act requires that our forces must be pulled out.

The law is not only unconstitutional but also unsound. It infringes on the authority of the President as commander in chief of the armed forces. Congressional-veto clauses in other laws but similar to the one in the War Powers Act have been ruled unconstitutional by the Supreme Court. It is with good reason that the Founding Fathers put authority over the armed forces into the President's hands. Congress is incapable of acting as commander in chief. As de Gaulle once said, "Parliaments can only paralyze policy; they cannot initiate it."

Given the realities of the world, the United States will sometimes need to use force in actions short of all-out war and will have to be able to act quickly and decisively. While 535 would-be commanders in chief dissect the merits and demerits of the intervention, the President will have to keep glancing over his shoulder to check the clock while fighting to defend American interests. Anyone who has witnessed the gridlock on Capitol Hill over the budget deficit and other critical issues in the last few years knows that the most likely action would turn out to be no action. As a result, by doing nothing—or by filibustering to ensure that outcome—opponents of the President's actions can achieve the same result as if their view prevailed in both houses of the Congress.

Those who passed the War Powers Act believed that the United States should rule out the use of force in the world. While such forbearance might be considered an act of virtue in the West, the Soviets and other potential adversaries consider it a sign of weakness and a green light to press forward with their aggression. A unilateral American renunciation of the use of force would provoke the use of force against us. In the U.S.–Soviet contest, Gorbachev has the freedom to conduct a freewheeling foreign policy. If we restrict the President's ability to act, America will be like a prizefighter boxing with one hand tied behind his back.

Covert operations. Overt economic or military aid is sometimes enough to achieve our goals. Only a direct military intervention can do so in others. But between the two lies a vast area where the United States must be able to undertake covert actions. Without this capability, we will be unable to protect important U.S. interests.

There are those who argue that the United States should not engage in covert operations, especially after the disaster of the Iran-contra affair. The administration's opening to Iran did not become a fiasco because it was a covert operation. It did so because it was ineptly conducted. A covert operation must serve an important strategic purpose. Initially, the contacts with Tehran sought the worthy objective of a rapprochement with Iran. The administration went astray as soon as it allowed Israel and Iran to introduce the question of arms sales into the negotiations, especially because only a rank amateur could imagine such deals staying secret for long in the Middle East. Arms transfers should only follow, not precede, a diplomatic opening. (Almost a decade passed after the rapprochement with China before the United States sold weapons to Beijing.) This error was compounded when the administration let its obsession with the fate of the hostages in Lebanon lead to the bartering of American lives for American weapons. It became a debacle when National Security Council staff members chose to divert profits from the Iranian arms deal to the Nicaraguan contras.

It would be a fatal mistake for the United States to renounce covert action as a foreign-policy instrument. We must ask ourselves whether giving up this capability would be sensible given the fact that the Soviet Union continues to exploit it. Through covert action, the Kremlin arms communist insurgencies, funds communist and other leftist parties, disseminates disinformation, trains international terrorists, assassinates opponents, to name just a few of its activities. We do not and should not emulate the Soviet

Union's behavior. But if we were to abandon covert action as an instrument of foreign policy, we would be in effect donning a straitjacket in our competition with Moscow.

Successful covert operations seldom receive publicity, but they have often protected vital American interests. One took place in 1953, when the Eisenhower administration gave covert support to help the Shah take power in Iran. The Shah displaced an incompetent left-wing government which had been blissfully ignoring Soviet efforts to exploit Iranian instability to propel the communist Tudeh party into power. Eisenhower's covert operation produced a regime in Iran that served not only American interests but also those of the Iranian people and of our friends and allies in the region for a quarter of a century.

Another has been in operation over the past eight years. The United States has sent hundreds of millions of dollars in covert assistance to the resistance in Afghanistan. That covert operation not only has created the possibility of rolling back a forward position of the Soviet empire, but also has inflicted such cost on the Kremlin that its leaders will have to think twice before again embarking on such an adventure in the future.

Contrary to popular mythology, most covert operations do not involve support for insurgent groups. More often, a covert operation involves giving money to individuals or groups who support American objectives. An example was our support for democratic political forces in Europe immediately after World War II. A continent was in ruins, and the Soviet Union was funneling huge resources into exploiting the situation to bring communists to power in countries like Italy. Our financial support to those who sought to rebuild democracy in Western Europe was absolutely indispensable to keeping our allies free.

Those who deride the need for the United States to be able to conduct covert operations should ask themselves whether we should have accepted a communist Iran in 1953, whether we should abandon the Afghan resistance today, or whether we should have looked the other way as the Kremlin foisted totalitarian dictatorship onto the peoples of Eastern Europe in the late 1940s.

After the Iran-contra affair, many advocate imposing new restrictions on covert actions. Some say we should stop helping insurgencies and only give military assistance to governments in power. But this policy not only would doom the United States to a purely reactive policy around the world but also would abandon those who want to fight for their freedom. At the same time, those who advocate this approach often reluctantly make an exception in the case of the Afghan resistance because Moscow brazenly invaded their country. The assumption is that somehow the Afghan resistance leaders are more legitimate than those of other anticommunist insurgencies. But the resistance leaders were no more elected than those of the contras. This is not to say that the Afghan leaders are not their people's legitimate leaders. They clearly are. What it does mean is that we must judge whether to support anticommunist insurgencies on a case-by-case basis.

Others argue that everything the United States has been doing by covert actions should be done overtly. That is impractical. In the case of supporting freedom fighters, if we were to acknowledge our assistance we would heighten the conflict to the government-to-goverment level, and our friends would soon be accused of acting as American puppets. But arming, training, and supporting freedom fighters are not typical covert actions. Far more often, covert actions involve things like support for a democratic political movement or funding labor unions or newspapers in a repressive state. We serve worthy ends through covert actions, but our activities would be instantly compromised if we acted overtly.

Still others believe the government should undertake covert actions only if they are legal, are vetted through congressional committees, are supportive of U.S. policy, and would be supported by the American people if they became public. No one would contest the first three conditions. But American foreign policy in general, and covert action in particular, should not be determined by the vagaries of public opinion. Most of the time, if our covert actions became known, they would be endorsed by the American people. But there will be exceptions. When President Roosevelt covertly provided assistance to Britain early in World War II, he not only violated the Neutrality Act but also acted contrary to the public's overwhelming neutralist sentiment. But in retrospect we know he was right. We must accept the fact that we elect our leaders to lead the country, not to follow the opinion polls.

While all these restrictions fail to pass the test of common sense, we did learn from the Iran-contra affair that the National Security Council should not be involved operationally in covert actions. To succeed, such activities must be deniable. They must be conducted in a way so that the United States can plausibly deny its involvement. But if covert actions are run out of the Old Executive Office Building, that becomes impossible. We must, however, keep a distinction between covert actions and secret negotiations. A President should be able, if he wishes, to use his national-security adviser as his negotiator. Often, particularly in sensitive talks with totalitarian leaders, the NSC head would be a better choice than the Secretary of State.

Our inability to keep a secret represents the greatest threat to our capability for covert action. Given the widespread dissemination of classified information and the relentless sniffing of the hundreds of Pulitzer hounds in the media, it is a wonder any covert actions remain secret. But the problem lies not just in Congress. Officials in the NSC, the Central Intelligence Agency, the State Department, and the Defense Department all leak out information. The answer is not to force those suspected of leaking to take lie detector tests. We should not destroy someone's career on the basis of a test that is hardly foolproof. Instead, the President should reduce drastically the number of people in the executive branch who have access to information about covert activities.

He should establish a new special "need to know" classification covering information which, if exposed, would risk the lives of those involved in a covert operation. Only statutory members of the NSC should be given authority to put this classification onto materials and documents. The present system, under which literally thousands of low-level bureaucrats can stamp a document top secret, is ridiculous. Those found guilty of releasing information about truly sensitive covert operations—regardless of motivation —should receive mandatory prison sentences. The present espionage laws are not adequate to cover such actions. Someone who leaks information out of spite or because of bureaucratic infighting

RICHARD NIXON

should receive the same sentence as someone who provides the information to a foreign power with the intention of hurting the United States.

In addition, Congress must create a single joint intelligence oversight committee of no more than eight members, staffed by professionals, to receive briefings on covert activities. In the long term, we must cultivate among the American people the attitude that those who leak secrets should be discharged in disgrace rather than receive a badge of honor, as did Daniel Ellsberg.

While the United States must have those six key capabilities, it must also have the skill to implement a strategy that uses each at the right time. We must understand where and how each instrument should be employed.

Our first task is to distinguish between vital interests, critical interests, and peripheral interests. No country has the resources to defend all its interests with its own forces all the time. Strategy means making choices, and making choices means enforcing a set of strategic priorities. We must react with flexibility in tactics to Soviet threats, but we must do so with a set of priorities firmly in mind.

An interest is vital if its loss, in and of itself, directly endangers the security of the United States. The survival and independence of Western Europe, Japan, Canada, Mexico, and the Persian Gulf are vital interests of the United States. The loss of any of these to the Soviet Union would imperil our own security. We have no choice but to respond with military force if necessary should the Kremlin attempt to dominate these areas.

A critical interest is one which, if lost, would create a direct threat to one of our vital interests. If Moscow were to achieve domination over South Korea, the Kremlin leaders would be in an ideal position to threaten Japan. If they were able to dominate Pakistan, they could put their naval power on the doorstep of the Persian Gulf. If they were able to consolidate their Nicaraguan beachhead in Central America, they could begin the campaign to destabilize the region as a whole, including Mexico.

We must recognize that the United States often must treat critical interests as if they were vital because a Soviet move against them could only be a prelude to the main challenge. If Britain and France had done so when Hitler moved against Czechoslovakia—which Neville Chamberlain called "a far away land populated by a people with whom we have nothing in common"—they would not have had to go to war ten months later over the German invasion of Poland. If we wait to oppose Soviet expansionism until Moscow threatens vital U.S. interests, we will soon find those interests at risk—and will have to defend them under the worst of circumstances.

A peripheral interest is one which, if lost, would only distantly threaten a vital or critical interest. While we would not want to see a pro-Soviet government take power in a country like Mali, we cannot conclude that such an event would endanger important American interests or those of our allies.

Our overall strategy must calibrate what we will do to protect an interest of strategic importance. We should not send in the Marines to defend a peripheral interest, but we must not flinch from doing so to defend a vital interest. We must match the level of our commitment to the importance of our stakes in a region. We should then match our capabilities—and the will to use them—to the threat we face.

Our top priority must be our vital interests. U.S. policy-makers often allow themselves to be sidetracked by peripheral issues. While we have more at stake in Canada and Mexico than in any other countries, seldom do they get attention commensurate with their importance. Canada is a member of NATO and our largest trading partner. We should seek to involve the Canadians more actively, not only in the pursuit of greater prosperity through such measures as the recently signed free-trade agreement, but also in the search for greater Western security and global stability. Canada has a great deal at stake in the world—and has much to contribute to the world. It is not in our interest to have Canada stand on the sidelines rather than cooperate with us on our common concerns.

Mexico's economic crisis represents one of our greatest long-term security threats. We can ignore the problem only at our peril. While the United States cannot solve Mexico's problems, we cannot afford to treat them as a sideshow. Our policies today simply tread water. That eases relations in the short term but courts disaster in the long term. As a result, we must take on the problem head on. Simply rescheduling debt indefinitely only postpones a reckoning and will eventually land the Mexican people in grinding poverty. We must start to develop, with Mexican leaders, a program to get at the root economic problems, rather than improvising temporary solutions to one crisis after another.

As a rule, if faced with a Soviet military threat to its vital interests, the United States must be prepared to employ its own forces in their defense. As long as Kremlin leaders threaten the free world, we must not weaken our security ties with either Western Europe or Japan. But in our competition with Moscow that is not where we should expect the challenges from the Kremlin to arise. In the years before 1999, it will be in the Persian Gulf region that the Soviet threat to vital U.S. interests will be the greatest. It is also the region in which the United States is the least prepared to defend those interests.

In my book *The Real War,* which was published just after the Soviet invasion of Afghanistan in 1979, I called the Persian Gulf the "oil jugular" of the West. I wrote that if control over access to the region's reserves were ever to fall into Soviet hands, the Kremlin leaders could blackmail the West by threatening to strangle its oil-fueled economies. That is still true—and will continue to be true for at least the rest of this century.

Access to Persian Gulf oil is a vital interest of the West. It would be a fatal error to let today's low oil prices blind us to the fact that we depend on oil imports from the Middle East. Oil is still the most important energy source for the industrialized world, and imports account for over half of the oil consumed in the Western industrialized economies. Moreover, Western dependence on imported oil is certain to grow, not diminish, for the rest of this century

In 1973, when the OPEC embargo produced gas lines which stretched for miles, the United States imported a third of its oil. In 1985, after a decade of concerted efforts to conserve energy and reduce our dependence on foreign energy sources, we still bought

27 percent of our oil abroad, while Western European dependence on imported oil stood at 63 percent and that of Japan at 100 percent. Although the United States imported most of its oil from areas other than the gulf, Western Europe imports about a third and Japan about two thirds of theirs from the area. Along the entire 7,000-mile route from the Persian Gulf to Japan, there is one oil tanker every 100 miles bound for Japanese ports.

Without oil imports from the Persian Gulf, our allies would tumble into an economic free fall. They would suffer a collapse that would make the Great Depression look like a mild downturn in the leading economic indicators. No one should mistakenly believe that the United States would escape unscathed—for when oil prices go up they go up for everyone.

Our dependence on oil from the Persian Gulf will almost certainly increase. American oil production will continue to decline, and American oil consumption will continue to increase as our economy grows. Since coal, natural gas, or nuclear power cannot make up the shortfall between supply and demand, we will find ourselves importing more oil. The U.S. Energy Department estimates that in 1995 the United States will import about 50 percent of its oil, while Western Europe will import about 70 percent and Japan 100 percent. Since the countries of the Persian Gulf hold 66 percent of the free world's proven oil reserves, they will supply the lion's share of oil imports of the industrialized democracies in the future.

As long as the Western economies are fueled by oil, the Persian Gulf area and its resources will remain a vital interest of the West. The Middle East had long been the crossroads where Asia, Africa, and Europe met. Now, with oil acting as the lifeblood of modern industry, the Persian Gulf has become the oil jugular of the West.

Kremlin leaders have always understood that fact. Soviet interest in oil has always drawn Soviet interest to the south. Early in World War II, in negotiations to carve up the world with its allies in Nazi Germany, Stalin's Foreign Minister told his counterparts that in addition to its objectives in Europe "the area south of Batum and Baku in the general direction of the Persian Gulf" was "the center of the aspirations of the Soviet Union." When Berlin acceded to that formulation, Stalin ordered his general staff to draw up plans for the invasion of Iran. In its opening pages, the war plan described Moscow's motivation with striking clarity in a quotation from Stalin: "In the final analysis, this is what it is all about: Who will own the oil fields and the most important roads leading to the interior of Asia?"

After Nazi Germany turned its armies on the Soviet Union in 1941, the Kremlin invaded northern Iran to prevent German advances in the region, while Britain and the United States moved their forces into southern Iran. But after the war, as both Britain and the United States withdrew their troops on schedule, Moscow tried to carve off northern Iran by announcing that in the territory under Soviet control the Autonomous Republic of Azerbaijan and the Kurdish People's Republic had declared independence from Tehran. The Kremlin immediately granted them formal recognition. Soviet units and Soviet-supported rebel military forces then tried to march on the Iranian capital. Stalin stopped and withdrew only after President Truman—at a time when the United States held a monopoly in nuclear weapons—delivered an ultimatum to Moscow. This critical decision by Harry Truman was as important as his decision to provide aid to Greece and Turkey in preventing Soviet domination over Western Europe.

What is ominous is that Moscow has a greater incentive to push to the south today than it did in 1945. After World War II, Soviet oil fields were still in their prime, with production on the upswing. In the mid-1980s, oil production in the Soviet Union peaked and then began to decline, with little prospect for a recovery. That is why the Soviet Union is pressing forward with nuclear energy despite the Chernobyl disaster. It is also a powerful reason—apart from achieving dominance over Western Europe and Japan—to seek control over the Persian Gulf.

In the late 1970s, the Kremlin deployed a pincer movement against the gulf. One pincer came from the southwest. In 1978, Soviet transports airlifted twenty thousand Cuban troops into Ethiopia, not only to assist its communist government in its war with Somalia, but also to establish military facilities across the Red Sea from Saudi Arabia. Later that year, a pro-Soviet group in South Yemen took power, thereby giving Moscow a beachhead on the Arabian Peninsula. South Yemen soon launched an overt military attack on North Yemen. From South Yemen, terrorists launched operations against Saudi Arabia and guerrillas conducted attacks in a border province of Oman. The other pincer came from the northeast. In 1978, a military coup put into power the Afghan Communist Party, which quickly signed treaties with Moscow. When a popular rebellion threatened to topple the communist regime, the Soviet Union invaded the country, putting its fighter-bombers within reach of the Strait of Hormuz from their newly acquired Afghan bases. From both directions, Kremlin leaders were extending their reach to get their hands on the oil jugular.

From 1953 to 1979, Iran under the Shah served as the principal pillar of Western security in the region. When the British withdrew from "east of Suez" in the 1960s, the United States, with over 500,000 troops in Vietnam, could not step into the breach. It was the Shah who filled the vacuum of power. He undertook a massive program to modernize his armed forces. His navy patrolled the gulf, and his army represented a powerful obstacle to any Soviet thrust. He protected Saudi Arabia and the other vulnerable sheikdoms in the region. He worked with other gulf states to create regional security arrangements. When the Shah's government fell in 1979, it produced a new vacuum of power—at the very same time Moscow was achieving the capability to fill it. Had the Shah survived it is highly unlikely that the Soviets would have invaded Afghanistan.

Today the United States is the only country that can safeguard Western interests in the Persian Gulf. None of the pro-Western gulf states is strong enough to do the job. None of our European allies have the forces or the will to do so. We, therefore, must step up to this vitally important issue, but so far we have not.

We must act on the military front to improve our capability to project American power into the gulf. We have made significant progress in this area. President Carter created the Rapid Deployment Force. President Reagan has upgraded the RDF into the U.S. Central Command, and Congress has appropriated billions of dollars for its forces. But we have not yet done enough. The Pentagon has made a disproportionate share of overall congressional budget cuts in the forces which would defend the Persian Gulf. As a result, the United States will not soon meet the goal of being able to deploy four divisions in the gulf within thirty days.

We cannot defend our interests in the gulf—or deter a Soviet move against them—if we cannot get our forces there. We need to invest substantially more in our airlift and sea-lift capability. It therefore must be made a top-priority item in our defense budget in the eleven years before 1999.

We must also act on the diplomatic front to forge closer ties with the countries in the region. It is impossible for the United States to intervene in the Persian Gulf without access to air bases in Saudi Arabia and other smaller gulf states. We need to base air forces there so that we can protect our ground forces as they establish a beachhead. Without air superiority, an American landing in the Persian Gulf would become a replay of the British landings at Gallipoli in World War I.

Improving our ties with these states requires the United States to undo the damage done by the Iranian arms deal. For our friends in the region, Khomeini's Iran is a much greater threat than even the Soviet Union. We must therefore assure them that the Iran fiasco was an aberration which will not be repeated. But we also must become actively engaged in efforts to settle the Palestinian question. It is this issue and our close ties with Israel that lead the gulf states to keep relations with the United States at an arm's length.

Even if we take these needed steps, our vital interests will be at risk unless the United States has the will to defend them. The perception that however powerful its armed forces may be, the United States will never use them is a dangerous one. It adds to the risk of war because it tempts aggressors to believe that aggression can succeed at little cost. Yet that is the exact perception that liberal candidates for President in 1984 encouraged when they took turns promising never to send American forces to fight for the Persian Gulf. Whoever makes that kind of pacifist pledge in 1988 will disqualify himself from being considered as a responsible leader of the United States and the free world.

In the current crisis in the Persian Gulf, the United States cannot afford to be disengaged. What happens in the Iran–Iraq war today profoundly affects our ability to safeguard the region from Soviet intervention in the future. If ever there was a war in which both parties deserved to lose, it is the Iran–Iraq war; if ever there was a war in which the United States could not afford either party to lose, it is also the Iran–Iraq war. An Iraqi defeat would lead to Iranian fundamentalist domination of Kuwait, Saudi Arabia, and the entire gulf region. An Iran bled white by massive losses of manpower would become vulnerable to Soviet subversion and intimidation.

In this war, we should seek a solution that provides peace without victory, while having no illusions about the ability of our diplomats to bring it about quickly. In the meantime, however, we should strengthen our friends in the gulf. We should encourage and assist recent moves toward greater regional defense cooperation, including the reintegration of Egypt not only in the Arab world but also as a potential military ally of the Arab gulf states. We must continue our involvement in escorting reflagged tankers in the gulf, for our presence gives our friends the confidence needed to spurn Iranian threats. We must remain ready and willing to launch stiff reprisals on military and economic targets in Iran for any attacks on our vessels.

At the same time, after months of fruitless debate, it is time for Congress to put up or shut up on the issue of invoking the War Powers Act. If members of Congress intend to try to intrude on the proper role of the President in foreign affairs, they should vote the question up or down. If they cannot muster the votes—and no one believes they can—they should stand aside and let the President operate without interference. As it is, Khomeini has been taking potshots at our tankers and naval forces in the hope of triggering the War Powers Act and starting the sixty-day clock for a U.S. withdrawal. The endless congressional debate, while well intentioned, only serves to bring our servicemen in the gulf under fire.

In addition to its vital interests in the Persian Gulf, the United States has critical interests in other countries in the Third World. We have an enormous stake in the economies and natural resources of these countries. Some also occupy key strategic positions which make them major prizes in the American–Soviet competition. Most important, it is in the Third World that we can expect to see the greatest gains and losses in the U.S.–Soviet competition.

Since the end of World War II, there have been 120 wars in which 18 million people have been killed—and over forty of them are being waged today. Except for the conflicts in Northern Ireland, the Falkland Islands in 1981, and Greece in 1947, all these wars have taken place in the Third World. The sharpest conflicts between the United States and the Soviet Union have occurred in the Third World. The most important battles in the American–Soviet competition are not along our borders but in remote villages and small countries whose names few Americans know. It is there that people and territory will be won and lost in the American–Soviet struggle.

In pinpointing Soviet aggression today, it is no longer enough to look for the smoking gun: we must now look for the hidden hand. While the Soviet Union is not responsible for all the conflicts in the Third World, it has started several and seeks to exploit most of them. We must recognize the role the Soviet Union and its surrogates play in instigating and supporting insurgencies against noncommunist governments—and take the appropriate counteraction.

To protect our interests in the Third World, we must learn how to respond to three situations: (1) a noncommunist government under attack by communist subversion; (2) a noncommunist government at peace but vulnerable to a communist insurgency; and (3) a communist government under attack by anticommunist forces.

When a friendly noncommunist government finds itself threatened by a communist insurgency, the United States should be predisposed to help it meet that threat. Without a sustained effort along the front lines in the battle between freedom and communism, the United States cannot compete effectively with Moscow.

We must become involved in these conflicts not only on behalf of our own interests, but also in support of the interests of the people of threatened Third World countries. British historian Paul Johnson wrote that "the essence of geopolitics is to be able to distinguish between different degrees of evil." Those who oppose U.S. involvement to stop the spread of communism in the Third

World because they do not like the noncommunist regimes we at times have to support fail to understand that point. We do not like dictatorships. But we must recognize the difference between communist dictatorships and noncommunist dictatorships. A noncommunist dictatorship allows some freedoms; a communist dictatorship allows none. A noncommunist regime allows some opposition and consequently creates the chance for peaceful change; a communist regime allows no opposition. A noncommunist government might support our foreign policy; a communist government will oppose it.

Soviet-supported communist regimes seek to export their repression, while noncommunist governments do not. North Vietnam's communist leadership did not rest content until it ruled all of Indochina. Cuba has fomented communist revolution in Latin America for thirty years. It succeeded in Nicaragua in 1979, and the Nicaraguan communists, in turn, took up the task of subverting El Salvador and other Central American states.

While U.S. friends and allies might not have perfect records on human rights, theirs are without exception better than those of Moscow's clients. Cubans were better off under Batista than under Castro; the Vietnamese were better off under Thieu than under Hanoi's communists; Cambodians were better off under Lon Nol than under Pol Pot. Since 1945, twenty times as many people have been killed by communist governments as have died in wars to stop communism. We must remember that a communist peace kills more than an anticommunist war.

Our support for noncommunist governments under communist attack should be guided by a policy which came to be known as the Nixon Doctrine after I announced it in Guam in 1969. It states that in the future, unless a major power intervened in a Third World conflict, the United States should not commit its combat forces. We should provide military and economic aid to friendly states in whatever amounts necessary to defeat Soviet-supported insurgents, but the country under attack must undertake the responsibility for providing the troops to mount its own defenses. If a country cannot mobilize the capability and the will to fight and win after receiving our aid and training, sending our own troops to do the fighting would at best provide only temporary success. Once we withdrew, the enemy would take over.

Many misinterpreted the announcement of the Nixon Doctrine as a decision by the United States to withdraw into isolation, leaving the countries of Asia and the rest of the world to fend for themselves. That was not the case. The Nixon Doctrine was not a formula for getting America *out* of the Third World, but for providing the only sound basis for America to stay *in* the Third World. I knew that after the Vietnam War it was going to be impossible to involve American forces in a war against guerrilla forces. The Nixon Doctrine made it possible for the United States to continue to play a responsible role in helping our friends and allies defend their independence against communist aggression. American aid to the government of El Salvador is an example of the Nixon Doctrine. We provide arms, economic aid, and training, but El Salvador provides the combat forces.

When a Third World government is under attack by communist guerrillas, the task of pacifying the country is extremely difficult. But the United States has had enough experience with this problem that we can avoid mistakes of the past by following seven basic guidelines:

First, we must not destabilize the leadership of our ally. Unless this leadership is hopelessly corrupt, hopelessly incompetent, or both, the United States should exercise great caution before tampering with it—and should act only if a better alternative exists. Strong leadership is essential in counterinsurgency. If our ally has strong leaders with a degree of popular support, we should give them great latitude for action in dealing with the insurgency. They usually understand better than we do what needs to be done in their country. The worst mistake we made in Vietnam was to instigate the coup against President Diem in 1963. While his government had serious flaws, his removal produced political instability, which in turn undermined South Vietnam's military capability. As a direct result, we had to assume the primary burden for fighting the war. If someone depends on us to put him in power, he will continue to depend on us after he is in power.

Second, we must seek to cut off supplies to the insurgents coming from outside sources. Unless an insurgency enjoys the total support of the people or the government is inept and weak, it is impossible for its troops to keep up the fight without outside aid. Captured weapons and ammunition can give the guerrillas the capability for hit-and-run raids or to defend a few rural strongholds. But a sustained offensive campaign requires the logistical support of an external power. We must therefore make it a military priority to cut off those outside supplies before they reach the insurgents.

Third, we must supply whatever amount of military aid is needed to defeat the insurgents. We must not skimp on a country's survival. We should adopt the principle of doing at least as much for our friends and allies as the Soviets do for theirs.

Fourth, we must require our ally to reform its armed forces, if necessary, to command the support of the people. Counterinsurgency is a political war as much as a military one. A political victory is a precondition for a military one. We must not allow the communists to gain popular support because of brutalities committed against the civilian population by the military. That will lead to a political defeat and, in turn, to a military defeat. Not only will the communists gain recruits and support, but also the United States will find it politically impossible at home to continue to back its ally. But we must pursue military reform with flexibility and patience. A difficult task in the best of circumstances, overhauling the armed forces in wartime without undercutting their effectiveness is a tightrope act which risks a fall to defeat.

Fifth, we must encourage our ally to adopt a strategy to defend the country at the village level. U.S. military-training programs should avoid the mistake of restructuring our ally's forces on the American model. Armies need to be equipped to fight the guerrilla threat they face. Our military is well suited to fight conventional wars but not unconventional guerrilla wars. It has too much confidence in devising technological solutions to military problems and, left to itself, will soon equip our Third World allies with high-performance fighter-bombers and heliborne assault teams. We must remember that in a guerrilla war an infantry platoon in each village will defend the people better than a mechanized battalion in each province.

Sixth, we must promote economic progress at the same time as we pursue military victory. Communism attracts few supporters on its own. Its appeal stems from the way communists exploit the sufferings of a people. We can argue that communist promises of a better life are deceitful and that a communist government will be still more oppressive than the present one, but that will have little effect on people locked in the debasing poverty of the Third World. We must look at the world from their perspective. For them, the status quo is indefensible. If the communists talk about their problems while we talk only about the communists, they will opt for the communists. We must wage a campaign to create economic progress as part of a political offensive to help achieve a military victory.

Seventh, we must be prepared to sustain our support over the long haul. Few guerrilla wars last less than a decade, and many have been fought for over a generation. Americans are an impatient people. We expect results quickly. But it is unreasonable to expect a government to defeat a guerrilla force overnight. If our friends and allies cannot count on us to stay the course, we will soon have none left.

When a friendly noncommunist Third World government faces no guerrilla threat, the United States should not assume all is well. The quiet could be the calm before the storm. In these cases, our strategy must be preemptive. We must defuse the issues of poverty and oppression which give communism its superficial appeal. We should seize the opportunity to make a peaceful revolution in the Third World now or confront the necessity of dealing with violent ones later. While we have learned to project power around the world better than any other nation in history, we must now learn to project progress just as dramatically.

Whenever a crisis breaks out in the Third World, we can almost always in retrospect see scores of warning signs of trouble ahead. We need to develop an early-warning system to detect hot spots before the fires of revolution break out. We should then offer an active, workable alternative to the status quo at one extreme and to communism at the other. We need to practice preventive political medicine before the patient is infected with an incurable revolutionary virus.

It is tempting for many in the West to push for instant democracy as a solution to all Third World problems. Their answer calls for pressuring governments to meet our own strict standards for human rights and for breaking ties with regimes which fail to measure up. After the United States helped to ease out President Duvalier in Haiti and President Marcos in the Philippines, they advocated applying the same formula to Pakistan and South Korea.

Their argument is right in identifying *part* of the problem but wrong in prescribing the solution. An authoritarian government is seldom popular, but in the Third World a democratic government is seldom possible. A democratic system is like a complicated timepiece. Just as the clock needs both its mainspring and its system of interconnected gears to keep time, a democratic system needs not only a popular desire for self-government but also the political, economic, and cultural institutions which make a democracy work. Those institutions took hundreds of years to evolve in the West. We should not expect them to take root overnight in the Third World.

We should always encourage progress toward democratic government and greater respect for human rights. That policy is in the interest not only of the peoples of the Third World. It is also in the interest of the United States, because a freely elected government is a stronger and more reliable ally. But we have to recognize that democracy by our standards is seldom possible in the Third World. When that is the case, we must apply a pragmatic formula in deciding which governments to support.

To qualify for our support, a nondemocratic government must meet four conditions. First, it must grant at least some human and political rights and must provide some prospect for peaceful change through the political system. Authoritarian governments allow some rights, like freedom of religion, while communist totalitarian regimes prohibit all rights. If we break relations with all the countries which fail to measure up to American standards of freedom and justice, we will have to cut ourselves off from two thirds of the world. Rather than isolating ourselves from the world, we should use whatever influence we have with these governments to improve their respect for human rights, while exercising care to distance ourselves from truly onerous regimes to avoid becoming tainted in the eyes of their peoples by our association with their oppressors. For example, applying economic sanctions as some advocated would have destroyed our ability to influence the government of South Korea to move toward greater democracy through the adoption of electoral reforms. Heavy-handed attempts to impose on other countries may be good politics in the United States, but they usually make bad policy abroad.

Second, it must provide competent leadership, especially in economic matters. A people will accept a temporary curtailment of political rights as the price of economic progress. But it will not quietly endure the twin burdens of political repression and economic stagnation. If our strategic interests require close ties with authoritarian governments, we should use our influence to get them to adopt the kind of economic policies that will produce genuine progress for the people. We must also recognize that economic progress alone is not enough. Economic progress without freedom, like freedom without economic progress, can survive in the short run. But in the long run neither can survive without the other. We should use our influence to ensure that both go forward together.

Third, it must have a competent military establishment capable of maintaining internal order and preventing the rise of a communist insurgency. We sometimes must support an unpopular government, but we should not link ourselves too closely with one which cannot defend itself should a communist movement take hold. If we do so, we will be sitting on a powder keg with a fuse running into the Soviet Politburo. We will find ourselves at the mercy of Moscow, and Kremlin leaders are not notable for their mercy.

Fourth, we should support an authoritarian government only if there is no viable democratic opposition leadership available. Wedding ourselves too closely to an authoritarian regime polarizes the political setting against the United States. We force moderate political figures who want to open up the political system to ally themselves with the extreme left and to attack the United States. If we need to work with authoritarians, we must at least keep up contacts with the opposition, while at the same time quietly but firmly pressing the government to adopt political reforms which will protect human rights and expand freedom.

Those four criteria should govern our relations with noncommunist authoritarian governments in the Third World. But our policies in the Third World must reach beyond our political ties. While we should seek to prevent communist expansion in the Third World, our policies also seek to expand freedom.

One of our problems is that we have created the impression that the United States becomes actively involved in the Third World only when *our* interests are threatened by communist aggression. We must now develop policies that address *their* interests. We should demonstrate that even if there were no communist threat we would actively seek to lessen the burdens of poverty, injustice, and corruption that have been their lot for generations. In addressing these concerns, we will serve not only the interests of the people of the developing world but also our own. We will deprive Moscow and its clients of the issues they seek to exploit in their competition against the United States.

When the people of a communist-ruled country rise up to overthrow their oppressors, the United States faces the difficult question of whether to send them support or not. Some say it would be immoral to sit on the sidelines. Others say it would be immoral to get involved in a civil war. Both are partially right. Our choices must be the product of a hardheaded, pragmatic understanding of whom we should help.

On the one hand, President Reagan is right in arguing that as a matter of *principle* we should always support those fighting against communist aggression. When the thirteen American colonies broke with Britain, George III held no political prisoners in a Gulag. Moscow's clients in the Third World have made this their specialty. If France was justified in helping the American Revolution out of the most cynical motivations, the United States is justified in helping anticommunist revolutions out of the most altruistic motives.

On the other hand, the opponents of the Reagan Doctrine correctly point out that the call to "support any friend and oppose any foe in defense of freedom" is good rhetoric but poor policy. It would involve the United States in every corner of the world opposing anyone who infringed on human rights, regardless of American interests or American capabilities. As painful as this may be for Americans who understand the suffering imposed by totalitarian tyranny, we must recognize that we cannot support every anticommunist revolutionary movement which appeals for our help.

These two points of view can be reconciled if we make a calculated appraisal of when we should apply the Reagan Doctrine. A careful application of the doctrine makes strategic sense. It is a logical extension of the idea of self-defense because, at minimum, it will hinder further Soviet aggression from those Third World countries it gained in the 1970s. It could reverse those gains because they lie on the periphery of the Soviet empire—where vital Soviet interests are not at stake. It does not involve our own forces. The Reagan Doctrine is a low-risk, low-cost policy.

Conservatives and liberals concur on supporting anticommunist forces when the communist government took power after an overt invasion by a foreign power. Just as the French resistance in World War II had the sympathy of the American people, the Afghan resistance and Cambodia's noncommunist forces fighting Vietnamese occupying armies have near-universal support.

But sharp disagreements arise when anticommunist revolutionaries seek to bring down a government which took power through the victory of a Soviet-supported insurgency. Some argue that in these cases the Reagan Doctrine constitutes interference in the internal affairs of another country and therefore violates international law. That argument rests on legalisms. Since no world government enforces it, international law must be founded on reciprocity. As soon as one side's actions depart from the norm, the other is no longer bound to it. Moscow has been supporting what it calls "wars of national liberation" since the end of World War II. We are therefore free to do the same, whatever the advocates of international law might argue. We cannot abide by Marquis of Queensberry rules when Moscow is hitting us below the belt.

To qualify for our help, an anticommunist revolutionary movement should meet three conditions: 1. It must be in the interest of people of the country involved. 2. It must be in the interest of the United States. In general, this is the case, for to deny help to our friends fighting for freedom while accepting the fact that the Soviets aid their comrades fighting for tyranny is strategically indefensible. 3. It must have a reasonable chance of success. If an anticommunist revolution cannot possibly prevail, we must not encourage freedom fighters in effect to commit suicide.

The fact that a country has a communist government does not by itself justify American support for an anticommunist rebellion against it. China is an obvious example. Beijing denies its people many freedoms we cherish, and a noncommunist government would clearly be in the interest of the Chinese people. But the government of China does not today threaten the United States, its friends, or its interests. On the contrary, China provides an indispensable counterweight to the Soviet Union. In addition, as the suppression of recent student protests showed, not even demonstrators, much less freedom fighters, have a chance to succeed against China's firmly established communist government.

Poland is another example. Few nations have suffered as tragic a history as the Polish people over the last two centuries, and no country deserves its freedom more than Poland. It would be in the interest of the Polish people and of the United States to support an anticommunist insurgency. But the sad fact is that it would stand no chance of success. As we learned in East Germany in 1953, Hungary in 1956, Czechoslovakia in 1968, and Poland in 1981, the Soviet Union will do whatever is necessary—including a brutal military invasion—to suppress an insurgency seeking to liberate one of its satellites in Eastern Europe. It would be a moral and strategic mistake to help a revolution against a tyrannical communist regime and then stand helplessly by as it is crushed by Moscow.

We should decide whether to help anticommunist revolutions on a case-by-case basis. We cannot support all the world's freedom fighters, but we must not turn our backs on any of them. If we casually dismiss those who oppose the totalitarians of the world, we will have lost our soul as a nation.

Once we decide to support an anticommunist cause, we cannot do so halfheartedly. We must not supply freedom fighters with enough arms and ammunition to fight and die for their country but not enough for them to liberate it. That would be the height of immorality. They are willing to make the ultimate sacrifice in the cause of freedom. We should give them the tools so they can finish the job. If we do not, we will be short-changing not only our friends but also ourselves.

While we must accept the fact that a great power does not always win, we must understand that if we take no risks we will never win. Victories require risks. At the same time, we must recognize that there are no permanent victories in the American–Soviet struggle. If they lose a battle, communists do not quit, but fall back to regroup for another day. Too often, after a defeat, Americans assume that the game is over, when in reality it has just moved into a different phase.

An ebb follows every tide in history. In the 1970s, the Soviets rode a rising tide in the Third World. But once in power, communists have failed to generate the genuine popular appeal necessary if the tide is to continue to rise. Yet, if the United States fails to support anticommunist revolutionaries with the Reagan Doctrine, this red tide will never ebb. If we accept all Soviet victories as permanent and irreversible, we will make communism the wave of the future.

We should apply these foreign-policy doctrines to current conflicts in Central America, Southwest Asia, southern Africa, and Southeast Asia.

In Central America, while vital U.S. interests are not directly at stake in the conflicts in Nicaragua and El Salvador, these struggles do involve the critical American interests of preventing the Soviet Union from securing a beachhead in the region. That would put the Kremlin a few shorts steps away from threatening the Panama Canal and Mexico. These vital interests might not be immediately at risk in the Central American crisis, but they are ultimately at risk.

In Nicaragua, our interests are not a matter of whether the government in Managua respects human rights and says nice things about the United States. A dictatorship, even a totalitarian one, does not threaten American interests per se, and the anti-American rhetoric of a country like Mexico is annoying but harmless. Our interests were engaged only when Nicaragua forged links with the Soviet bloc and became a base for Soviet expansionism in Central

America. The problem is not the fact that the Sandinista government is communist but that the communist government of Nicaragua is inherently expansionist.

There are those on the left who dispute the fact that Nicaragua is a threat to its neighbors. They have to concede that the Sandinistas have built up the largest military force in the history of Central America. But they argue that it was created solely for the defensive purpose of fighting the U.S.-supported anticommunist contras. They are doubly wrong. They ignore the fact that the Nicaraguan buildup *predated* the rise of the contras, and they miss the major point that the real threat to Central America from Nicaragua is not an overt invasion with conventional forces but covert subversion with unconventional forces.

Nicaraguan communist leaders would not dispute this fact. They freely admit, and even boast, that they seek "a revolution without frontiers" in Central America—a clear admission that they intend to impose communism on neighboring countries. It was cause and effect, not coincidence, that a geometric escalation of the guerrilla threat to El Salvador followed the Sandinista victory in Nicaragua. If Nicaragua becomes a safe haven and an arms conduit for communist revolutionaries, we can look forward to decades of messy counterinsurgency warfare in the region. Moscow will be able to conquer Central America at its leisure.

If the United States fails to act against this threat now, it will face a far graver threat later. Those who counsel a policy of containment against Nicaragua urge, in effect, that we wait until our security problems become acute before we act. That approach could undermine the entire American position in the world. Containment works only against overt attack. It does not work against subversion. If Nicaragua succeeds in sparking communist revolutions in other Central American states, our reaction would be to seek to contain them as well. Sooner or later, we will hear the same voices which now call for drawing the line at the Honduran border advocating a policy of containment for a communist Mexico by drawing a line at the Mexican border.

That would be a strategic disaster for the West. The only reason the United States can deploy 350,000 troops in Europe and 40,000 troops in Korea is that it does not have to defend any of its borders. If the Nicaraguan communists consolidate their power at home and export communism abroad, the United States will have to redeploy its forces, drawing back a substantial portion of our forces in Europe to defend our southern flank. It is significant to note that Managua's military buildup has already forced the United States to deploy two thousand troops on a semipermanent basis in Honduras.

The United States cannot accept a government in Nicaragua that is tied to the Soviet Union and that seeks to subvert neighboring countries. That is exactly what the current regime intends to do. Our goal therefore must be to induce the Sandinistas to change their aggressive policies toward their neighbors.

Many believe that the states of the region should settle their differences through the peace plan of Costa Rica's President Oscar Arias. President Reagan has accepted the plan, but the United States must avoid repeating the failures of the Contadora peace talks. Nicaragua used those negotiations to buy time to build up its military position. For six years, the two sides talked past each other. The Reagan administration and the democratic states of Central America wanted an agreement that called for the Sandinistas to negotiate with the contras about the political future of Nicaragua. The Sandinistas wanted an agreement that required the United States and its friends to cut off assistance to the contras. While well intentioned, the Arias plan risks falling into the same deadlock.

At the other extreme, there are those who argue that the United States should just bite the bullet and intervene with its own forces in Nicaragua. If we invade, there is no doubt that the United States has the power to prevail, and prevail quickly. Nicaragua's army is large and well armed for the Third World. But its ranks are filled mostly with unwilling conscripts who have fought poorly against the contras, and its supply lines to Cuba and the Soviet Union would be severed immediately. Unlike in Grenada, the United States would suffer significant casualties. An intervention would not, however, be another Vietnam. We would win.

Our problems would come not in winning but in deciding what to do once we had won. However effective the contras may turn out to be as a guerrilla force, they are not a government-in-waiting.

If the United States intervenes, it should be ready for a long stay. It took the Allies six years to set up a government in West Germany and for the United States to do so in Japan. It would take longer in Nicaragua.

Since negotiations alone cannot reach a genuine solution and since a long-term U.S. military involvement is an unsatisfactory option, the only way to stop Sandinista aggression is to couple peace talks with renewed support for the anticommunist contras. Nicaragua's communist leaders are fanatical men with conquest on their agenda. They are bent on bringing down all the fledgling democracies in Central America. We will not win them over with kindness. Unless the United States puts some kind of pressure on the Sandinistas, they will have no reason to change their policy of aggression through subversion.

U.S. aid to the contras has been in the interest of the Nicaraguan people. Some people support the government, but the majority oppose it. Nicaraguans from every sector of society joined the revolution against Somoza in order to establish a democratic government. Instead, they have gotten a tyranny worse than Somoza's. The Sandinistas have trampled on human rights, held fraudulent elections, harassed the church, closed down the press, intimidated the internal opposition with state-supported mobs, and tightened their grip on power with shipments of arms from the Soviet Union. The communist government has stolen the people's dream of democracy and has earned their enmity.

In addition, pressure from the contras lessens the repression by the Sandinistas. When the United States sent almost $300 million in economic aid to Nicaragua in the first year after the revolution, the Sandinistas took their greatest strides in building the foundations of totalitarianism. When that aid ended and American aid to the contra movement commenced, they eased the pace. But when Congress cut off our assistance to the contras, the Sandinistas escalated their repressive efforts to achieve total control over the Nicaraguan people. The most frivolous argument against aid to the contras is the chant "No more Vietnams." The way to avoid another Vietnam is to aid the contras now, rather than to be faced later with the necessity to send in U.S. forces to eliminate a Soviet base in the Western Hemisphere.

There are those who say that the contras have no chance to win. Whether they are right or wrong depends on the definition of victory. If it means marching on Managua in less than a year, they are right. If it means forcing the Sandinista leadership to negotiate a settlement, they are wrong.

With continued American support, contra forces have the staying power to wage a prolonged guerrilla war of attrition. With over twenty thousand troops in the field, the contras already have a more powerful army than the Sandinistas did when Somoza was toppled. Nicaragua's regular army has about sixty thousand troops and has received modern Soviet equipment, but has not performed well in combat. Even when the contras received no official U.S. military assistance, they were able to blunt the attack of Sandinista forces on contra base camps in Honduras. Government units have failed to stop the contras from infiltrating thousands of troops and tons of arms and ammunition into Nicaragua. The military bottom line is that Managua cannot prevent the contras from undertaking a major guerrilla campaign.

If we give the contras adequate support, the Sandinistas will not be able to count on the Soviet Union to come to the rescue. As the Cuban missile crisis demonstrated twenty-five years ago, Kremlin leaders would never risk a direct confrontation with the United States ten thousand miles away from the Soviet Union. They cannot project their conventional power over such great distances. And despite their increased nuclear capability compared with 1962, they are not going to risk nuclear war with the United States in order to save their clients in Managua. If push comes to shove, they will leave the Nicaraguan government to fend for itself. That fact creates major leverage for the United States.

We need to have a two-track policy. On the one hand, we should give the talks under the Arias plan a reasonable chance to succeed. On the other hand, however, our commitment to these negotiations cannot be open-ended. There must be a deadline.

The terms of the Arias plan call for all countries in Central America to end their civil wars by adopting democratic forms of government in which antigovernment insurgents can participate. Our friends in the region—Costa Rica, El Salvador, Honduras, and Guatemala—already comply with those conditions. But Nicaragua does not. We must ensure that President Arias and the other Central American leaders hold the Sandinistas' feet to the fire on the crucial issue of establishing a genuine democracy in Nicaragua. We should also insist that Nicaragua scale down its enormous armed forces and that its huge shipments of Soviet-bloc weapons be discontinued. For the Soviets alone to discontinue their aid would not be enough. Cuba and the other communist-bloc countries would pick up the slack. If the negotiations fail on these points, we must be prepared to move to the second track: military pressure on Managua.

We must be realistic about the motivations behind the political maneuvering of the Sandinistas. They have one objective in mind: to disband the contras. American political figures who meet with Sandinista leaders and who then prattle about how sincerely the Nicaraguans want peace are unbelievably naive. Daniel Ortega and his sidekicks want peace only if it means a victory of his communist government over his anticommunist opposition.

Unfortunately, in accepting the Nobel Peace Prize, President Arias urged that the United States immediately end all aid—military and nonmilitary—to the contras. This would bring a communist peace to Nicaragua—a peace which would mean death for the contras, desolation for the Nicaraguan people, and a new wave of communist aggression through subversion against the free nations of Central America.

Sandinista leaders adopted a shrewd political strategy. They skillfully created the appearance of political progress in Nicaragua in order to induce Congress to cut off funding to the Nicaraguan freedom fighters. As a result, they released about one thousand political prisoners, permitted the church radio station to resume broadcasting, allowed *La Prensa* to reopen, and even entered indirect negotiations with the contras. But the Sandinistas still hold more than four thousand political prisoners, prohibit news programs on the church radio station, and censor the press. Most important, in their indirect talks the Sandinistas are willing to discuss only the terms of surrender for the contras, rather than sitting down to work out the procedures for instituting democratic elections.

To counter this, the Reagan administration should pursue every available legal means to keep the anticommunist forces alive. This is needed to pressure the Sandinistas in the negotiating process and to prepare for the likely event that the talks fail. Those in Congress who want to kill the cause of democracy in Nicaragua should keep in mind that whenever the legislative branch seizes the executive's authority over foreign affairs they will be held responsible for the consequences. The administration's Wrightscapade put the contras on a slippery slope. If the Sandinistas consolidate their control in Nicaragua, the consequences will include communist insurgencies and heightened instability throughout Central America. And the blood will be on the hands of the Congress.

If the Arias plan fails, Congress must renew military aid to the contras—and on a far larger scale than we have so far done. But we should not leave the defense of our critical interests in Central America solely in the hands of a proxy force like the contras. We should use our own forces to quarantine Nicaragua. We should prevent its expansionist and repressive communist government from receiving further shipments of arms and supplies from the Soviet Union and Cuba. Since they came to power the Sandinistas have been igniting fires throughout Central America. It makes no sense for the United States to run around putting out the fires while allowing the arsonists to continue to get their hands on the supplies to light still more.

We must declare a new version of the Monroe Doctrine. We should state that the United States will resist intervention in Latin America, not only by foreign governments, but also by Latin American governments controlled by foreign powers. A military quarantine of Nicaragua would be part of that policy. It would prevent Managua from subverting our friends in the region. It would also enable the contras to put the greatest pressure in the shortest time on the Sandinistas to agree to a settlement creating a genuine democratic process in Nicaragua, which is the only viable long-term solution to the crisis in Central America.

In Southwest Asia, the key American–Soviet conflict is the war in Afghanistan. After the Soviet invasion in 1979, Egypt's President Anwar Sadat ominously observed, "The battle around the oil stores has already begun." His comment was right on the mark.

If the Kremlin succeeds in consolidating its control over Afghanistan, it will have put itself into a perfect position from which to threaten our vital interests in the region. Moscow will be able to use Afghanistan as a base from which to destabilize Pakistan and Iran. That would give the Soviets total dominance over either the maritime approaches to the Persian Gulf or the gulf itself. Moscow would have won control of the oil jugular. We must treat the Soviet–Afghan war not as a peripheral conflict in a faraway place but as a crucial battle in our competition with Moscow.

At its present level of engagement, the Soviet Union has won only a stalemate. Eight years of fighting have put the Soviets no closer to final victory than they were at the outset. Since its armies have been unable to run the Afghan resistance off the battlefield, Moscow has adopted a strategy of attrition. It seeks to wear down the will of the Afghan people to resist with brutal attacks on the civilian population. There is not a village in the entire Afghan countryside which has escaped attack by Soviet aircraft. But even this campaign of terror bombing has not buckled the Afghans. Gorbachev and his colleagues know that they face a long, up-hill fight to consolidate their control over the peaks of the Hindu Kush.

Therefore, the Kremlin has been trying to find a shortcut to victory. Moscow is trying to undercut outside support for the resistance, and that makes Pakistan the key to the war. Assistance from foreign countries, such as the United States, China, and oil-rich Middle East countries, reaches the Afghans principally through Pakistan, and the Soviets have leveled tremendous pressure on Islamabad to cut off the aid pipeline. In 1987, air strikes by Soviet and Afghan government jets and helicopters killed hundreds of people in Pakistan, and Soviet-supported terrorists planted over 250 bombs in Pakistani cities. Soviet forces have also armed separatist tribes in the Afghan–Pakistani border areas.

While Moscow has waged war, it has talked peace. It has put up a smokescreen of peace offers to soften the West and to create domestic pressure within Pakistan to sign a deal on Moscow's terms. For six years, UN-sponsored negotiations between Afghanistan and Pakistan worked toward a settlement of the war. The tentative agreements have two key provisions. The first states that as soon as the parties sign an agreement the aid to resistance must be cut off. The second states that after the signing the Soviet Union would have a certain amount of time to pull out its forces. While it took only two days to put their forces in, the Soviets have been demanding a year or more to take them out. That would give Moscow time to decimate the resistance before its forces would have to depart.

We must pursue two goals in Afghanistan—a pullout of Soviet forces and self-determination for the Afghan people. Neither our interests nor those of Pakistan and the Afghan resistance would be served if we settle for the first without the second. To achieve our objectives, the United States must work on both the military and diplomatic fronts. We must aid the resistance, protect Pakistan, and negotiate with Moscow.

We should provide as much military and financial assistance to the Afghan resistance as they can effectively use. So far, we have not. We must increase our assistance both in quantity and in quality. The decision in 1986 to provide a sophisticated U.S. antiaircraft missile—the Stinger—has made a significant impact on the war. This should have been done six years earlier. We must not try to fine-tune the level of pressure on the Soviets, turning up the intensity of the war in small increments. If we want to induce the Soviets to strike a deal, we should give as much assistance to the Afghan resistance as it can effectively deploy.

An increase in our aid to the Afghans is in the interest of the United States and Pakistan because raising the military and political cost of the war is the only way to pressure the Soviets to accept a diplomatic solution. It is in the interest of the Afghan people because a diplomatic solution is the only way to liberate their country. It has a chance of success because there has been a direct correlation between the flexibility of the Soviets at the negotiating table and the intensity of the fighting on the battlefield. It is not coincidental that Moscow's recent willingness to reduce its withdrawal timetable from six years to one year came after the United States provided Stinger missiles to the resistance.

We must also protect Pakistan against Soviet efforts at intimidation. We issued a pledge in 1959 to come to the assistance of Pakistan in the event of a communist attack. Today, we must make good on that promise. Congress must not cut our military and economic assistance package to Pakistan, notwithstanding its concerns about whether Islamabad is developing the capability to build nuclear weapons. We should accede to Pakistan's request to buy airborne radar aircraft so that its air force can shoot down marauding Soviet and Afghan-government jets and helicopters. We must recognize that if we cannot secure Pakistan against Soviet intimidation we cannot secure a just settlement of the war in Afghanistan.

While the government of President Zia ul-Haq is not a perfect democracy, it does meet the four conditions for American aid. It allows some freedoms, including freedom of the press, and has a parliament which creates the possibility for change through the electoral process. It has a competent government which has a good record on economic growth. It has a strong military which is capable of keeping order. The current opposition leadership would be a disaster for Pakistan if it succeeded in winning power.

On the diplomatic front, we must not allow Moscow to win at the negotiating table what it has failed to win on the battlefield. Afghanistan is not a minor issue, like cultural-exchange programs, which should be tossed into a summit as a sweetener. It is a crucial conflict that will determine who wins the U.S.–Soviet competition.

We must first dispel two misconceptions about how to deal with the issue of Afghanistan. The first is that the Soviets want any settlement they can get. On the contrary, they intend to use a settlement to get what they want. Moscow's goal is to withdraw after a communist government is firmly entrenched. Gorbachev's proposal for a protracted withdrawal period is designed to enable Soviet forces to crush a resistance starved of ammunition and supplies before packing up to leave. The second misconception is that if we provide enough assistance to the resistance the Afghans will be able to expel the Soviets from the country. However brave and determined resistance forces may be, they cannot win the war in the sense that the Allies did in World War II. Moscow can win militarily if it is willing to stay the course. Our friends in the Afghan resistance therefore can only liberate their country through a political settlement.

We must make achieving a fair settlement a top priority item on the U.S.–Soviet agenda. We have the leverage to succeed. Moscow can win if Kremlin leaders are willing to pay the price—but we can raise that price. We should scrap the U N talks on Afghanistan and pursue the issue in bilateral talks. These talks must address the key issue: the future domestic and international political status of Afghanistan. We should concede that the Soviet Union has one—but only one—legitimate interest in Afghanistan: It is that Afghanistan be a nonaligned country. Neither the Soviet Union nor any other country has a right to determine the nature of Afghanistan's political system.

That is the basis of a fair settlement. A transitional government, composed of Afghans who are not members of either the Communist Party or the resistance and perhaps headed by the former King of Afghanistan, could rule while Soviet forces pulled out. After the withdrawal, an election or a national tribal council could decide the future system of government. This government should be pledged in advance to a nonaligned status internationally, and the United States, China, and the Soviet Union should all sign an agreement to guarantee that status.

We must accept no agreement that gives the Soviet Union a withdrawal period longer than about half a year. Moreover, we must not cut off American aid to the resistance until the Soviet Union has removed all its forces from Afghanistan, though we could phase down our aid as the Soviets reduced their forces. After the withdrawal, the agreement should call for the Soviet Union to stop aid to its communist clients at the same time the United States stops aid to the resistance. And if the Soviet Union breaks the arms embargo, the United States must respond in kind. Any policy that fails to measure up on these points would be a sellout.

Such a settlement would protect the interests of all parties involved in the war, including the Soviet Union's. Moscow is not threatened by a free and neutral Finland. It withdrew its postwar occupation forces from and accepted the neutrality of Austria under a treaty worked out with the United States in 1955. For sixty years before the Afghan communists took power in their 1978 coup, a nonaligned but free Afghanistan had been acceptable to Moscow. Gorbachev should accept a restoration of that formula today.

We should actively pursue such a settlement in direct U.S.–Soviet negotiations. But we must also understand that it will never come about unless we protect Pakistan from Soviet intimidation and help the Afghans increase the cost of the Soviet occupation. If Gorbachev would like to cut his losses in Afghanistan, we should accommodate him—if he accepts a fair settlement, but not if a Soviet military withdrawal is a smokescreen to retain political control.

Antigovernment insurgencies exist throughout southern Africa, but Angola is the most important case. The region itself represents a critical interest for the West. It contains vast deposits of strategic minerals, such as platinum, chromium, manganese, and cobalt, upon which the industrial economies of the West depend. In some cases, the only alternate source is the Soviet Union. Unless we want to pay monopoly prices to the Kremlin, the United States must seek to minimize Soviet influence in the region.

In the late 1970s, the Soviet Union exploited the fall of the Portuguese empire to establish several communist states in southern Africa. In Angola, the communist members of a three-party government broke up the coalition and ordered up 35,000 Cuban troops through their friends in the Kremlin to assert their control over the country. Still worse, from the point of view of Western interests, these forces were used in a brief invasion of mineral-rich Shaba province of neighboring Zaire. Only a combined French-American intervention prevented a Cuban victory.

One of the other parties in the initial postcolonial coalition government, known by its acronym UNITA, then took up arms against the communists in Luanda. Congress prohibited U.S. assistance to UNITA through the Clark Amendment of 1976, leaving UNITA no other option than turning to South Africa for material aid. With the support of a substantial segment of the Angolan people, UNITA quickly secured control over a third of Angola, with only the shield of Cuban proxy forces preventing UNITA from laying siege to the capital. In 1985, when Congress repealed the Clark Amendment, the Reagan administration resumed assistance to Angola's freedom fighters.

We should continue and increase that support. It is in our interest to increase the costs of keeping Cuban forces, for no other means exists to induce the Kremlin to pull them out. It is in the interest of the Angolan people to bring an end to the communist rule that has turned their county into an economic wasteland. UNITA's leader, Jonas Savimbi, seeks not unconditional surrender but rather a coalition government. His program calls not for more centralized planning but a market-based economy. Moreover, UNITA stands a good chance to succeed. In the last two years, major Cuban- and Soviet-led military thrusts into UNITA territory have failed abysmally, partly as a result of air strikes by South Africa but mainly because of UNITA's strength. In any case, while Moscow could conceivably sustain its losses in Afghanistan indefinitely, it is certainly an open question whether over the long haul Cuba can endure its casualties in Angola.

In Southeast Asia, the key conflicts in the competition between the United States and the Soviet Union are the war in Cambodia and the insurgency in the Philippines.

Since Vietnam invaded Cambodia, a consensus exists in the United States that the Cambodian resistance deserves our help. While wearing down the Vietnamese occupation forces is in our interest, we have to accept the fact that Cambodia is a peripheral interest for the United States. Also, since communist Khmer Rouge forces make up the majority of the Cambodian resistance, a victory could put into power the same people who killed over two million Cambodians from 1975 to 1978. That would not be in the interest of the Cambodian people. There is little chance we can succeed in helping establish a noncommunist government, because the amount of supplies we would have to deliver to take on the Vietnamese would be tremendous. The sad fact is that we simply

143

do not have the capability to push the Vietnamese out. This is an area in which China, rather than the United States, should take the lead.

The Philippines are a critical interest for the United States. Our Subic Bay naval base and Clark Air Force Base are the two largest American military installations outside the United States. They are indispensable for our presence in the Pacific and our capability to project power into the Indian Ocean and the Persian Gulf. And there are no suitable substitute locations for those bases anywhere in Southeast Asia. The United States cannot afford a defeat by anti-American forces in the Philippines.

We made the right decision in standing aside while the forces behind Corazon Aquino displaced the government of President Marcos. In his first years in power, Marcos was an outstanding leader of his country and a loyal ally of the United States, but after several years of success his government failed. While he did permit a great degree of freedom, he had blocked the possibility of reform through elections. That would have certainly led to a political explosion if he had stayed in power. While he did not invent corruption—which has been a way of life in the Philippines and still is—he had allowed his cronies and his family to enrich themselves beyond all reasonable limits. While almost all free countries were enjoying rapid economic growth, the Philippines became an economic disaster area, with government-backed monopolies blocking individual initiative. While the communist New People's Army rapidly gained strength, he neglected the need to build up and improve the competence of the military. If Marcos had stayed in power, the situation would have steadily—and quickly—deteriorated.

We also had an alternate leadership in the Philippines that held out the hope of turning these trends around. But whether President Aquino will succeed is still an open question. A revolution creates instability, and the communist-led NPA can profit from instability. It is not yet clear that the new leadership is up to the challenge. What is clear is that the United States cannot make the mistake of believing that the departure of Marcos has solved all our problems. We need to help the Philippines get back on their feet. We must increase our economic aid, assist the new government in devising the right economic policies to encourage growth, and help reform and reequip the Filipino armed forces so that they can turn back the communists.

Whenever the United States involves itself in replacing one leader with another, it also takes on the responsibility to ensure that the new government will do better than its predecessor. We have pledged to help the Philippines. But we have yet to commit the kinds of resources which President Aquino needs to do the job. We must do so, for the future of the South Pacific and our future as a Pacific power are at stake.

Our competition with Moscow must not be limited to the non-communist world. To accept the proposition that the communists have a right to compete with us in the free world but that we have no right to compete with them in the communist world is a recipe for defeat. We must adopt policies to engage the Soviets in the kind of competition between our systems that will foster peaceful change in theirs.

We cannot win the U.S.–Soviet struggle unless we go on the offensive—but on a peaceful offensive. We should develop a strategy for peaceful competition with Moscow on the other side of the Iron Curtain, not only in Eastern Europe but also within the Soviet Union itself. We must recognize that, in the long term, peaceful competition will be just as important to the outcome of the American–Soviet struggle as keeping up our military deterrent.

Our most difficult problems arise in finding a way to wage this competition within the Soviet bloc. Given the Kremlin's control over these countries, we are competing at a decided disadvantage. But a temporary disadvantage does not decide a contest. While we have no perfect means to compete with Moscow in the Soviet sphere, we must not abandon the imperfect means which are available. While the thirty-one Soviet army divisions in Eastern Europe prevent Moscow's satellites from breaking out of orbit, the aspirations of their peoples and the superiority of our system and our ideals make them gravitate toward the West.

There are those who consider the countries of Eastern Europe to be a lost cause. In this view, however regrettable the betrayal at Yalta may have been, Moscow's subjugation of these countries is an unalterable fact of life. They argue that military change is too dangerous and that peaceful change is impossible. They are right on the first point but wrong on the second. Nothing in this world, not even a well-entrenched communist government, is immune to the forces of change. Eastern Europe today differs profoundly from Eastern Europe in 1950; Eastern Europe in 1999 will differ profoundly from Eastern Europe today. What we do will affect what kind of change takes place. If we accept the view of those who would write off Eastern Europe, it will be harder for the forces for positive change to prevail. We cannot *determine* what happens in Eastern Europe, but we can *influence* events there. If we adopt responsible policies to compete with Moscow in Eastern Europe, we can help shape and accelerate the process of positive change.

Soviet control, though great, is not total. The Soviet Union and the countries of Eastern Europe are not a monolithic bloc. The peoples of these countries totally reject Soviet domination. Not even the communist leaders of Eastern Europe and those of the Soviet Union have identical interests. Soviet military power does severely limit the scope of independent action, both domestically and internationally, on the part of East European leaders, but personal, political, national, and even ideological differences have developed—and will develop—between the Soviet Union and its East European clients.

We must base our policy on a sophisticated understanding of the motivations of the three key political groups in Eastern Europe: the leaders in the Kremlin, the peoples of Eastern Europe, and the communist leaders of the countries of Eastern Europe.

Moscow's leaders are ruthless imperialists who want to control Eastern Europe. It is part of their empire, and they want to keep it. A desire for imperial expansion is as ingrained in the Kremlin's way of thinking as the desire for freedom is in ours. While the Soviets gloss over their imperial domination with talk about the "fraternal camp of socialist countries," it is nothing more than window dressing. In 1968, when Alexander Dubček, the communist leader of Czechoslovakia, presented Brezhnev with reforms to liberalize his country while retaining the socialist system and staying in the Warsaw Pact, the Soviet leader cast aside the pretense. "Don't talk to me about 'Socialism,' " Brezhnev told Dubček. "What we have, we hold."

But at the same time the Soviets cannot exert total control over every detail of government policy in every East European country. They have tremendous power to decide who holds office in their satellites. Through that power, they can determine basic political and economic policies of these countries. But they have much less control over the fine points of policy. Moscow will not throw its clients out of office over small matters, because it wants stability. Unless they are willing to purge major East European communist leaders or intervene with military force, the Kremlin leaders often have to live with their clients' decisions, even if they do not approve.

While the governments of Eastern Europe are Soviet allies, the peoples of Eastern Europe are *our* allies. More than anyone else, those who suffer from Soviet oppression know the need to stop Soviet expansion. Many analysts tout today's anticommunist freedom fighters as an unprecedented development. It is not. We must remember that the East European peoples did not go quietly into the totalitarian night. Hundreds of thousands who opposed the imposition of communism on their countries were killed during and after World War II. Tens of thousands more have since fought and died for the liberation of their native lands.

Few today remember the opposition the Soviet Union met when its forces invaded Hungary in 1956 and Czechoslovakia in 1968. We often read about how Soviet tanks rolled into these countries, as if the Hungarians, the Czechs, and the Slovaks simply rolled over at their sight. That is a myth. If we are to understand Eastern Europe today, we must keep in mind that East European resistance to Soviet military forces has been as impressive as that of the Afghans today.

I was in Austria on the Hungarian border soon after Moscow invaded the country in 1956. It took 200,000 Warsaw Pact troops three weeks of fighting to put down the popular uprising. Soviet forces killed 25,000 Hungarians, wounded 150,000, and imprisoned 20,000, many of whom were later executed. Two hundred thousand refugees fled into Austria. Large parts of the Hungarian army defected to the resistance. But the fight was a mismatch. Hungarians fought with rifles, grenades, and Molotov cocktails against Soviet T-54 tanks. Many areas of Budapest suffered more damage than they had in World War II. In an interview with correspondents on the scene, I called Khrushchev the "butcher of Budapest." The epithet stuck because it fit.

In Czechoslovakia in 1968, it took 500,000 troops weeks to restore Soviet control over the country. Without any arms or military equipment, the resistance hamstrung Soviet forces for weeks. Crowds sat in front of tanks. A brave few stuffed tin cans down the gun barrels. Throngs milled around the central radio and television station to prevent the invaders from taking them over. Civilians undertook a systematic campaign of passive resistance. Soviet morale plummeted as the people totally ostracized the troops. With near-universal popular adherence to the resistance call for "not a drop of water for the occupiers," Soviet units were handicapped by a severe shortage of drinking water.

It is those popular uprisings, not the champagne toasts at Warsaw Pact conferences, that represent the fundamental political reality of Eastern Europe. Hungarians, Czechs, Slovaks, Poles, East Germans, Romanians, and Bulgarians are strong peoples, and they are our allies in the U.S.–Soviet competition. Our strategy for peaceful competition must capitalize on their strength.

East European communist leaders are pulled in opposite directions by two factors, their desire for legitimacy in the eyes of their peoples and their dependence on the Soviet Union to stay in power. These governments are not legitimate. They were imposed by Soviet arms, and they are maintained by Soviet arms. No one in these countries—not even the members of their governments—would dispute these facts. As a result, East European communist leaders have a desperate desire to be seen as legitimate rulers. It is the central preoccupation of every East European communist leader I have ever met.

This acute insecurity came through with eloquent clarity in the narrative of the climactic events of the Hungarian uprising in the memoirs of András Hegedüs, the Stalinist Prime Minister of the country at the time. He wrote: "I . . . got to my feet and looked out of the window: I could see that the head of the demonstration had reached the middle of the Margaret Bridge [on the way to the government's building]. It was a terrifying sight. Even if I had not seen it coming, I should then have realized that here was national resistance developing against the central leadership and against the policies of the old leaders, including myself. I saw quite clearly—this is it, the people are coming.''

East European communist leaders face a difficult dilemma. Legitimacy can come only from greater national independence or better economic performance. Independence requires policies that distance the country from the Soviet Union. Economic growth requires reforms that depart from the Soviet model. Either would clearly displease the Soviet leaders—and it is at their pleasure that the rulers of Eastern Europe hold office. This basic tension produces different kinds of communist leaders in Eastern Europe. Some, like Hegedüs, tie themselves inextricably to Moscow. Most seek to create a margin of independence without severing their lifeline to Moscow or prompting a Soviet invasion. And like Dubček, a few genuinely want to change the system from within.

Eastern Europe today is ripe for positive peaceful change. In 1983, I traveled throughout Bulgaria, Romania, Hungary, and Czechoslovakia and met with several Eastern-bloc leaders and hundreds of private citizens. One message came through loud and clear: doctrinaire communism was dead as a motivating force. That was clear in the sullen manner in which common people pursued their lives. It was even clearer in the conversations I had with East European leaders. They recognized the fact that a fundamental incompatibility existed between the interests of their countries and those of the Soviet Union and that the Soviet model of economic development was irrelevant in Eastern Europe.

Soviet-style economic planning has failed to provide the peoples of Eastern Europe even with the basic necessities of life. In stark contrast to their neighbors in Western Europe, these countries have literally entered a period of economic decline. In the 1980s, their economies have grown less than one percent per year. Since their populations have been growing at a more rapid pace, the standard of living has been dropping. The countries of Eastern Europe have run up against a hard but inalterable fact: Rigid bureaucratic planning cannot create a dynamic economy. East Euro-

149

pean countries must undertake fundamental economic reforms. Without them, they will sink into the quicksand of economic stagnation. To try to muddle through will only mire them more deeply.

There has been a total loss of faith among East European communists. Most today are careerists and bureaucrats. The will and confidence of the communist parties have been broken. Many of their leaders want to deviate from the Soviet economic model and to improve their own relations with the West in order to open up possibilities for internal reform. The rising generation of East Europeans are not ideologues but pragmatists—and pragmatism creates openings for peaceful change.

This is particularly true with Gorbachev in power. He has alienated East European leaders by calling for greater coordination among Eastern-bloc economies and by ending the Soviet subsidies on some exports, like oil. But his policy of Glasnost will reduce, not increase, his control over Eastern Europe. His call for greater openness in public criticism will lead inevitably to pressure within East European countries and communist parties to put more distance between themselves and Moscow. Gorbachev might intend his Glasnost campaign to serve as a safety valve for popular dissatisfaction and as a weapon against his political foes. He might not mean his rhetoric to be taken literally, but it will be so understood in Eastern Europe.

If the Soviet Union and its clients respond to the challenges before them with half measures, they might make marginal progress for a time, but they will not be able to energize the peoples in Eastern Europe to support their governments. That failure will generate still more pressure for greater changes. Since World War II, the tectonic plate of Soviet imperialism has been pushing against that of Eastern European nationalism. These forces have produced tremors in the past, but unprecedented pressures will build up along the fault line in the 1990s. Without genuine reform, a political earthquake in Eastern Europe is inevitable in the years before 1999.

Gorbachev has announced a willingness to allow his East European satellites to pursue independent approaches to internal reform. But he has also made clear that two limits must be observed. The communist system must remain intact, and ultimate control by the Soviet Union must remain unquestioned. What he fails to realize is that stagnation in Eastern Europe stems not just from the idiocies of communist economic systems; it also results from the heavy hand of Soviet imperialism. Before the American Civil War, freemen in the North produced far more per capita than slaves in the South. Oppression, not only of individuals but also of nations, breeds social and economic stagnation. East European peoples will not break out of this inertia until they achieve a real degree of control over their national destinies.

Our challenge is to formulate a strategy to increase the chances that from these inherent pressures will emerge positive peaceful change. We must first clarify what our policy should *not* be. We must not make it our goal to create states in Eastern Europe which are aligned against and openly hostile to the Soviet Union. Nor should it be our policy to destabilize these countries by supporting freedom fighters within their borders. Given the Soviet Union's overwhelming military superiority in the region, that would be nothing more than offering freedom fighters up for slaughter.

Our long-term goal should be to create independent states that have open societies domestically and that pose no threat to the Soviet Union. In a sense, our goal is to "Finlandize" the countries of Eastern Europe. Our policy should be to encourage the people of Eastern Europe to push for incremental increases in their freedom and to create incentives for their governments to grant those freedoms and to push for incremental increases in their independence from the Soviet Union. Moscow cannot invade an East European country every time its people increase the scope of free communications or every time its government allows market forces to exert more influence in determining economic prices. We need to help foster a process of accumulating small, marginal gains. It might seem frustrating, even futile. Yet, it is the only way that these countries will ever achieve a measure of national freedom.

How can the United States encourage this process? A precondition for peaceful change is military deterrence. It is essential that the Soviet Union not be perceived as the supreme military power. As soon as the West demonstrates that it cannot be cowed into submission, the peoples of the East will seek to assert themselves more actively. If the West cannot muster an adequate military deterrent to Soviet intimidation, we cannot expect East European peoples to defy the Kremlin.

Beyond deterrence, our strategy for peaceful change in Eastern Europe must have four elements. First, we must seek a relaxation of American–Soviet tensions. While many anticommunists in the West have reviled the policy of détente which I adopted as President in the early 1970s, the anticommunists in the East supported this approach wholeheartedly. International tension strengthens a dictatorship, and a relaxation of those tensions weakens a dictatorship. No one would deny that our policy of détente in the 1970s contributed greatly to the events which led to the rise of the Solidarity movement in Poland.

Even one of the fiercest, though most responsible, critics of détente, Richard Pipes, conceded this point in writing about its effects on the Soviet system. He wrote that détente "undoubtedly accelerated the process by which society in the USSR began to resist controls." He added that, for the Soviets, "To proclaim the Cold War over—even while repeating ad nauseam that the struggle between the two systems must go on to the bitter end—is to put in question the need in Russia for a repressive regime." If détente had this effect in the Soviet Union, its impact in Eastern Europe was tenfold greater.

A relaxation of tensions undermines the rationale for communist governments. As it is, the communists of Eastern Europe have a lot of explaining to do. They have to explain why they have subordinated themselves to Moscow, why they repress political and intellectual freedom, why they cannot overcome economic backwardness, and why they permit social privilege based on political position. They justify all of this in terms of the supposed military threat from the West. Better American–Soviet relations make this argument unsustainable. Communist rule is exposed as the rule of naked force. This inexorably pushes the communists to seek legitimacy through reform or greater national independence.

Second, we must seek to maximize Western contact with the peoples of Eastern Europe. A relaxation of superpower tensions facilitates greater contact. But we must vigorously pursue it. We should increase our trade and our cultural-exchange programs with

Eastern Europe. We should devote more resources to foreign radio broadcasting into the area. The more contact we have with the East, the more we open it to the force of the example of the West. That is a force which even the communist elites will have difficulty resisting.

Moreover, these countries face great problems for which the Soviet Union has no solutions to offer. In the years before 1999, for example, Eastern Europe will confront a major ecological crisis. While the West has grappled with the problem of industrial pollution for twenty years, Soviet-bloc countries have totally ignored it. The nightmare forecasts of American environmentalists in the 1960s could very well come about in Eastern Europe in the 1990s. Beset with its own ecological problem, Moscow has nothing to offer Eastern Europe in this area. We in the West do—and we should take the initiative because through our actions we can significantly improve the quality of life of the peoples of Eastern Europe.

Third, we must seek a reduction in American and Soviet conventional forces in Europe. The less military force the Soviet Union has in Eastern Europe, the less control it has over Eastern Europe. Moscow has no troops in Romania, and Romania will not give Moscow the right to station any there in peacetime. That has given Romanian President Nicolae Ceausescu the ability to diverge from Soviet positions on international issues. While no one would claim that his domestic policies are anything but severely repressive, no one can deny that he has carved out a real measure of national independence in foreign policy. We must therefore make conventional arms reductions a major focus of arms control.

Fourth, we must seek to work with East European communist leaders who want to implement genuine reforms. There are those who argue that a communist is a communist and that all East European leaders are beyond the pale. In this view, the United States should break all contacts with these regimes. That is the worst mistake we could make. It is essential that we always keep in mind that some of the greatest challenges to Soviet control over Eastern Europe have arisen *within* the satellite communist parties. Marshal Tito sprang Yugoslavia from the Soviet bloc in 1948. Imre Nagy led the Hungarian rebellion in 1956. Wladyslav Gomulka faced Khrushchev down on the key issue of agricultural collectivization in Poland in 1956. Enver Hoxha split Albania away from the Soviet Union in 1961. Ceausescu distanced Romania from the Soviet line on some international issues in the 1960s. Dubček brought about the Prague Spring in 1968. Edward Gierek's regime agreed to negotiate an agreement with the Solidarity movement in Poland in 1979. Janos Kadar has instituted a gradual liberalization of the Hungarian economy during the 1980s.

This does not mean that East European communist leaders are closet Jeffersonian democrats who can hardly wait to hold town meetings. But it does mean that we should not ignore the possibilities inherent in the conflicts between Soviet communists and East European communists. The key is to differentiate between those leaders who are interested in genuine reform and those who are not. We should calibrate our policies to their behavior. If an East European regime adopts more liberal policies or distances itself from Moscow, we should encourage its leaders with better economic relations with the West, which their countries need so desperately.

Hungary is an excellent example. General Secretary Kadar, whom Khrushchev appointed after the Soviet invasion of 1956, has widely liberalized his country's economy. He has not worked miracles but he has produced positive change. The Budapest I saw in 1963 could only be described as drab and dreary. When I returned in 1983 it was bright and lively—an eloquent example of what just a little freedom can do. Kadar allows Western television and radio stations to broadcast their programs unjammed into the country. It is now even possible to buy some Western newspapers in Budapest. These reforms have greatly improved the quality of life for the Hungarian people—and they create the basis for future governments to adopt still more reforms on a pragmatic basis. We must welcome such positive change because we have a stake in its success. We should never adopt policies—such as wholesale isolation of the Eastern bloc—which would abort them at the outset.

Our strategy for peaceful competition in Eastern Europe must be grounded in pragmatism. It is not an all-or-nothing venture. Like Lenin, we must be willing to adopt a strategy of taking two steps forward and one step back. Some East European countries have already made significant progress. Each wave of reform consolidates previous reforms and opens the way for still more in the future. In the early 1950s, the great issue in Poland was whether the Kremlin could force its clients in Warsaw to collectivize agriculture. Poland held Moscow off. Today, after successive waves of peaceful change, the issue of land ownership is not even subject to debate. Solidarity expanded the frontiers of freedom to an unprecedented extent. Even through the imposition of martial law, the Polish government failed to restore the previous status quo. Warsaw has had to accept the existence of thousands of independent publications. With the Solidarity leadership still active, it has even had to accommodate itself to a de-facto organized political opposition. Stalin must be twirling his mustache in his grave.

Promoting such peaceful change is how we can compete with Moscow in Eastern Europe. Maintaining control over these countries will be a perpetual problem for the Kremlin. Freedom is an acquired taste. Unlike the Russians, East Europeans have tasted freedom in the past—and they still have a taste for it. How far peaceful change can carry the countries of Eastern Europe toward genuine independence and internal freedom is an open question. We must not render that question moot by failing to do what we can to promote it.

We should also extend this peaceful competition into the Soviet Union itself. To many Americans, this sounds like a kind of hostile act. But it is not. Soviet commentators now regularly appear on American news broadcasts, peddling the Soviet line on international issues. The United States must not refrain from beaming news and information into the Soviet Union. We have every right to do so under international law, and we should exercise this right. If we adopt a policy of unilateral restraint in the war of ideas, we will forfeit one of our most effective tools in the American–Soviet competition.

Our goal should be to encourage the decentralization of power in the Soviet Union. That must be a long-term goal—but it is within reach. While Kremlin leaders hold thousands of political prisoners, the era of Stalinist mass terror has ended. Without terror, Moscow simply cannot exert the same kind of total control. This has loosened up the system and has opened up far greater opportunities for individuals and groups to deviate from the edicts of the central government. Our broadcasts into the Soviet Union should promote a gradual push on the part of the Soviet peoples to lessen control by Kremlin leaders.

There are those who argue that such reform is impossible in a totalitarian power like the Soviet Union. They are wrong. While change comes at an excruciatingly slow pace, it does occur—and we must seek to affect the direction it takes.

Radio Liberty is a good beginning. But our broadcasts must direct far greater attention to the non-Russian nations of the Soviet Union. Moscow rules the last multinational empire on earth. Russians constitute barely half the total population. The other half includes Ukrainians, Uzbeks, Byelorussians, Kazakhs, Tatars, Azerbaijanis, Armenians, Georgians, Moldavians, Tadzhiks, Lithuanians, Turkomens, Kirghiz, and dozens of others. There are over one hundred distinct nations in the Soviet Union. Our radio broadcasts should address these peoples in their native languages and should provide them with information about their own regions and histories which the Russian-dominated government refuses to disseminate.

Virtually all of the non-Russian nations consider the Soviet government to be rule by the Russians and for the Russians. These peoples know that Russians permit only token representatives of other nations to hold top slots in the central government. They still remember that Russian armies conquered their lands, that Russian colonists quickly moved in, and that the Russian minority now dominates key government and economic positions at the provincial level. They would be a highly receptive audience for our message calling for decentralization of power in the Soviet Union. If Kremlin leaders had to devote more of their attention to satisfying the demands of these peoples, the world would become a more peaceful place.

Americans often forget how powerful and enduring the memories of historical injustice can be. They mistakenly believe that the non-Russian nations incorporated into the Soviet Union have assimilated themselves into Russia, just as immigrants do when they come to the United States. But fifty million Ukrainians, for example, have never forgotten that they are the largest nation in the world without a state. They remember that the Kremlin killed over eight million Ukrainians in the collectivization of agriculture and the political purges of the 1930s. They remember that their national repression was so severe that in World War II, when Hitler's Germany occupied the region, the Ukrainian Insurgent Army, composed of forty thousand guerrillas, fought against *both* the Soviets and the Nazis. We can be certain that the Ukrainian desire for national self-determination will not soon ebb.

Moslem peoples in Soviet Central Asia are no different in this respect. They have not forgotten that over a million and a half people died from starvation when Stalin withheld food supplies from Central Asia in his brutal quest to consolidate Soviet control over the region during the 1930s. They know that Russian colonists dominate their local governments. They know that the Kremlin has decided to focus the program for economic renewal on the European areas of the Soviet Union, dooming their homelands to economic stagnation and their peoples to poverty. They know that future generations will either have to migrate elsewhere in search of jobs or face unemployment.

These historical memories and current political realities make the peoples of Central Asia a potential force for peaceful change. They consider communism to be an alien, oppressive ideology, and they are susceptible to the influence of the worldwide resurgence of Islam. They know that Soviet troops are committing genocide against the people of Afghanistan—with whom the Central Asians have far more in common ethnically, culturally, and religiously than they do with the rulers of the Kremlin. Soviet power has subdued these peoples temporarily. But nationalism, the most powerful political force in the twentieth century, is not dead in the Soviet Union. After Gorbachev replaced a Kazakh provincial leader with a Russian, riots involving tens of thousands of people swept the city of Alma-Ata for several days. Even Soviet officials conceded these were "a manifestation of nationalism." With a population of 55 million—and with a growth rate far exceeding that of the Russians—the Central Asian peoples will be a force to reckon with in the years beyond 1999.

Americans have only one historical experience remotely comparable to those of the non-Russian nations: the Civil War and

Reconstruction. While hundreds of thousands of deaths in that war hardly compare to several million deaths through Soviet oppression, the Civil War did create an enduring regional split in the United States. Over a hundred years passed before the South was reintegrated into the national life of the United States, and memories and prejudices which trace back to the Civil War still persist. With less than a century elapsed since the conquest of the non-Russian nations by the communist leaders in Moscow, those national resentments remain white hot. If anyone believes otherwise, he is whistling as he walks by the graveyard.

Our only way to engage in peaceful competition inside the Soviet Union is through foreign broadcasting and cultural-exchange programs. While our broadcasts should not promote rioting or other violence, we should direct attention to the question of nationalism and should encourage these peoples to press for their national rights. Within the Soviet system, there is a constant bureaucratic war between the Russians and the non-Russian peoples over resources and the key political positions in the outlying provinces. If Kremlin leaders make concessions in this struggle as a result of growing non-Russian national awareness, the door for positive peaceful change will have been opened.

Our strategy for peaceful competition must also take advantage of Gorbachev's policy of Glasnost. While many in the West have been fearfully wringing their hands over this new approach, those who do so in the East are more justified in their fears. Winston Churchill once observed, "Russia fears our friendship more than our enmity." He understood that one of the greatest dangers to the Soviet system is contact between their ideas and ours, their peoples and ours, their society and ours. This proximity invites unwelcome comparisons. It breaks the Kremlin's monopoly on information. It plants seeds of thought that will someday blossom into peaceful change.

We must adopt policies to maximize this contact. We should take Gorbachev at his word when he calls for more openness. Western leaders who appear on Soviet media or who address Soviet audiences should not mince their words about Soviet domestic and international policies. We must redouble our radio broadcasting into the Soviet Union. We also need to exploit new technologies in this effort. We should make it our goal in the years before 1999 to put into orbit a satellite capable of beaming television programs throughout the Soviet Union.

Nikita Khrushchev threw down the gauntlet of global competition in the 1950s. For thirty years, Moscow has been competing with the United States across the board. It is time the United States and the West pick up the gauntlet and adopt a comprehensive strategy to compete with Moscow. We must maintain the strength necessary to protect our vital interests around the world. We must develop the capability for measured responses to Soviet challenges against our more peripheral interests. We must compete with the Kremlin not only within the Soviet bloc but also within the Soviet Union itself. In the years before 1999, we need to deter Moscow and to learn to compete with Moscow. If we do both, we will have put ourselves in the best position from which to negotiate with Moscow.

5

HOW TO NEGOTIATE
WITH MOSCOW

If we deter the Kremlin leaders, we will be in a position to negotiate with them. If we compete effectively with them, they will *want* to negotiate. Deterrence, competition, and negotiation are equally important elements in our overall strategy to achieve real peace. But a difference exists among them. While we can successfully deter and compete with Moscow without negotiations, we cannot successfully negotiate without effective American policies for deterrence and competition.

In negotiating with the Soviet Union, we must keep three points in mind. First, only after we take whatever actions are necessary to deter Soviet aggression can we negotiate agreements to stabilize the strategic balance. Arms control cannot substitute for deterrence, but it can supplement it. Second, only after we take whatever actions are necessary to defend American interests around the world can we negotiate understandings to stabilize regional conflicts. Unless we stand up to protect Western interests, Kremlin leaders will have no incentive to sit down with us at the bargaining table. Third, negotiated agreements between the superpowers will not put an end to the American–Soviet conflict. Negotiations can lead to limited cooperation, but limited cooperation does not mean an end to competition.

That does not mean negotiations are unimportant. They can reduce the risk of a nuclear war between the superpowers. They can also have a profound effect on the fate of millions of people. We must remember that Moscow won Eastern Europe without firing a shot. Stalin's victory came across the conference tables in Tehran, Yalta, and Potsdam, not on the battlefields of Central Europe. In the years before 1999, we therefore need to be able to negotiate effectively with Moscow. In order to do so, we must understand why we should negotiate, what we should negotiate, how we should negotiate, and how we should conduct negotiations at the level of American–Soviet summits.

There are two extreme views on the question of whether we should negotiate with Moscow.

At one extreme, some argue that any negotiations with the Kremlin are useless at best and dangerous at worst. They point out, correctly, that our goals for negotiations are totally different from those of Moscow. They cite Stalin's aphorism, "A diplomat's words must have no relationship to action; otherwise, what kind of diplomacy is it?" Soviet leaders use negotiations to win victory without war; too often we use negotiations only to achieve peace without victory. Negotiations for them are a means to an end; for us they tend to be an end in themselves.

Those who hold this view also argue that the negotiating process itself is skewed in favor of the Soviet Union. While Kremlin leaders can totally ignore the views of the Soviet peoples, popular hopes and expectations for better East–West relations put enormous pressure on Western leaders to make unilateral concessions in order to conclude agreements. In addition, they point out that Soviet leaders are diabolically clever, duplicitous, and untrustworthy. They have relentlessly preyed upon Western hopes for peace, ruthlessly exploited ambiguities in the language of treaties, and repeatedly violated agreements in order to further their interests.

There is an element of truth in these contentions. But five overriding reasons exist why their basic prescription for American policy—the less negotiating with Moscow, the better—needs to be rejected.

First, it would be irresponsible for the two superpowers—each with the capacity to destroy the other and the rest of the world—not to explore every way possible for reducing the risk of nuclear war. Communication does not produce peace, but it does enable each side to get a clear measure of the other and thereby reduce the risk of a miscalculation leading to war. Without communication, we would put our relations in a highly combustible atmosphere of semibelligerency, with both sides building up armaments without restraint while firing salvos of hot rhetoric. Our interests would inevitably rub together in the powder kegs of the world like the Middle East, possibly sending off a spark which would ignite a nuclear war.

Second, it would be difficult politically to sustain the policies necessary for deterrence and competition without a negotiating initiative. If an American President maintained a posture of diplomatic belligerence while the Soviet leadership beckoned for him to come to the negotiating table, his policies would be incomprehensible to the American people. They do not expect a breakthrough in U.S.–Soviet relations, but they do expect their leaders to make every reasonable effort to reduce the risks of the nuclear world. As a result, a President who opposes negotiations per se would see his policies inevitably undercut in Congress.

Third, it would be impossible to hold together the NATO alliance in the absence of an active policy of negotiation. Alliances are primarily held together by fear. The threat of Soviet expansionism has been a major factor in holding NATO together for forty years. But today in Europe the fear of nuclear war has eclipsed the fear of Soviet aggression, even though the Kremlin's military power is massively greater than it was when NATO was founded. Gorbachev's brilliant public-relations "peace" campaign and President Reagan's belligerent rhetoric about the Soviets during his first term have contributed to this problem. This has prompted a majority of Europeans, except in France, to believe that Gorbachev is more committed to peace than Reagan.

To keep the alliance together, therefore, we must appeal to reason, not just fear. We could never have made the initial deployment of Pershing II and cruise missiles in 1983 without the parallel track of negotiations to reduce the level of intermediate-range nu-

162

clear forces in Europe. Our policies must convince the peoples of Western Europe that the dual threats of Soviet aggression and nuclear war exist and that the United States and the alliance have adopted the measured and prudent policies to deal with both. American–Soviet negotiations are indispensable toward that end. Hope for peace is essential if the people of Europe, as well as the United States, are to continue to support the military strength necessary to maintain the deterrence upon which stability depends. Over the long haul, the absence of hope for peace fuels the forces of appeasement.

Fourth, we must recognize the simple fact that even with communists, statecraft counts. Negotiations can make a positive difference. It was American–Soviet negotiations that led to the 1955 Austrian Peace Treaty, which brought about the withdrawal of Soviet occupation forces from half the country, including Vienna. Those who oppose all negotiation with communists opposed any contacts with communist China. But the world is a better and safer place with a strong and independent China that has good relations with the West than with a weak and pliant China tied to the Soviet Union.

Fifth, a reduction in East–West tensions divides the East more than it does the West. Since Moscow justifies its iron grip over the other members of the Eastern bloc and over the Soviet peoples as a necessary response to the East–West conflict, a policy of active negotiation undercuts that rationale. It becomes ever more difficult for the Kremlin to legitimize its oppression. That, in turn, leads to a subtle process through which the satellite states gradually increase their room for maneuver. A renewed Cold War, with a high level of international tension, would make positive peaceful change impossible. Confrontation strengthens a dictatorship. Contact and negotiation can weaken it.

At the other extreme, there are those who believe that through negotiations and agreements the United States and the Soviet Union can overcome their mutual misunderstanding and suspicion and bring about peace. That view is also wrong. We must disabuse ourselves of the notion that the differences between the Soviet Union and the United States stem from a giant misunderstanding and that they can be overcome through a grand compromise. We do not have differences because of our misundertandings. We have misunderstandings because of our differences. The American–Soviet conflict is rooted in the profoundly different ideologies, interests, and intentions of the two superpowers. We must understand that negotiations can never produce a permanent, perfect peace.

Gorbachev understands that, but the question remains whether Americans do. There are two kinds of peace: pragmatic peace, which means conflict without war, and perfect peace, which means a world without conflict. Gorbachev seeks only the first kind. Too often Western leaders sappily emote about the second. As a Leninist, Gorbachev does not believe in the possibility of perfect peace as long as noncommunist states exist in the world. In my meeting with him, he plainly acknowledged that some differences between the two sides were so deep that they would probably never be settled. For him, the decision to forgo overt military aggression results not from dewy-eyed sentimentality but from a hardheaded calculation that the present balance of power, or correlation of forces as he calls it, makes such a policy unprofitable. He engages in negotiations not to open a new era of perfect peace—which he considers an illusion—but to improve the Soviet military and political position in the world.

That approach is most evident in arms control. If the Soviets are behind numerically, they demand equality. If they are ahead, they demand equal cuts that improve their relative position. If the United States is poised to exploit its superior technology—as with the SDI—they demand that such advances be banned. If the United States is prepared to modernize some of its weapons systems, they demand terms which have the effect of preventing or minimizing those deployments. Meanwhile, new Soviet deployments are nonnegotiable or are allowed under the Soviet terms for an agreement, and Soviet research programs for new technologies, like strategic defense, are not even acknowledged to exist.

This is not to say that we should refuse to negotiate on arms control, but rather that we should sign only agreements that are in our strategic interest. There is a legitimate role for arms control. Without it, the number of U.S.–Soviet nuclear warheads will continue to multiply. Without SALT II, whatever its flaws, the Soviet

Union would have built even more destabilizing weapons systems than it did. Without arms control, there is the danger that the Soviets will sprint ahead in the arms race while the United States jogs along at a slow pace. Given our economic power, we can win an arms race with the Soviets—but only if we race. Given the vagaries of defense budget appropriations in a democracy, whether we will race is always an open question.

In negotiating, if we pursue an unrealistic perfect peace while Moscow seeks to capture concrete advantages, we will simply be making ourselves an easy mark for some of the best geopolitical hustlers in history.

Our approach to negotiating with Moscow must chart a course between these extremes. We need to negotiate, but we must be realistic about the limits of what we can achieve through negotiations. We must base our approach on a firm recognition that the U.S.–Soviet conflict is not a problem but a condition. A problem can be solved; a condition can only be treated. Our struggle with Moscow will not change until the aggressive nature of the Soviet Union changes. If such a transformation ever does occur, it will come about over the course of generations. We must not delude ourselves into thinking that an American President can transform the Kremlin's character by personal charm or by sliding a more attractive set of negotiating points across a conference table. If there is one lesson I have learned over the forty years I have been in the political arena, it is that negotiating with a Mikhail Gorbachev is a lot different from negotiating with a George Meany.

While we cannot negotiate an end to the American–Soviet conflict, we must not underestimate the potential importance of negotiations, both in competing with Moscow and in tamping down the danger that our competition could lead to war. Soviet leaders consider negotiation to be a key tactic in their struggle with the United States. American leaders too often tend to equate superpower agreements with progress toward perfect peace. In negotiations, our purpose too often is just to strike a deal; theirs is to strike a deal that serves their larger strategic purposes. As a rule we should not model our actions on the Kremlin's statecraft, but we must in the years ahead match the Soviet capacity to integrate negotiation into overall strategy.

———

We must begin by defining the kinds of issues we should negotiate about and the kinds of goals we should set. There are two basic types of U.S–Soviet issues. The first are those in which our interests conflict and therefore cannot be resolved through negotiations. For these, the only realistic purpose of negotiation is to reduce the chance that our differences will erupt into armed conflict. The second are those on which our interests run parallel. In these cases, negotiations can potentially produce agreements that will serve our common interests.

In the first category, the key issues are arms control and the political conflicts, like the Middle East, the Persian Gulf, Afghanistan, and Central America, that could lead to the use of arms. Soviet objectives on these issues are military superiority and geopolitical expansion, and ours are military stability and political self-determination for the peoples of those regions. There is no middle ground—no difference to split—between those propositions. Our differences are simply irreconcilable. With or without negotiations, the Soviets will pursue their goals with their characteristic relentlessness, and we must be sure that we do so as well.

On these issues, we must seek to negotiate not permanent solutions—such goals are unachievable—but to restrain the means by which both sides pursue their conflicting goals. We will never succeed in negotiating a once-and-for-all arms-control agreement and certainly never succeed in eliminating nuclear weapons from the face of the earth. But we can succeed, through tough, skillful diplomacy, in striking an arms deal that will stabilize the strategic balance so that neither side stands vulnerable to a first-strike attack. We will never succeed in negotiating a permanent settlement in the world's flashpoints. But we can arrive at a common understanding of the rules of engagement by which we conduct our continuing competition without resorting to nuclear war.

Human rights also fall into the first category. We seek to promote respect for human rights in the Soviet Union, but Kremlin leaders will never willingly grant their peoples freedoms that would result in opposition to and eventual overthrow of communist rule.

No communist regime will agree to commit suicide. A leak in the dike of censorship would produce a flood of recriminations against the party and the state. A crack in the door barring emigration would result in a tide of humanity seeking a better life abroad. We therefore cannot realistically demand in our negotiations that the Soviet Union adopt Western-style democracy or respect all the freedoms embodied in the Bill of Rights. But that does not mean that we should abandon the issue. In our private negotiations, we should press the Soviets to increase emigration, to release specific dissidents, to increase the flow of information from Western sources, and to live up to its obligations as a signatory of the Helsinki agreements. We cannot expect to achieve all that we want, but what we do achieve can mean a lot in the lives of the oppressed peoples of the Soviet Union.

In the second category of issues, there are important ones like increasing commercial ties, controlling the proliferation of nuclear weapons, reducing risks of accidental war, creating means for resolving incidents at sea, opening up cooperation to protect the environment. There are also less important but still significant issues, like expanding cultural exchanges. On these matters, the United States and the Soviet Union can reach agreements that will serve our mutual interests.

We might even be able to cooperate in combatting terrorism. While Kremlin leaders have actively aided terrorist groups over the last twenty years, the time may soon come when Moscow itself becomes a victim, and the rapid advance of technology may make that cooperation imperative. We live in an age when technological miniaturization could someday make it possible for not only countries but also individuals to break the nuclear threshold—a sobering thought for any country in which an unarmed Cessna airplane could land in the front yard of the Kremlin.

It would be a mistake to underestimate the number of possibilities for greater cooperation between the United States and the Soviet Union. But it would be a far greater mistake to overestimate the significance of that cooperation for the U.S.–Soviet relationship. In the 1970s, the fact that the renowned Bolshoi Ballet danced in Washington did not stop the Red Army from waltzing into Afghanistan.

Our track record of negotiating with the Soviets is not good. They are the best in the business at extracting the most from their adversaries while giving up the least in return. Churchill might have said about them that never have diplomats won so much for so little. It is therefore imperative that we develop a better understanding of how to negotiate, on both the strategic and the tactical levels.

To understand the strategic importance of negotiation requires an understanding of statecraft. Statecraft is something that Americans have traditionally failed to appreciate. None of the graduate schools that train our foreign-service officers, military leaders, and intelligence analysts teach comprehensive courses on statecraft. They produce graduates who know everything about small details and nothing about the big picture. None of our foreign-policy bureaucracies have any talent for statecraft. They are long on expert specialists but short on expert generalists. Yet in the years ahead no capability will be as important as statecraft.

What statecraft involves is not simply the intricacies of patching together a diplomatic communiqué or striking a trade deal, or the complexities of the military science needed to maintain deterrence at all levels of a potential conflict. Instead, statecraft is the capacity to integrate all our capabilities—military power, economic clout, covert action, propaganda, and diplomacy—into a policy that serves our overall strategy. As an element of statecraft, negotiation is the art of political maneuver at the highest level.

No administration, including my own, has ever explicitly developed—on paper—an American strategy encompassing our military, economic, and political instruments of power. Whenever we have articulated a national strategy, it has tended to be in terms of military power, slighting or ignoring our economic and political assets. Some Presidents have done better than others in shaping a more comprehensive strategy in practice. But we need to create a process for systematically developing American statecraft.

In negotiating with Moscow, we need to develop the capacity to craft proposals that both achieve our goals and create political pressures on the Soviets to accept our terms. In essence, it involves making an offer the other side does not want to accept but feels it cannot refuse. We need to present the Kremlin with choices structured so that rejecting them would hurt the Soviet Union politically but accepting them would run against Moscow's instincts. If Kremlin leaders turn us down, we gain in the political competition; if they take up our offer, we gain our objectives.

In the recent arms-control agreement on intermediate-range nuclear forces, Gorbachev proved to be a master at this kind of maneuver. When the United States proposed the zero option in November 1981, it did so not because policy-makers thought that such a solution served Western interests but because they expected the Soviets to reject the idea and be hurt politically for doing so. It was assumed that the proposal would score political points in Europe and would enable the United States to station INF forces in NATO countries. That tactic worked as long as the Soviet Union fell into the trap and remained obstinate at the negotiating table.

But Gorbachev soon figured out that a zero–zero solution ultimately favored Moscow, eliminating U.S. capabilities to retaliate from Europe without affecting Soviet capabilities to hit Europe. When he accepted the American offer, the Reagan administration felt it had no choice but to proceed with the agreement, despite the serious reservations of the Department of Defense, former NATO commander Bernard Rogers, and the allies in Europe. One of the principal reasons reluctant supporters of the accord used to rationalize their position was that refusing our own offer would be too costly politically in terms of public opinion in Western Europe. Through Gorbachev's shrewd negotiations, Moscow won its objective.

A bare-bones analysis of how to integrate negotiation into our overall strategy requires us to answer three basic questions:

1. What do we want from the Soviets? We should not enter negotiations willy-nilly. Instead, we need to define in very specific terms what we would like to bring about. In talks on strategic weapons, it makes no sense to pursue an across-the-board reduction of 50 percent in the arsenals of the two superpowers. Our primary goal should be to achieve a large cutback in Soviet first-strike weapons so that Moscow does not ever have enough for a

credible first-strike capability. In negotiations on the balance of forces in Europe, it makes no sense to pursue an elimination of tactical nuclear weapons, because they are needed to counter the Warsaw Pact superiority in conventional weapons. We should instead pursue reductions in their conventional forces to the point where NATO could, if necessary, defend itself without nuclear weapons.

2. What are we willing to give up to get what we want? Gorbachev is neither a philanthropist nor a fool. It is a waste of time to try to convince the Soviets that we should both pursue an abstract concept like strategic stability. They do not think in those terms. Gorbachev is not interested in what we think is "good"—but rather in what he thinks he gets. In order to achieve the zero–zero INF deal he wanted, he was willing to give up several times as many warheads as we did. If we do not have something to offer, it is a waste of time even to enter into negotiations. Kremlin leaders will strike deals, but they will never give anyone something for nothing.

3. What moves can we make to put political pressure on Soviet leaders to make the deal we want at the price we want to pay? That is not easy, but it is possible. It requires, first, that American policy-makers understand Soviet motivations and vulnerabilities. It also requires a keen sense of gamesmanship. Most of all, it requires an ability to package our proposals with a sense for public relations. We cannot negotiate successfully unless the peoples of the West support our initiatives. Otherwise, the pressure to make a deal at any price can overwhelm the better judgment of policy-makers. At the same time, a united front of Western powers—which a politically attuned proposal can galvanize—places maximum pressure for the Soviet Union to negotiate on our terms.

Zbigniew Brzezinski has spelled out an idea for conventional arms control—a deep reduction in tank forces in Europe and a tank-free zone in Central Europe—that fits the bill. While military experts need to flesh out the specifics of an actual proposal, it has great potential. It isolates the key problem, the offensive threat inherent in Moscow's overwhelming superiority in tank armies, and proposes a diplomatic response capable of mobilizing public support. It educates Western public opinion about the real threat we face on the conventional level. Most important, it puts the heat on the Soviets by focusing attention on the *Soviet* policies that threaten peace and that need to be changed. If Moscow rejects the idea of a tank-free zone, we should not back off from it. Instead, we should point out at every turn that Soviet leaders refuse to take steps to lessen the danger of a major war. We should constantly emphasize that as far as Europe is concerned the only reason we need nuclear weapons is because the Soviets have superiority in conventional weapons.

We should quickly move in that direction to take advantage of Gorbachev's statements at the Washington summit in December 1987 to the effect that the Soviet Union accepts the principle of asymmetrical reductions. He said that in areas where Moscow held an edge he would be willing to make greater reductions to reach a balance. We should use these statements for political leverage. President Reagan should tell Gorbachev about the American aphorism about "putting your money where your mouth is" and suggest that he put his tanks where his mouth is. The fundamental premise of an acceptable conventional arms-control agreement is that the Soviet Union must reduce its offensive tank forces so that a balance exists between NATO and the Warsaw Pact.

Unfortunately, such strategic thinking almost never surfaces in our foreign-policy bureaucracies. George F. Kennan's containment policy, which led to the Marshall Plan and NATO, was a notable exception. As President, I met many very able individuals who worked in the State Department, the Defense Department, and the Central Intelligence Agency, but I do not recall a single instance when those bureaucracies generated a truly innovative approach on a major issue. That is why we had to develop our initiatives in the White House. When presented with a problem, the bureaucracies dust off their folders and trot out their standard school solution. Their thinking is dominated by a curator's mentality. They treat current policy as if it were a museum piece to be preserved at all costs, and they view a new idea as a mortal threat to their prized artifacts. They are experts on tactics but neophytes on strategy. We must not fall victim to this fossilized thinking. It is a deadly prescription for competing with Moscow in a rapidly changing world.

It is not possible to implement good strategy without good tactics. But good tactics are useless unless they are part of a good strategy. Our strategy determines what negotiations we should go into, and our tactics determine what kind of deal we come out with.

An administration will never succeed in negotiations at the tactical level without establishing a solid foreign-policy process. Above all, this requires a President who understands the essentials of foreign policy in enough detail so that he can make an informed decision among the available options. Most of America's foreign-policy disasters in this century—for example, Wilson at Versailles in 1919 and Roosevelt at Yalta in 1944—have resulted when the President was naive about those with whom he was negotiating or was not adequately informed about policies vital to our national security. In the presidential election this year, Americans should make competence in foreign affairs the prime consideration in deciding for whom they will vote.

When we choose our leaders, we must remember that they are not candidates for sainthood. Personal character should always be a proper subject for debate and examination, but it is far more important to know whether a candidate has the strength and intelligence to hold his own across the table from Gorbachev than whether he might have smoked marijuana in college. If in the past sainthood had been a job requirement for high office in the United States, we would have denied ourselves outstanding military and political leaders. Cleveland had a child out of wedlock but served ably as President. Grant had been an alcoholic, but he was the general who led the Union armies to victory in the War Between the States. Lincoln suffered bouts with mental depression but freed the slaves and preserved the Union. Political pundits forever deride the quality of our leaders. But American politics has deteriorated to the point where any man who cherishes his private life has to think twice before stepping into public life and submitting himself and his family to murderous vendettas by sensation-crazed reporters and inquisitions by senators posturing for the television cameras.

Our foreign-policy process requires three key elements to function properly. First, it needs a strong central leader—a President who can draw the best from his advisers, who can glean the key information from his departments, and who can exercise independent judgment on foreign-policy questions. It may have been possible in the nineteenth century for a President to delegate foreign policy totally to his Secretary of State. But in that era the level of tariffs, not survival, was the big foreign-policy issue. With so much at stake, the President must be a hands-on leader.

A President must have a sense of history. Sir Robert Menzies, who served brilliantly as Prime Minister of Australia, aptly observed that in a leader an obsession with the "verdict of history" can "only serve to distract the statesman's attention from the stern need for decision and action." What was vital, in his eyes, was that a leader possess "a sense of history, a phrase which I use to describe a state of mind which draws inspiration and light from the recorded past, not a state of mind which is anxious to be regarded well in the unrecorded future." In negotiating with Kremlin leaders, we will never get where we want to go unless we have a keen understanding of where we have been and how we have gotten there.

Second, the President must appoint to the key posts of Secretary of State, Secretary of Defense, and Director of Central Intelligence individuals who have the background to lead, not follow, their departments. Those who make up the permanent bureaucracies in State, Defense and the CIA have ingrained ways of thinking that bias their analyses and recommendations. And they are experts at buttering up the boss. It is inevitable that an inexperienced appointee, no matter how able, will be captured—taken in by the departmental line—and will lose his usefulness to the President. He will become the bureaucracy's representative to the President rather than the President's representative in the bureaucracy.

Third, the President must retain a strong National Security Council system. After the Iran-contra hearings, it was the common wisdom among Washington's political pundits that the national-security adviser and his staff had grown too strong and should be demoted to the status of mere paper-pushers. Some put it bluntly: "Put the State Department back in charge of foreign policy." The next President could not make a greater mistake than to follow this advice. A President needs more than a clerk as his national-security adviser. He needs a strong individual who can organize the decision-making process, crystallize the policy options, and ride herd on the bureaucracies to keep them in line. While the President steers policy with his decisions, it is in the bureaucracies that the rubber meets the road. Without a national-security adviser to exercise hawk-eyed vigilance over the implementation of presidential decisions, the President will see a great deal of slippage between what he wants done and what in fact gets done.

Without these three ingredients, the policy-making process will become fragmented. The bureaucracies will be like wheels without an axle: they will still roll—but they will go off in their own directions. Most important, they will not provide the President with the kind of information and counsel he needs to choose the right tactical moves in negotiating with Moscow.

The next question is who should negotiate with the Soviets. The arcane debates in think tanks and university seminars and on television talk shows typically conclude that all negotiations should be conducted by the State Department. This is not possible when we are negotiating with Moscow. In such talks, we need to distinguish between those issues that should be handled in the formal government-to-government channel and those that should be taken up on a personal basis between one leader and another.

Government-to-government negotiations conducted primarily by the State Department can be effective only on issues where the two sides have common interests. In dealing with our allies, our diplomats routinely resolve most issues in official channels. That can be true in dealing with Moscow, but only on specific issues where our interests and those of the Kremlin are compatible. Measures to reduce the risk of accidental war or agreements to promote cultural exchange are the type of issues that fall into this area. Our diplomats are masters at devising compromises that benefit both sides, but when clashing interests rule out compromise that ability is irrelevant.

When we negotiate with Moscow on issues where American and Soviet interests are irreconcilable, we cannot achieve meaningful results through official diplomatic channels. The President must handle these negotiations on a head-to-head basis with the top Soviet leader. Raising these issues at the highest level conveys the importance we assign to our interests in these matters. It also recognizes the fact that no other forum offers even the shadow of a hope for progress. Some may still believe that real progress can be made on the tough issues like Afghanistan and Central America in meetings in which assistant secretaries of state and deputy foreign ministers read from prepared position papers. But those who hold this view are living in a dream world.

In dealing with communist regimes, we must bear in mind the differences between officials in the party and in the government. Decisions are made by the party, not in the government. Government officials are the handmaidens of party leaders. We can apply all the persuasive power in the world on a Soviet government negotiator, but he will not budge an inch on his own from his position on a major issue. In deriding a proposal for settling an issue at one meeting of foreign ministers, Khrushchev dismissed them as irrelevant, remarking that his Foreign Minister would sit on a block of ice if he told him to. That is still the case. To make progress in negotiations on critical issues, an American President must deal with the top Soviet Communist Party leader.

Gorbachev might choose to negotiate through his ambassador in Washington, his Foreign Minister, or some other personal representative. The President must be ready to do likewise. In some cases, he might want to use his Secretary of State, in others his national-security adviser, and in still others a special representative, perhaps even someone outside government. The key point is that the President must designate an individual whom Gorbachev will recognize as the President's personal representative. If the Secretary of State is selected, it must be clear that he wears the hat not of a cabinet department head but of the President's emissary. Gorbachev must understand that whoever has this assignment speaks for the President and reports only to the President.

These negotiations must take place in secret. Secrecy has a bad connotation in the United States. In our elite universities, political-science professors still warble with approval about Wilson's imperative about "open covenants openly arrived at." But they fail to understand that in most cases with the Soviets the only way we can conclude an open covenant is to arrive at it in secret. There is a world of difference between a secret treaty and secret negotiations. In a democracy, secret agreements on important issues cannot and should not be tolerated, but secret negotiations to reach important agreements are not only necessary but justifiable.

That is especially true in the case of negotiations with communist states. All totalitarians—not just the Soviets—are obsessed with secrecy. Without secret negotiations, there would have been no opening to China in 1972, and no peace agreement in Vietnam in 1973. Some may point out that in those two cases secret negotiations were appropriate because the United States did not have diplomatic relations with either China or North Vietnam. But even the SALT I accords with the Soviet Union would have been impossible without secret talks.

Secrecy is necessary for more fundamental reasons. First, by its nature diplomacy must be conducted beyond the range of cameras and microphones. Negotiating with Moscow is not like haggling with a rug merchant in an Oriental bazaar. Instead, it is a quiet, subtle process of feeling out the differing degrees to which various elements of the other party's position are negotiable, and of trying varying combinations of give-and-take. Each side has to be able to advance tentative proposals, to test out hypothetical alternatives, and to plumb the other side's reactions. Both sides need to have the opportunity to advance propositions without being bound by them. Negotiators can afford to do this only if they can do it in privacy.

Second, genuine negotiations require each side to compromise specific interests to advance both sides' general interests. That, in turn, requires concessions from both parties. When U.S.–Soviet negotiations have been conducted in highly visible forums, such as the thirteen-year-long Mutual and Balanced Force Reduction Talks in Vienna, they have produced nothing. It is far more difficult— and sometimes impossible—for one side or the other to make a major concession in public. If a side needs to back down from its initial position, it allows the internal opposition to *any* negotiated accommodation to crystallize and block further progress. That is true in the United States, but it is particularly true in the Soviet Union, where every concession must always appear as a victory. Either side can present a fair agreement as a package of beneficial trade-offs, but neither can ever package specific concessions as anything but detrimental.

That is why a President is well advised to establish a back channel outside the bureaucracy for negotiating with the Soviets. It is essential to have a private means to communicate with Kremlin leaders, outside formal channels and beyond the intruding lenses of television cameras. During my administration, the back channel involved discreet, regular meetings between Henry Kissinger and the very capable and experienced Soviet ambassador, Anatoly Dobrynin. These were critical in the early phases of our talks, when each side was exploring the position of the other. We made far more progress in those working sessions than we did in the highly publicized formal negotiations.

A back channel is indispensable in defusing potential crises before they become public and both sides are forced to dig in their heels. In 1969, the back channel enabled us to avert a major crisis over the Soviet attempt to construct a nuclear submarine base at Cienfuegos, Cuba. It also gave us a way to prevent the war between Pakistan and India from escalating into a major U.S.–Soviet conflict. The next President should establish a back channel with the Soviets. Since it minimizes the risk of leaks and the inhibitions on frank exchanges between the top leaders, it maximizes the chance of a successful resolution of contentious issues.

In the negotiations themselves, the United States must employ six key tactics:

Flanking actions. What we do outside our negotiating sessions is as important as what we do inside them. It is a geopolitical axiom that you cannot win more at the conference table than you can win on the battlefield. The same is true in other negotiations as well. If we do nothing more than table elegantly phrased proposals, we will achieve nothing in the negotiations. We need to take actions to outflank Moscow's position. In arms-control negotiations, we must deploy whatever weapons systems are necessary to assure our strategic security and must mobilize support for our negotiating position among the American people and among our allies. If we want the Soviets to agree to a withdrawal from Afghanistan, we must help the Afghan resistance raise the cost of Moscow's occupation of the country. The Soviets are tough negotiators. They will make agreements we want only if we create conditions which would put them in a worse position if they failed to do so.

Linkage. This tactic, linking progress on one issue to progress on another, is highly controversial. When I practiced linkage as President, the political pundits and the professional diplomats were virtually unanimous in their disapproval. But linkage remains absolutely essential to a genuine improvement in U.S.–Soviet relations.

Kremlin leaders will take the United States to the cleaners in superpower negotiations unless we impose linkage among issues. The two sides do not have the same degree of interest in progress on all issues. There are some, like trade, in which Moscow has more at stake. There are others, like resisting Soviet adventurism in the Third World, in which the United States has a stronger interest. Moscow is more than willing to negotiate solely on the former. If the United States acquiesces to that unbalanced approach—if it fails to link the two sets of issues—it will allow the Soviets to dominate the negotiating agenda and we will inevitably come out the loser.

Moscow will always reject explicit linkage, whether involving trade or arms control. Yet, while they will not adopt the principle of linkage, they will adapt to the fact of it. During my administration we linked the talks to ban anti–ballistic-missiles systems, a top priority for the Soviets, to those to limit offensive strategic systems, a top priority for us. If we had not insisted on linkage between the two, we would never have succeeded in concluding SALT I. The Soviets would have negotiated on the ABM Treaty and stalled on the interim accord on offensive systems, thereby gaining a free hand to continue their nuclear buildup. We also linked the progress in the negotiations on increases in East–West trade—which was a Soviet priority—to Soviet behavior in other parts of the world. When the Kremlin took actions that threatened our interests, we slowed the talks to a crawl. The Soviets soon got the message. They did not like it, but they did respond to it.

Linkage is inherent in the way the world works, but to benefit from linkage the United States must practice it. We must impose iron links between progress toward better overall relations and

Soviet global behavior. We must not move forward with arms control and increased trade if the Soviet Union persists in threatening U.S. interests with aggression in Afghanistan or by pumping hundreds of tons of arms into Central America. If we enter major agreements while ignoring Soviet conduct, we will be sending the wrong message to Moscow. We will be saying that aggression pays, and we will be facilitating our own destruction.

Ironically, the arms-control lobbyists who most oppose linkage have the most to lose if we fail to link issues. Linkage is a fact of international life. We can negotiate arms-control treaties in spite of Soviet expansionism. But there is no way the Senate will vote to ratify such treaties if at that time the Soviet Union is trampling over Western interests. After all, it was Moscow's invasion of Afghanistan that torpedoed any chance for ratification of SALT II. If we want genuine and enduring improvement in U.S.–Soviet relations, we must link progress in arms-control talks to progress in the political conflicts that could lead to the use of those arms.

Moscow has made arms control its first priority in U.S.–Soviet negotiations in part to distract attention from the vital political issues. We must not allow them to achieve this objective by treating the questions of Soviet expansionism and repression as secondary concerns and as unfortunate obstacles to progress in arms control. We must force the Kremlin to address our concerns, and linkage is our only means of doing so. If they are to benefit the cause of real peace, arms deals must be accompanied by changes in Soviet policy. As Brian Crozier wrote, "What the Soviets or their surrogates do in Central America or southern Africa is the substance; the arms deal is the shadow." If the Reagan administration goes forward on arms control without linkage, it risks creating a dangerous euphoria in which anyone who dares raise the issue of Soviet aggression around the world will stand accused of poisoning the atmosphere of U.S.–Soviet relations.

But linkage requires subtle execution. An American President cannot step before the cameras and announce that he intends to hold the next arms-control agreement hostage to Soviet capitulation on one or another issue. He must enforce linkage in private negotiations. This is particularly true on the issue of human rights. As a result of private pressure from my administration, the Soviet

Union increased Jewish emigration from 400 in 1968 to nearly 35,000 in 1973. When Congress passed the Jackson-Vanik Amendment explicitly tying trade to Soviet emigration, the Kremlin leaders slammed the door shut again. No powerful state will ever allow another nation to dictate its internal policies.

We need to press the Soviets on this issue, not only for humanitarian reasons, but also because Soviet human-rights violations affect the chances for improving overall American–Soviet relations. But we must undertand that private pressure, not grandstanding, has the best odds for success.

Economic power. Our biggest chit in U.S.–Soviet negotiations is our economic power. That is especially true with Gorbachev. He has made it clear that his top priority is to jump-start the Soviet economy. He knows that if he fails, the Soviet Union will be eclipsed as a great power in the next century. To succeed, he desperately needs access to new infusions of Western technology and credits. As a result, we possess greater negotiating leverage today than we have ever enjoyed before.

Trade should be a major subject on the agenda of the next U.S.–Soviet summit. The possibilities for increased trade are enormous. Our trade with China, which still has primarily an agricultural economy, was $10 billion last year. Our trade with the Soviet Union, a major industrial power, was about $2 billion. Economically, this does not make sense. But we must remember that it was only after China opened its doors to the West and discontinued its expansionist policies that bilateral trade took off. Trade in nonstrategic goods can also be a powerful incentive for the Soviet Union to adopt more humane policies at home and a less aggressive policy abroad. As our relations improve, the administration should ask the Congress to give the Soviet Union most-favored-nation status. This would open the door to a significant increase in Soviet–American trade in nonstrategic goods.

Moscow needs trade with the West more than the West needs trade with Moscow. We know it, the Soviets know it, and we should make use of it. The United States and the Soviet Union largely trade Western technology for Soviet raw materials. We can buy their products elsewhere if necessary, but they have no alternative suppliers for ours. That gives us leverage. We should use it to extract concessions from them on other issues. We should sell Moscow Western goods, but we should stamp them with a political price tag as well as an economic one. Gorbachev has a choice. He cannot trade and invade at the same time.

Trade should be a key element of our relationship with the Soviet Union. But we must disabuse ourselves of the myth that trade brings peace. Nations which traded with each other killed each other by the millions in World War I and World War II. Alone, trade cannot produce peace or prevent war. Many argue that if we increase trade with the Soviets, they will become less aggressive. But the Kremlin will not be bought off. In the late 1970s, they showed that they *would* both trade and invade. The bottom line is that economic relations can never substitute for deterrence or competition. If properly implemented, however, they can reinforce it.

If we are going to increase trade, we must do so in a way calculated to create incentives for the Soviet Union to desist from its aggressive policies. It makes no sense to give the Kremlin leaders what they most want without getting something we want in return. If we fail to use our economic power, it will show that the Soviets can win gains simply by improving the atmospherics of our relationship, even while seeking other gains through aggression. That is a precedent we cannot afford.

We cannot take advantage of our economic power without the cooperation of our NATO and Japanese allies. The collective economic power of the West dwarfs that of the East because our economic system works and theirs does not. NATO and Japan outproduce the Soviet Union and its Warsaw Pact allies by a ratio of over five to one. But we will fritter away that superiority if we do not coordinate our policies for trading with Moscow.

At a minimum, that coordination must involve a tight control over the export of militarily useful technology and an end to providing subsidized export credits to the Soviet Union. Beyond that, we also need to cooperate in regulating the level of East–West trade. It is imperative that we get our act together immediately. Gorbachev has been talking explicitly about greater trade as the economic consequence of reduced tensions. Soviet trade delegations have already started crisscrossing the West. We therefore need to establish a Foreign Economic Policy Board, not only in the United States, but also for the Western alliance as a whole. It would act as the vehicle for coordinating our use of economic power vis-à-vis the Soviet Union.

We made a major mistake when the Reagan administration removed the grain embargo imposed by President Carter after the Soviet invasion of Afghanistan without any corresponding concession. It was compounded when the United States signed a new grain deal with no linkage to other issues. It is also unfortunate that the administration's trade officials have followed the flawed axiom that the only limit on our trade with Moscow should be Soviet port capacities. The next administration should abandon that approach. It should first pull together the economic assets of the West and then sit down to negotiate with Moscow about the political conditions for an increase in trade.

Lenin contemptuously remarked that capitalist countries were so shortsightedly greedy that they would sell the Soviet Union the rope by which they themselves would someday hang. Unfortunately, some Western political leaders and businessmen fit the bill. They would sell the Soviets not only rope, but also the scaffolding and a how-to book for the hangman. We must reject the counsel of those whose narrow minds consider the bottom line as the only guide for our East–West trade policy. If we accept their view, a few in the West will profit financially, but only the Kremlin leaders will profit geopolitically.

Tenacity. In the revolutionary times of turn-of-the-century Russia, the Bolsheviks prevailed over other leftists by outlasting them in meetings. Lenin's followers would pick over the most trivial debating point *ad infinitum*, while the opposition tired and some of its delegates wandered away. As soon as the other side's numbers had dwindled sufficiently, Lenin's party would call a vote and would win, even though the Bolsheviks were a minority at the outset. Today's Soviet negotiators have not lost that talent for victory through verbal endurance.

Our diplomats have tended to make two fundamental mistakes in dealing with Moscow. First, they have tended to underestimate the adversary. They have often looked down on the Soviets as clumsy, boorish and uncivilized but have failed to recognize that style has nothing to do with capability. Stalin might not have been as stylish as President Roosevelt, but Stalin won Eastern Europe at Yalta. Our negotiators must prepare painstakingly for their encounters, and they must have tenacity, intensity, patience and stamina. Among his many talents, these were Henry Kissinger's major strengths in his negotiations with the Soviets, the Chinese, and the Vietnamese. Max Kampelman has demonstrated those qualities in his marathon arms-control negotiations in Geneva. It is not arguments across the table but political decisions from above that move Soviet negotiators toward concessions. But our team must be capable of fighting an indefinite holding action in order to induce the Kremlin to fall back from its initial positions. We should never negotiate against a deadline. If we appear to be in a hurry, the Soviets will gladly rush us into a bad deal.

Second, our diplomats have a pervasive tendency to negotiate with themselves on behalf of the Soviets. Every hard-line negotiating option discussed within the U.S. government encounters a chorus of derision on the grounds that "the Russians will never accept it." Gaggles of foreign-service officers, with assistance from their friends in Congress and the media, then urge modifications in our position—before negotiations even begin—to make our proposal more palatable to the Kremlin. That is utter folly. We must never modify our proposals based on whether its terms are acceptable from the Soviet point of view, but only on whether they are desirable from ours.

Moscow's diplomats are total professionals in the political trench warfare of U.S.–Soviet negotiations. They dig into their positions, devise scores of potential lines of debate as verbal fortifications, and fall back only after repeated frontal assaults by the opposition. Even then, our side will have to root out their positions one by one, because as they retreat on one front they will create false points of contention on another in order to win real concessions on a third. Soviet negotiators are among the world's ablest. They can certainly watch out for Soviet interests. We need not help them do so with preemptive concessions on our part.

If we have a strong, logical position, we should stand our ground. As a veteran Moscow correspondent, Joseph Galloway, wrote, "You should state your purpose, your aims, and your course clearly and firmly at the outset and then hew to that line with every ounce of determination and doggedness you can muster. If you bend even the smallest of your principles, you convince the other side that there is at least a chance you will bend on the larger ones. That is enough to keep the Russians working on you forever."

Our negotiators must learn to put our general interests over their desires to conclude an agreement. The SDI is a case in point. Within the foreign-policy bureaucracy, there is a constant harping about the need to make concessions to the Soviets on SDI in order to get a START agreement. They treat SDI as if it were a problem for us. In fact it is a problem for Moscow. We should not wring our hands and ask ourselves what we are going to do about SDI. Instead, we should sit back and ask the Soviets what *they* are going to do about their superiority in strategic nuclear weapons, which is the reason we are developing SDI.

Our cardinal rule must be, Give nothing without getting something in return. We must never give the Soviets a free ride. If we toss out concessions intended to win goodwill from Moscow, the Soviets will gather up the loose change and ask for more. As one experienced American negotiator once commented, the Soviets seldom pay for services already rendered.

Talk soft, act tough. Diplomatic machismo may make points at home but it serves no useful purpose abroad. The Soviets are masters of the bluff. As any poker player knows, one who uses the bluff can generally detect one when it is used by his opponent. The best way to deal with the Soviets is to talk softly and act strongly.

Unpredictability. Our diplomats tend to lay their cards out on the table before seeing the Soviets' cards. They should have in mind the golden rule of diplomacy in dealing with the Soviets: Do unto them as they do unto you. Gorbachev is a master at making the surprise move. We should be just as unpredictable as he is.

If we learn to combine a tempered tone and tough actions and to employ flanking actions, linkage, economic power, tenacious bargaining, and unpredictability, we can get good deals out of the Soviets on trade, arms control, and other issues. But the task of negotiating with Moscow does not stop there. It requires the United States to scrutinize Moscow's compliance with the agreement. That means, first of all, that all agreements must be written with extremely tight verification procedures. From the record of SALT I and SALT II, we have learned that the Soviets will ruthlessly exploit even the smallest of loopholes.

We must also recognize that the Soviets will stretch every agreement to the limit. They will do everything that is allowed—and whatever else they can get away with. We must respond accordingly. Those who claim that the SALT I agreement permitted the Soviet Union to push ahead of the United States in strategic systems misplace the blame. We fell behind in strategic nuclear weapons not because of the agreement but because of our failure to do everything permitted under the agreement. A whole range of strategic programs—the B-1 bomber, the MX missile, and the Trident submarine—were under way when SALT I was signed. But Congress cut back on their appropriations in the mid-1970s, and the Carter administration canceled some and stretched out the timetable for deployment of others. If we had done all we were allowed to do under SALT I, the window of vulnerability would never have opened up.

In addition, we must not put the issue of Soviet arms-control violations on the back burner while other negotiations proceed. President Reagan has rightly insisted that the United States take proportional steps to counter Soviet violations. Since the Soviets have broken through the SALT II numerical ceilings, the United States should do likewise. Since they have deployed more new missiles than permitted under SALT II, we should press forward with both the MX and Midgetman missiles. Since the Soviets encrypt the telemetry of their missiles in test firings, we should do the same.

We must insist in our negotiations on resolving the issue of compliance before entering new agreements. This is not just a diplomatic nicety. We must tirelessly point out to those who would brush this issue aside that it ultimately affects our national survival. At the same time, we must tirelessly point out to the Kremlin that if they refuse to deal with the issue of violations of past agreements, there is no way that the Senate will—or should—ratify future ones. If we hold to that position, the Soviets will eventually come around.

Those who oppose the idea of negotiating with Moscow also oppose summitry between the superpowers. Summits, in their view, not only have the drawbacks of negotiations in general, but they also benefit the Soviets disproportionately. With their unavoidable champagne toasts and diplomatic cordiality, U.S.–Soviet summit meetings legitimize the Kremlin leaders in the eyes of the world, regardless of the brutal policies they pursue in distant places like Afghanistan.

That view is understandable, particularly given our poor track record at summits. All too often, we have seen an American President captivated by the notion that if only he and his Soviet counterpart got to know each other and succeeded in developing a new tone or spirit in their relationship, then U.S.–Soviet problems would be solved and tensions would wane. This led to the vaunted "spirit" of Geneva in 1955, of Camp David in 1959, of Vienna in 1961, of Glassboro in 1967, and again of Geneva in 1985. But while these spirits improved the atmosphere of U.S.–Soviet relations, they did nothing to resolve the major underlying issues. When a summit is all spirit and no substance, the spirit evaporates fast.

We need to face the hard reality that spirit and tone matter only when leaders of nations with similar and compatible interests have a misunderstanding that can be resolved by their getting to know each other. Such ephemeral factors are irrelevant when nations have irreconcilable differences, as do the United States and the Soviet Union.

But that does not mean that American–Soviet summits serve no beneficial purpose. Summits can play a decisive role in serving peace. But they contribute to a genuine improvement in East–West relations only if both leaders recognize that tensions between their countries are caused not by misunderstanding but by diametrically opposed ideological and geopolitical interests. Most of our differences will never be resolved. But the United States and the Soviet Union have one major goal in common: survival. Each has the key to the other's survival. The purpose of summit meetings is to develop rules of engagement that can prevent our profound differences from leading to an armed conflict that would destroy us both.

We must recognize that despite forty-four years of peace a world war remains possible. From the least to the most dangerous, there are seven potential causes of such a conflict: (1) a calculated decision by the Soviet leadership to launch a first-strike attack on the United States; (2) an attack on NATO forces by Warsaw Pact forces or on Japan by the Soviet Union; (3) war by accident, in which one side launches a nuclear attack because of some kind of mechanical malfunction; (4) nuclear proliferation, which could put nuclear weapons into the hands of a leader of a minor revolutionary or terrorist power who would be less restrained from using them than the major powers have been; (5) a Soviet preemptive strike to liquidate the Chinese nuclear arsenal, a war which would inevitably drag in the United States; (6) escalations of small wars in areas where the interests of both superpowers collide, such as the Middle East and the Persian Gulf; and (7) a miscalculation in which a leader of one superpower underestimates the will of his counterpart to take the ultimate risk to defend his interests.

The United States and the Soviet Union have a mutual interest in reducing the danger and risks represented by all seven scenarios. Superpower summits can play a constructive role in mitigating each one of them. If properly conducted, such meetings can facilitate the cooperation necessary to reduce the risk of accidental war and to stem the proliferation of nuclear weapons. They also provide a means to make clear our determination to resist Soviet aggression against Western interests, thereby lessening the risk that Moscow will put our will to the test.

Summits present an American President with a unique set of opportunities and challenges. At the summit, he has the chance to break the glacial pace of negotiations between American and Soviet bureaucracies. Such meetings are also the hearth in which he can forge the linkage between various U.S.–Soviet issues. They are the forum in which his Soviet opposite number—for better or worse—takes his measure of the United States. But the summit also has its perils. A President might blunder into a Soviet diplomatic trap. Or he might inadvertently set a tone for U.S.–Soviet relations that produces a counterproductive public euphoria about the possibility of finally ending the superpower struggle.

During forty-two years in public life, I have watched nine U.S.-Soviet summits and participated as President in three. In looking back at our successes and failures, I believe that in practicing summitry the next President should keep five key rules uppermost in mind:

Do not expect good personal relations with a Soviet leader to produce better state relations. There can be no more dangerous illusion than the belief that a charismatic American President can charm his counterpart into desisting from aggressive policies around the world. Soviet leaders are expert at playing to this American blind spot. Manlio Brosio, who served for six years as the Italian ambassador to Moscow, saw through the charade. "I know the Russians," he told me in 1967. "They are great liars, clever cheaters, and magnificent actors. They cannot be trusted. They consider it their duty to cheat and lie."

Almost every President starting with Franklin D. Roosevelt has at some point fallen prey to the belief that a special personal relationship with the top Soviet leader would facilitate a diplomatic breakthrough that would, in turn, pacify the U.S.–Soviet relationship. All were utterly disillusioned when the Soviets toasted us with one hand while stabbing us in the back with the other. We must recognize that the road to diplomatic disaster is paved with naive intentions.

That does not mean that personal diplomacy makes no difference. It is indispensable in the chemistry of summitry, but if handled improperly it can also explode in our faces. We must learn that the essential element is not sentimental friendship but hard-headed mutual respect. A President need not try to prove his manhood with chest-pounding belligerence toward the Soviets. Instead, he should strive for a serious and businesslike attitude in negotiations, granting the Soviet leader the respect due the leader of a global superpower. But at the same time a President should keep an acute awareness that separating the two sides are irreconcilable differences that cannot be bridged through personal diplomacy between their leaders.

In dealing with Gorbachev, it is particularly important for a Pres-

ident to keep a realistic attitude about the role of personal diplomacy. Gorbachev is a master at charm. In interviews, he has
transformed some of America's toughest reporters into lapdogs.
But we must recognize that, as a master of charm, Gorbachev
cannot be affected by charm. He knows all the tricks because he
has employed them a hundred times. If a President tries to prevail
through charm, he will win not friendship but contempt.

*Do not pretend that even a successful summit will bring about a
permanent peace.* Successful summits tend to breed euphoric expectations, but no single meeting between American and Soviet
leaders can transform the world and put an end to the U.S.–Soviet
rivalry. Euphoria is an illusion that breeds disillusion and invites
irresolution. In fact, utopian hopes hurt the United States and our
allies. It is a goal of the Soviet Union to foster a euphoria about
better U.S.–Soviet relations because that in turn facilitates an increase in East-West trade and a reduction in Western defense
spending. If we allow—or encourage—such euphoria, Kremlin
leaders will not only get what they want but also get it at a dis-
count. We must not make the mistake of believing that Gorbachev's willingness to relax tensions means he has abandoned
hardheaded self-interest as his guiding light.

As President, I was well aware that our highly successful summit
meeting in 1972 might spawn euphoric expectations among the
American people. Even though I knew I stood to benefit politically
from such euphoria, I tried to tamp it down and to keep our successes in perspective. I did so particularly because Brezhnev had
repeatedly underscored to me that a relaxation of tensions would
not end Soviet support for what he called wars of national liberation in the Third World. In a speech before a joint session of
Congress immediately upon my return from Moscow, I frankly
stated that we did not "bring back from Moscow the promise of
instant peace, but we do bring the beginning of a process that can
lead to a lasting peace." I added, "Soviet ideology still proclaims
hostility to some of America's basic values. The Soviet leaders
remain committed to that ideology." My words proved to be inadequate. Despite my warnings, euphoria did develop in the Congress and in the media. I was not surprised when the communists
acted like communists in the Mideast in 1973. But it was a shock

to many Americans who thought we had entered a new era of peace and goodwill. Unfortunately, the euphoria did not fully dissipate until the Soviet invasion of Afghanistan in 1979.

After the Washington summit in December 1987, euphoria swept the capital. President Reagan's postsummit address to the American people was a well-balanced and very responsible assessment of U.S.–Soviet relations. But some administration officials fed the fires of euphoria, predicting rapid progress on complex issues and depicting the dawn of a new era in world affairs. That kind of exaggerated rhetoric weakens our negotiating position by raising domestic expectations. All future Presidents who participate in summits should keep their staffers on a shorter leash.

We must bear in mind that no agreement signed at a summit will eliminate the threat of Soviet aggression. At best, it can only reduce the possibility of that threat's escalating into armed conflict. While we should seek agreements that serve our interests, we must never assume that any agreement changes the nature of the American–Soviet conflict or the aggressive character of the Kremlin's global intentions.

Do not go to an unprepared, "quickie" summit meeting. Accepting an invitation to an unprepared summit meeting is tantamount to accepting an invitation to a diplomatic disaster. Moscow thrives on these kinds of meetings because it can exploit the publicity for propaganda without making any substantive concessions. When announced, a quickie summit creates anticipation that breeds unrealistic hopes. When it inevitably fails, it creates unrealistic fears and disillusionment. While they might be a short-term political plus, shoot-from-the-hip summits result in our shooting ourselves in the foot and in damaging the prospects for better U.S.–Soviet relations in the long term.

We should have learned this lesson from our experiences with summits in the 1960s. After the Vienna summit in 1961, some of the President's most ardent media supporters reported that Khrushchev manhandled a woefully unprepared Kennedy, who was still reeling from his failures at the Bay of Pigs and in Berlin. The summit contributed to Khrushchev's inaccurate view that Kennedy was a weak President and thereby encouraged the Soviet leader to decide to press his near-fatal gamble to put missiles into

Cuba the following year. At the quickie summit in Glassboro in 1968, Johnson achieved nothing, except to help the world forget the recent brutal Soviet invasion of Czechoslovakia.

The meeting at Reykjavik in 1986 is a prime example of how not to conduct a summit. Never has so much been risked with so little forethought. In one meeting with Gorbachev, President Reagan actually negotiated about eliminating not only ballistic missiles but also all other nuclear weapons on the basis of a scrap of paper on which an aide had scrawled a couple of talking points. Had it not been for the fact that the President, to his great credit, adamantly refused to trade away the SDI, the United States might have cast aside the core of Western defense strategy—all without consulting its allies or even the Joint Chiefs of Staff. Ironically, even if no weapons are ever deployed as a result of the SDI, it has already once saved the West from disaster.

In the end, the unprepared summit at Reykjavik achieved nothing in terms of Western interests. First, it allowed the Soviets to get off the hook for their recent kidnapping of American journalist Nicholas Daniloff. Second, it enabled Gorbachev to paint the SDI as the principal obstacle to a sweeping arms-control agreement. Third, its loose talk about eliminating nuclear weapons sent shock waves through the West. No summit since Yalta has threatened Western interests so much as the two days at Reykjavik. It is almost inevitable that any freewheeling summit will career toward disaster.

Do not allow arms control to dominate the summit agenda. At a summit, a President must give proportional weight to the entire spectrum of U.S.–Soviet issues. In fact, a summit agenda should place top priority not on arms control but on the potential flashpoints for U.S.–Soviet conflicts. After all, it is not arms but the political differences that lead to their use that cause wars. The failure to devote sustained attention to these political differences sends the wrong message to Moscow. Kremlin leaders watch their counterparts closely at a summit. Our choice of issues carries a signal: What we address is what we think important. If we skirt an issue, they will assume we are giving them a free hand on it.

Conflicts in the Third World are the most important issues to raise. Soviet leaders must be made to understand that it would be both irrational and immoral for the United States and the West to accept the doctrine that the Soviet Union has the right to support so-called wars of national liberation in the noncommunist world without insisting on our right to defend our allies and friends under assault and to support true liberation movements against pro-Soviet regimes in the Third World. We cannot realistically expect the Soviets to cease being communists dedicated to expanding their influence and domination, but we must make it clear at the summit level that military adventurism will destroy the chances for better relations between the United States and the Soviet Union, thereby nullifying any potential benefits Moscow might derive from reduced tensions.

The Reykjavik summit in 1986 and the Washington summit in 1987 were primarily arms-control summits. Gorbachev succeeded in his efforts to block progress, and in fact any real negotiations, on any other issues. At the next summit, the United States should insist that equal priority be given to the causes of war as is given to the arms that could be used to wage war. Arms-control talks are important and can serve our interests. But they should proceed in tandem with and be expressly linked to the other issues on the agenda. A relaxation of tensions that is based exclusively on arms control and that allows Soviet expansionism to run unchecked will lead not to real peace but to false hopes and runaway euphoria.

Do not negotiate with a deadline. We tend to make foreign policy in four-year cycles. A typical American President aspires to overhaul our policies vis-à-vis the Soviet Union and to settle all outstanding questions before the next presidential election. He is a man in a hurry and is visibly concerned with the ticking clock. Kremlin leaders are acutely aware of the pressure that time puts on a President and are capable of exploiting it ruthlessly. Our top leaders must therefore be more realistic in what they hope to achieve. No single President will solve all the issues, and no single issue will be solved for all time by any President. At the summit, we must be willing to walk away without a deal if the terms are not right. It is a fatal mistake for any American President to negotiate with a deadline. After all, Gorbachev's negotiating deadline is about twenty-five years.

Institute annual summits. If a President hews to these five basic guidelines, he can go toe-to-toe with any Soviet leader at the summit. As part of his overall negotiating strategy, he should seek to establish a process of annual summit meetings with the top Soviet leader.

Annual summits are useful for three reasons. First, since both leaders will want substantive agreements for a summit, the fact that one is scheduled gives added impetus to negotiations mired in the bureaucracies. It is one of the best ways for the United States to put the heat on the Soviets to budge from their entrenched positions. While this should not be carried to the point of seeking an agreement for the sake of an agreement or of negotiating against a deadline, scheduled annual summits can help break negotiating logjams. Second, the regular discussion of political differences on an annual basis reduces the possibility that one leader will miscalculate the reaction of the other. Each will have ample opportunity to stake his ground and demonstrate his will to defend his interests. While the two leaders might not like each other, they will understand each other. It will therefore lessen the chance that a miscalculation by one will result in a war neither wants. Third, the fact that a summit is scheduled will inhibit aggressive moves by the Soviet Union in the run-up to the meeting. Neither leader wants to be accused of poisoning the atmosphere prior to a summit.

Some might be tempted to conclude that it is hopeless to expect a democracy to come out on equal terms in negotiations with a totalitarian dictatorship. But in the past we have reached sound agreements. The Austrian Peace Treaty of 1955, the Limited Nuclear Test Ban Treaty of 1962, the Berlin agreement of 1971, and the SALT I Treaty of 1972 all represented significant progress in U.S.–Soviet relations. In each case, however, we must remember that the agreement did not mark an end to the superpower conflict but simply took a step toward setting up a process to live with the continuing conflict.

If we recognize their limitations and if we adhere to proper guidelines for their conduct, negotiations with Moscow can serve a useful purpose—in effect providing rules of engagement for competition without war. But we must not pursue negotiations in isolation from the other aspects of overall strategy. We can go forward with talks only if we do what is necessary to maintain deterrence and keep up our competition. To negotiate without maintaining a deterrent leads to gradual accommodation and capitulation. To negotiate without continuing to compete leads to acquiescence to Soviet aggression. If we learn to combine the three —deterrence, competition, and negotiation—we will be in a position to achieve real peace in the years beyond 1999.

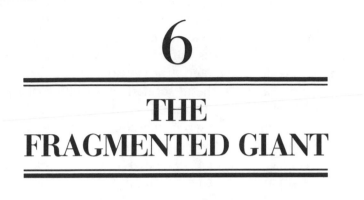

6

THE
FRAGMENTED GIANT

In the years beyond 1999, the balance of power in the world will reflect less and less the dominance of the United States and the Soviet Union and more and more the rising importance of three other global geopolitical giants: Western Europe, Japan, and China. The future of the world rides to a large degree on whether these other power centers contribute to the strength of the East or the West. Therefore, in the years before 1999, the United States must undertake a concerted effort to integrate the world's three rising power centers into a broad coalition to deter Soviet aggression and create a stronger world order.

There are those who would contest that view in the case of Western Europe. They do not believe that NATO matters anymore. They sum up the shift in world power by describing the nineteenth century as the century of Europe, the twentieth as the American century, and the twenty-first as the Pacific century. They argue that Europe is finished as a major factor in world affairs. No European country by itself can qualify as a superpower. Even Great Britain, France, and Germany, the nations which once were the world's premier military and economic powers, are soft and decadent, unable to see their own interests, much less to mobilize the willpower to defend them. Their leaders are obsessed with satiating the appetite of their rapacious welfare states rather than playing a constructive world role. Those who view Europe in this way, as a collection of geopolitical has-beens, conclude that the United States should therefore cast Europe aside and either turn to the Pacific or go it alone in the world.

In one respect, this view is correct: The two world wars of the twentieth century have exacted a heavy toll on the European nations. In World War I, all the absolutist monarchies, the political systems of half of Europe, were uprooted. In World War II, the seeds of destruction were sown in the colonial soil of all the great European empires. As de Gaulle told me in 1969, "In World War II, all the nations of Europe lost; two were defeated." Europe entered the postwar period as a continent suffering from historical exhaustion. In the first half of the century, its peoples had barely survived two devastating wars, and their instincts told them to withdraw from the world and to adopt a more parochial outlook.

But the critics of Europe ignore the positive side of the ledger. Britain and France are no longer rivals, and France and Germany are no longer enemies. Western European countries have made great strides in integrating their economies and have taken the first halting steps toward political unity. While for almost a century it was customary to describe Turkey as "the sick man of Europe," it is now well on the way to vigorous economic and political health and provides more divisions for NATO than any other country. After remaining neutral in World War II, Spain adopted a democratic government and has joined NATO, and, despite the dispute over the future of U.S. air bases, socialist Prime Minister Felipe González remains committed to remaining in the alliance.

While the fragmented giant of Europe still has a long way to go before it achieves genuine unity, we should not ignore the fact that the countries of Western Europe have come a long way since 1945. We can safely predict that these countries, which clashed in dozens of crises in the one hundred years before 1945, will not go to war against one another again in the next century. That has not happened since the Pax Romana fifteen centuries ago.

Moreover, it is still in the interest of the United States to remain in NATO and to maintain the U.S. military presence in Western Europe. The population of Western Europe is greater than that of the United States and almost as great as that of the Soviet Union.

With one-fourth the territory of the United States and one-eighth that of the Soviet Union, our NATO allies have a total GNP almost equal to ours and more than 50 percent higher than the Soviet Union's. Western Europe's peoples are highly educated and capable of exploiting the enormous promise of high technology. Most important, for the first time in history all the West European nations have democratic governments.

Thus, for the United States, Western Europe continues to be the single most strategic piece of territory in the world. It contains over a quarter of the world's economic power and represents the forward line of defense against the Soviet Union. Yet, a profound crisis today threatens the future of the Atlantic Alliance. Harold Macmillan saw this coming thirty years ago when he told me, "Alliances are held together by fear, not love." Ironically, today while the Soviet threat is greater, the fear of Soviet aggression is less. When it was established in 1949, the North Atlantic Treaty Organization represented an appropriate response to the threats we faced in 1949. But since then the world has changed. If NATO cannot adapt, it will not survive. It needs to grow to meet the new challenges we face, or it will perish.

The crisis of NATO has grown out of the profound transformation of the world in the last forty years.

When the leaders of the original twelve NATO states gathered in Washington to sign its charter in 1949, each grounded his decision to join the alliance on four common assumptions:

1. Moscow posed a dangerous military threat to Western Europe. In the late 1940s and early 1950s, Western leaders were haunted by the nightmare of scores of Red Army divisions sweeping across Europe to the English Channel. European communist parties compounded the image of Soviet hostility by dutifully toeing the party line from Moscow and vigorously denouncing any West European participation in the Marshall Plan. As a result, no democratic leader—not even those of Europe's socialist parties—denied the danger. Among the democratic parties of Western Europe there was unanimity on one point: military aggression by the Kremlin was a real threat.

2. Moscow's superiority in conventional forces could be countered with American nuclear superiority. In 1950, the NATO countries had fewer than 600,000 ground troops, while the Soviet Union had 1.5 million. But the leaders of the West stood firm in the face of the Soviets' two-to-one conventional superiority, because of overwhelming U.S. nuclear superiority. The United States had in its arsenal three hundred nuclear bombs, while Moscow had only tested its first crude nuclear explosive less than a year before. Thus, the members of NATO assumed that nuclear weapons could guarantee Western Europe's military security for the foreseeable future.

3. U.S. economic strength compared with Western Europe's enabled the United States to bear a major share of the financial burden of conventional defenses in Europe. In 1950, the U.S. economy represented over half of the world economy, while the countries of Western Europe were still suffering from the economic devastation of World War II. America had reached its economic zenith; Europe was still digging out of the rubble. Western Europe had to demobilize in order to devote its resources to economic recovery. As a result, the United States stepped in to fill the breach, deploying more than 435,000 ground troops in Europe by 1953 and expending more than $60 billion in 1987 dollars on the Marshall Plan.

4. The military threat from Moscow was focused on the European continent. In the immediate postwar years, the members of NATO assumed that the major target of the Kremlin's aggressive designs was Western Europe. If Moscow unleashed a war of aggression, they believed, its divisions would roll across the European plain. Moreover, the Soviet Union was not yet a global superpower. Moscow did not have then the capacity to project military power beyond the countries on its borders. Thus, the threat was only to Europe, and the response needed to come in Europe.

None of those assumptions are held in common by all the leaders of NATO countries in 1988.

First, a profound disagreement has developed between NATO leaders on the opposite sides of the Atlantic over how great a threat the Soviet Union poses to the West. Generally, Americans believe that the Soviet threat remains as great as or even greater than ever. They point to the massive buildup of Soviet strategic and conventional forces—as well as to the continuing domination of Eastern Europe and the string of geopolitical gains Moscow tallied up in the 1970s—as proof of the Kremlin's hostile intentions toward the West.

Many in Western Europe agree with the American view of the East–West conflict. They remember the Berlin crisis in 1948, when only an airlift by the Western powers prevented Moscow from starving the city's western sector. They remember the malicious delight with which Khrushchev built the Berlin Wall, the only wall in history put up not to keep invaders out but to keep its own citizens from escaping. They are well aware of the grimness of life under communism in Eastern Europe. Most of all, they know that the Warsaw Pact's forces always train to fight an offensive, not defensive, war.

But in recent years there has been a tendency among West Europeans, especially but not exclusively those on the left, to see the Soviet Union in a different light. The more responsible critics of the U.S. point of view believe that Americans are overreacting to a real but exaggerated threat. They argue that the Soviet threat is not so overwhelming and immediate as to require a frantic response. They point out that communism in the Soviet Union is not a historical success story. Given the Kremlin's great internal problems and its increasing difficulty in holding its East European empire, the Soviet Union is not in a position to threaten seriously Western Europe. Only a madman in the Kremlin, in their view, would consider launching a war of aggression across the central European plain. And the threat of a Soviet nuclear attack is minimal, because ruling over a Europe of destroyed cities and dead bodies would not be a rational war goal of any sane leader. They therefore believe that American anxiety and the American call for more vigilance and military preparedness represent an overreaction of an immature world power.

The less responsible European critics of America take this analysis a step further. They believe that the United States is a greater threat to peace than the Soviet Union. They argue that Western Europe should opt out of the East–West struggle. Their heated rhetoric accuses the United States of forcibly conscripting Western Europe in its Cold War with the Soviet Union and insidiously refers to American troops in Western Europe as "occupation forces." They believe that a third world war is more likely to result from U.S. recklessness than from Soviet aggression. Unfortunately, two major European socialist parties, the Labour Party in Britain and the Social Democratic Party in West Germany, have succumbed to these views. Their platforms in recent campaigns have called for the complete removal of American nuclear forces from Europe and other steps which would lead directly to the dissolution of NATO.

This problem will undoubtedly get worse before it gets better. NATO is a victim of its own success. Western Europe has enjoyed unprecedented stability, prosperity, and security largely as a result of the alliance. As Michael Howard has observed, "It takes only one generation of successful peacekeeping to create the belief that peace is a natural condition endangered only by those professionally involved in the preparation for war." NATO's success in deterring a Soviet attack has led many to question whether a threat existed in the first place. With the new Gorbachev leadership in Moscow more attuned to public relations, the problem will become greater. Some public-opinion polls already indicate that West Europeans believe that the actions of the United States threaten peace as much as or more than those of the Soviet Union. If this becomes a trend, it will make not communism but neutralism the wave of the future in Europe.

The second major change has come in the overall East–West strategic and conventional balance of power and has had profound consequences for NATO's strategy for defending Western Europe.

On the conventional level, the Soviet Union continues to enjoy a decisive margin of superiority. In Europe, the Warsaw Pact has 2.7 million troops, 47,000 main battle tanks, and 5,400 tactical aircraft. NATO has 2.4 million troops, 23,000 tanks, and 4,000 aircraft. The Warsaw Pact has huge potential reserves in the Soviet Union, which are only a few miles away, while NATO's reserves in the United States are four thousand miles away. While NATO's forces have the advantage of technological superiority, they lack an integrated command structure and must defend a front 4,200 miles long, while fully integrated Warsaw Pact forces need only to break through at a single point. Moreover, the countries of Western Europe have been so lax in maintaining military readiness that NATO would quickly run out of ammunition in a conventional war.

The greatest concern is that, unlike the early years of the Cold War, the United States today does not have unquestioned nuclear superiority to counter the threat of Moscow's armies. From 1945 to 1949, the United States had a monopoly on nuclear weapons. From 1949 to the mid-1950s, it had a monopoly in the means to deliver a significant nuclear strike on the other side's territory. From the mid-1950s to the mid-1970s, it had a significant, but eroding, margin of nuclear superiority. In the mid- to late 1970s, the Soviet Union first achieved parity with the United States in strategic weapons, and then pressed forward to forge a significant degree of superiority in land-based ballistic missiles.

When the United States enjoyed absolute nuclear superiority, it adopted the doctrine of "massive retaliation." According to this doctrine, if Soviet forces broke the trip wire in Central Europe, the United States would respond, not only by firing tactical nuclear weapons at attacking Soviet armies, but also by unleashing the full force of American strategic forces on the Soviet Union itself. But we could threaten a massive nuclear retaliation only because Moscow did not yet have the capability to respond in kind. Once the Soviet Union developed a major strategic arsenal of its own, an American nuclear retaliation to conventional aggression would in turn involve millions of American casualties in a matter of hours. Thus, the threat of massive retaliation became a threat to commit mutual suicide—and therefore lost its credibility.

As a result, the United States and its NATO allies adopted the doctrine of "flexible response" in the 1960s. In the event of a Soviet conventional attack, it called for NATO forces to stop the enemy with whatever forces were necessary—but at the lowest possible level of violence. If conventional forces could not stop the Warsaw Pact attack, NATO would use first battlefield nuclear weapons, then intermediate-range-theater nuclear forces, and finally American strategic weapons as a last resort. U.S. leaders would therefore be able to respond with flexibility to the situation on the battlefield.

That shored up the security of Europe despite the erosion of American nuclear superiority. Since NATO could certainly stop Soviet armies in their tracks with battlefield and theater nuclear weapons, the doctrine of flexible response left the ultimate burden of deciding to escalate to the level of all-out strategic nuclear war squarely in the Kremlin. Soviet leaders therefore had to include the risks of *total* war in their calculation of the risks of launching *any* war. That, in turn, undercut the possibility that Moscow could exploit the threat of its conventional superiority to blackmail Western Europe.

Theater, or intermediate-range, nuclear forces—U.S. missiles and bombers based in Western Europe that can strike deep within the Soviet Union—were recognized as the linchpin of the doctrine of flexible response. Only these forces could execute the vital mission of destroying Soviet conventional reinforcements long before they reached the front. Moreover, only these weapons could keep deterrence in Europe credible. Strategic parity had diminished the credibility of the threat of a U.S. strategic retaliation to a conventional attack. To bolster deterrence, the United States therefore needed to develop the capability to threaten to retaliate against the Soviet Union from Europe.

NATO as a whole recognized that fact. For this reason, the West European members of NATO requested in 1979 that the United States station ground-based cruise missiles and Pershing II missiles in Europe. Our allies knew that in the event of war NATO bombers not only would be unable to penetrate Soviet air defenses, but also would be desperately needed for conventional bombing missions at the front. They further knew that U.S. sea-based missiles were not accurate enough to hit military targets in the Soviet Union. These ground-based missiles were therefore critical to deterrence in Europe. That was why the West European governments—despite enormous antinuclear street demonstrations—were willing to pay the political price for deploying these U.S. missiles in 1983.

With these weapons in Western Europe, NATO's strategy to deter a Soviet aggression became a seamless web. Moscow knew that, even if it succeeded initially, a conventional invasion would inevitably lead to nuclear strikes on the territory of the Soviet Union—a risk the leaders in the Kremlin would not dare court.

Without these missiles, however, a gap would open up in NATO's deterrent. At best, it would become far from certain that the United States would employ its strategic arsenal—and therefore ensure a massive counterattack on American cities—to prevent the conventional defeat of NATO. At worst, it could leave the countries of Western Europe vulnerable to intimidation and blackmail in a crisis. Moscow might therefore prevail in Europe without firing a shot.

That was why Gorbachev made elimination of U.S. intermediate-range missiles in Europe his top priority in arms control. He desperately wanted the agreement he recently signed with President Reagan, certainly not out of the motive some gullible observers attribute to him—that of saving money which he can apply to much-needed domestic projects. Nuclear weapons are cheap, and the savings will be minimal.

Some naive arms-control enthusiasts have contended that Soviet acceptance of the zero–zero option is a victory for the West because Gorbachev gave up four times as many warheads as we did in Europe. They fail to ask themselves, "Why?" Gorbachev is not a philanthropist, and he is not a peacenik. Russians are the best chess players in the world, and the key to chess is to play for position early and always to think ahead several moves, anticipating and planning for the opponent's most likely countermoves. United States negotiators were obsessed only with the move in front of them—to reduce the number of nuclear weapons. Gorbachev was focusing on another part of the strategic chessboard: his goal was to decouple NATO and particularly the West Germans from the United States. He succeeded in demoralizing our staunchest friends in Germany and in getting plaudits from the antinuclear activists. With the recent arms-control agreement, Gorbachev did not win Europe—but did improve the Soviet strategic position for doing so at some point in the future.

The third critical change since the formation of NATO has been in the distribution of economic wealth. The reason American leaders chose to shoulder a disproportionate share of the burden of defending Western Europe in the immediate postwar years was that the Europeans themselves did not have the economic resources to do so. But that condition has changed. Western Europe has long since been rebuilt from the ruins of World War II. Today it stands as an economic equal to the United States, with its GNP of $3.5 trillion only slightly behind the $4 trillion U.S. economy. Moreover, the United States, given its large government deficits, is no longer in a position to pick up most of the tab for keeping the Warsaw Pact armies on the other side of the inner-German border.

Yet, despite its capacity to do so, Western Europe still contributes a great deal less proportionately to the common defense. The United States spends about 7 percent of GNP on defense, while the countries of Western Europe expend only about 3.5 percent. As former NATO Commander Alexander Haig has repeatedly pointed out, we should not underestimate our allies' contribution to the defense of Europe. They provide the bulk of NATO's forces, and they maintain a system of military conscription, while the United States does not. But it is no exaggeration to say that in absolute terms Americans spend more to defend Western Europe from Soviet attack than Europeans do.

Finally, the fourth basic change since the creation of NATO has been the deep divisions that have developed among the members of the alliance over Western policies outside Europe. In 1949, since all agreed that the likely axis of a Soviet advance ran through Europe, there was little thought given to countering Soviet expansion elsewhere. But apart from the contentious question of colonialism, all NATO members generally agreed that they shared common global interests, including that of preventing the spread of communism. As a result, when communist insurgencies arose in Malaysia and Indochina, the British and the French expected allied support in defeating them. When the North Koreans invaded South Korea, the United States expected the allies to send troops into that war.

But that comity broke down in the 1950s and 1960s and has virtually disappeared today. One of the greatest blows to allied cooperation outside Europe came when the United States decided to oppose the British and French effort to reclaim the Suez Canal militarily after Nasser nationalized it in 1956. President Eisenhower had cause to oppose them: Britain and France had kept him in the dark, even lied to him, about their plan to seize the canal, and he did not want to appear to be supporting brazen imperialism. And they could not have picked a worse time for their action, coming as it did two weeks after we had condemned Khrushchev for sending Soviet troops into Hungary and one week before the American elections in which Eisenhower was running on a platform of peace and prosperity.

I supported the decision at the time, but in retrospect our opposing British and French efforts to defend their interests in Suez was the greatest foreign-policy blunder the United States has made since the end of World War II. I have reason to believe that Eisenhower shared that assessment after he left office. The bottom line was that we failed to empathize with our allies and to calculate the long-term damage this would cause to the solidarity of the West. For them, the Suez Canal represented a critical interest. The failed Suez intervention had a disastrous net effect: our allies ceased to play their roles of world powers and began a precipitate retreat from the positions they had held around the globe.

As they withdrew, we either had to take their place or had to risk seeing the Soviet Union do so. Moscow took its cue, and the focus of the Soviet threat shifted. By the mid-1950s, NATO had secured the central front in Europe—so the Kremlin then shifted its attack to the flanks. New expansionism would come in the developing world, as Moscow sought to move into the vacuum of power left by the retreating European empires. Over the ensuing decades, the Soviet Union became a formidable global power, with the capability to project its power around the world and to threaten Western interests and access to strategic sea-lanes, oil reserves, and mineral deposits. It was a challenge NATO never before had to face—and one for which the alliance has yet to develop a sound strategy.

Moreover, as our European allies ceded their responsibility for shaping the course of events in the world, some political leaders became increasingly irresponsible in the positions they took on key East–West conflicts in the Third World. In the Vietnam War, some Europeans denounced as immoral the U.S. effort to prevent the brutal totalitarian warlords in Hanoi from taking over all of Indochina. They also came to pursue a reduction of tensions in Europe as a kind of absolute value, to be sought as an end in itself, regardless of whether Soviet actions elsewhere threatened Western interests. Soviet proxy wars in Africa, in their view, merited no response. After the direct Soviet invasion of Afghanistan in 1979, they took no actions apart from verbal denunciations. Even Moscow's suppression of the Solidarity movement in Poland in 1981 drew only hot rhetoric and lukewarm action.

Today, there is unprecedented dissension within NATO about issues outside Europe. Our allies would not allow us to resupply Israel from their territory during the Yom Kippur War in 1973. Margaret Thatcher was sharply criticized by those who opposed her decision to allow the United States to use British air bases as a jumping-off point for the strike on Libya in 1986, and France denied our bombers the right to pass over French territory en route, thus forcing them to fly thousands of extra miles. Today, NATO allies have only reluctantly agreed to cooperate with the United States in protecting freedom of navigation in the Persian Gulf, and U.S. efforts to prevent a Soviet beachhead in Central America receive little support and meet with much uninformed carping criticism.

The major problem NATO now faces is not the threat of Eurocommunism but rather the pernicious effect of Eurocriticism. It has robbed NATO of goodwill among members of the Congress. In the 1970s, NATO was attacked by liberal isolationists, who almost succeeded in passing the Mansfield Amendment to cut back U.S. forces in Europe. Today, the opposition to NATO comes from the conservatives. They believe not only that our allies are getting a free ride on defense spending, but also that the alliance restrains the United States in acting to defend its interests in the Third World. They have even gone so far as to argue that NATO weakens the West and undermines the national security of the United States. The overwhelming bipartisan support of NATO in 1949 has evaporated.

Given these four profound changes in the assumptions that undergirded NATO from the start, it is clear that this is not the garden-variety crisis which has led every few years to calls for "an agonizing reappraisal" of the alliance.

There is a real danger of a psychological decoupling in NATO. No alliance can survive if its members dispute its central purpose for existing. No alliance can survive if its members refuse to share fairly the financial burden of their collective security. No alliance can survive if its members disagree on the nature of the threat to their security. No alliance can survive if its members question the sincerity or the good intentions of some of their partners.

Unless the United States and its West European allies address these problems, we will look back in 1999 and see that the disputes of today were the first signs of the final disintegration of NATO.

As President, I sought to make 1973 the Year of Europe in order to focus the energies of my administration on resolving the problems which had arisen from changing times. We did not achieve the progress I thought was possible, and no administration since has made a concerted effort to deal with these issues. Therefore, whoever succeeds President Reagan in 1989 should dedicate his first year to solving the problems in the Atlantic partnership. The next President will be strongly tempted to put at the top of his agenda the Soviet–American relationship. Some will urge that he seek an early summit meeting with Gorbachev. This would be a mistake. Before seeking better relations with our adversaries, we should repair our relations with our friends. This means consulting seriously with our major NATO allies before meeting the Soviets, rather than perfunctorily informing them afterward.

Upon entering office, the next President should gather the NATO heads of government to initiate ministerial-level negotiations on the issues that divide us. These negotiations should reforge the bonds of the alliance and culminate in a NATO strategic summit at the end of the year. This would be a most fitting commemoration of the fortieth anniversary of NATO—and will enable the alliance to reach its fiftieth anniversary in 1999 with renewed vitality and purpose.

It is vital that we strengthen, not weaken, the alliance. Europe is still the major geopolitical target of the Kremlin. A Finlandized Europe would give a massive boost to the economic power of the Soviet Union and would lead to an economic disaster for the

United States. Nor can the United States afford to sink into self-satisfied neo-isolationism. It needs the help of its allies to defend Western interests around the world. As Franklin Roosevelt said in 1945, "We have learned that we cannot live alone, in peace."

Moreover, to break with Europe would be to rend the fabric of our history. We are largely a composite of European peoples and ideals. We share values, faiths, and cultural and philosophical heritages with Europe. Our military alliances and our close economic and cultural relationships are expressions not only of a common external threat, but also of our common heritage.

In a new Year of Europe, we must focus our energies on recasting the strategic underpinnings of NATO. In recent years, the alliance has become a master at producing meaningless communiqués by mating ambiguity with obfuscation. Its leaders have preferred to paper over disagreements rather than hammer out a clear accord. It is time to set forth with crystalline clarity our common understanding of the threats to NATO's security and our common strategic response. Putting it bluntly, there is a new threat, and we need a new NATO to meet it.

We first need to reach agreement on the nature of the adversary. Many claim that the Soviet Union under Gorbachev is no longer a dangerous threat to the West. That view is wrong. There is no evidence—so far—that he has changed the geopolitical thrust of Soviet foreign policy. He has not let up on the Soviet military buildup. He has not cut back on supporting Soviet client states in the Third World. He has not changed the status of Soviet satellites in Eastern Europe.

If Gorbachev does change the Soviet Union at home—and pacifies its foreign policy abroad—the West should welcome his actions. But we must be sure that we wait for him to make these changes before we give him the credit for doing so. We should not reward him with a change of our policy toward him until he changes his policy toward us. He cannot have it both ways—a relaxation of tensions with the West while he still engages in actions which threaten Western interests.

We must also agree on the nature of the Soviet threat. The fact is that Moscow threatens the security of the West both on the central front in Europe and in the Third World. It is easy to recognize the threat in Europe, for it comes in the form of over 100 divisions primed and ready to roll west. But the difficulty in detecting the hidden hand of Moscow in the Third World makes the threat no less real. While American superhawks need to concede that not all anti-Western movements and insurgencies result from Soviet actions, West Europeans need to accept the fact that some do and that the West must respond to this indirect aggression.

We must all recognize that while the Soviets' long-term major target is Western Europe, their immediate threat is to nations whose natural resources are indispensable to the survival of Europe. The Soviet Union can dominate Europe without waging war in Europe. The fact that there has not been a war in Europe in forty years is proof that NATO has been the most successful alliance in history. But while the Soviet Union has not waged war directly against NATO in Europe, it has successfully waged war indirectly against NATO in the Third World over the past forty years. It continues to do so. If NATO does not develop a strategy to meet that threat, the Soviets will achieve their goal of dominating Europe without attacking it directly. NATO's conventional armies in Europe will, in effect, have been a Maginot Line which the enemy has enveloped and made useless.

The major countries of NATO must therefore delineate the critical interests of the West around the world and develop a cooperative approach to defending them. We must stop at nothing less than a renewal of our strategic alliance. We must rethink basic strategy, reorganize the West's military forces, and reforge the linkage that once existed between overall East–West relations and Moscow's actions around the world.

The defense of Europe remains the core mission of NATO. A war in Europe is highly unlikely, but that does not mean that a war cannot occur. No one thought the assassination of an Austrian archduke would trigger a four-year world war which would kill over 14 million people. Most thought that this horrendous conflict was "the war to end all wars," only to see another world war break out twenty years later. War has no greater ally than those who claim that war will never come.

Therefore, in thinking about the defense of Europe, we must not begin by assuming that war can never happen. If no chance exists for a Soviet invasion, the United States has far better ways to spend the more than $100 billion in its defense budget allocated directly to European defense. Apart from the threat posed by the Warsaw Pact, there is no rationale for NATO. But if war is possible—even if highly unlikely—we must not let our guard down simply because the current Soviet General Secretary has a warm smile and a firm handshake.

NATO must first grapple with the role of nuclear weapons in the defense of Europe. These weapons have been both a blessing and a curse to Europe. NATO's nuclear arsenal has given Western Europe an inexpensive means to counter Soviet conventional superiority in the postwar years. This helped the Europeans economically. But when West Europeans failed to rethink their dependence on nuclear deterrence after their economic recoveries, the sole pillar of their security became nuclear weapons. Europeans sold their souls to the nuclear age. Their decision hurt them politically by undercutting their global role. These once-great world powers demoted themselves to the ranks of the world's regional powers.

But NATO cannot do away with nuclear weapons given the present balance of conventional forces. Without them, the alliance would in the event of war face the prospect of choosing between a conventional defeat and an all-out strategic nuclear war. Resolving that dilemma is a more difficult task given the new arms-control agreement. It is therefore imperative that as the process of dismantling the U.S. and Soviet intermediate- and short-range nuclear forces begins we take a hard look at how NATO can maintain nuclear deterrence.

First, we must resist the political temptation to make our goal in arms control the elimination of all nuclear weapons in Europe. Inevitable political pressures in Europe to take the new arms-control accord a step further and ban battlefield nuclear weapons have already arisen. But scoring easy political points courts a strategic disaster. A denuclearized Europe has been a long-standing Soviet objective. Moscow knows that an American threat to launch an all-out strategic war in response to conventional aggression is not credible. A total ban on nuclear weapons in Europe would further strain the already-frayed American trip wire in Europe. It would leave U.S. allies prey to Soviet conventional military intimidation.

Second, we must strengthen the link between American nuclear forces and European defense. The new arms-control agreement will eliminate U.S. missiles in Europe over the next three years. That gives NATO enough time to adjust its military posture to maintain deterrence. We should increase the number of bombers capable of executing nuclear strikes deep within Warsaw Pact territory. We should deploy additional sea-launched cruise missiles on U.S. warships assigned to NATO. We should also dedicate some of the new U.S. Trident II submarines, with their very accurate hard-target warheads, to serve exclusively as part of our NATO commitment.

Third, we should renounce the Reykjavik formula calling for the elimination of all nuclear weapons in ten years. The next administration must make a conscious break with this naive notion. For the foreseeable future, nuclear weapons and the threat of nuclear war will exist. That is a basic fact of international life. Like it or not, nuclear weapons must be part of our strategy to deter war. No deeper blow has ever been dealt to allied confidence in the United States than by the incorporation of the nuclear-free fantasy into the American negotiating position at Reykjavik. The rhetoric of Reykjavik should be replaced by the realism of Margaret Thatcher, who told Gorbachev in 1987, "A world without nuclear weapons may be a dream. But you cannot base a sure defense on a dream. A world without nuclear weapons would be less stable and more dangerous for us all."

We must also renounce the irresponsible rhetoric of denouncing nuclear deterrence as immoral. It is simply wrong. We would not need nuclear weapons for deterrence in a perfect world. We should in any case minimize our dependence on them. But given the realities of the world, we must have nuclear weapons to deter potential aggressors from launching a war or forcing surrender without war. That is a moral goal pursued by the best means practically available.

Fourth, we must find ways to integrate West Germany into our strategy of deterrence. It was West Germany—under Social Democratic Chancellor Helmut Schmidt—that initiated the request in 1979 that U.S. intermediate-range missiles be stationed in Western Europe. The new arms-control agreement pulls out those missiles, as well as the Soviet equivalents. But every target in Western Europe is covered by the thousands of long-range missiles in Moscow's inventory. The elimination of intermediate- and short-range weapons does not reduce the Soviets' nuclear threat to either Europe or the United States. It does remove NATO's capability to respond to a Soviet attack on Europe with nuclear weapons from Europe. With no nuclear weapons of its own, West Germany is particularly vulnerable to the nuclear and conventional blackmail of the Soviet Union. The next administration must find ways to reassure the Germans on this issue.

Fifth, we must improve NATO's conventional forces in order to raise the threshold which would require the use of nuclear weapons. NATO's conventional inferiority is the reason the United States deployed nuclear weapons in Europe. In the event of war, NATO today would find it difficult to avoid escalating immediately to the strategic nuclear level to hold off the Kremlin's conventional forces. But that need not be the case. NATO could reduce the possibility of having to make that awesome decision by rectifying the current imbalance of forces on the conventional level. In fact, the research fallout from the Strategic Defense Initiative holds the promise of developing new conventional weapons that will help restore the balance in Europe. We should recognize, however, that increasing NATO's conventional forces is not a substitute for, but a strengthening of, nuclear deterrence. It substantially lengthens the nuclear fuse.

Western Europe would benefit politically, as well as militarily, by raising the nuclear threshold. The fear of nuclear war has corroded the morale of Europe. It was inevitable that a defense policy based on a threat with such cataclysmic consequences could not be sustained. Europeans have come to feel threatened by their own defense. They therefore should adopt a strategy based on a credible conventional defense of Western Europe. Our allies will feel more secure—and therefore more confident—if they have a defense that defends rather than relying on one that might turn out to be an empty cannon.

For a policy of deterrence to have credibility, Europeans must be reassured that the benefits of carrying out the policy will exceed the costs. The present nuclear deterrent does not meet that test. The fear of nuclear war is greater than fear of the Russians. A credible conventional defense backed by a nuclear deterrent would meet that test.

In developing its strategy, NATO must reject the enticing but dangerous concept of "no first use" of nuclear weapons. The Soviets push this line because they know that NATO's strategy is solely defensive. No serious observer believes that NATO would launch an offensive conventional attack on Warsaw Pact forces. On the other hand, the Soviets' strategy is openly offensive. The sole purpose of NATO strategy is to deter a Soviet attack. Renouncing first use of nuclear weapons would eliminate a major element of deterrence. Soviet military planners must be made aware that if NATO's conventional defense fails they run the risk of nuclear retaliation.

An initiative for the conventional defense of Europe can come from the United States—but the political actions to bring it about must come from Europe. Today, the U.S. military presence in Western Europe has reached its highest level in three decades. There is no chance that American spending on NATO will rise. There is a great danger that it will be substantially cut. If West Europeans value the American military presence, they must act now or risk losing it.

Hawks have joined doves in arguing that the United States should withdraw a substantial portion of American forces from Western Europe in order to compel action on the part of the Europeans. As long as Americans pay the freight, they point out, West Europeans will be willing to go along for the free ride. That view is already pervasive in Congress. At a time when the U.S. presence in Europe has hit its high-water mark, the support in Congress for maintaining that presence has hit its low-water mark.

There is nothing more dangerous to NATO than the smug attitude among many Europeans that the United States would never dare pull out of the alliance. I would warn Europeans against that view. As President, I fought repeated battles in Congress to stave off the Mansfield amendments to cut sharply United States forces in Europe, and I just barely won. I believe in the importance of Europe and in the necessity for the United States to support NATO. But I also know the Congress. The fact is that Europeans have won few new friends and have disillusioned many of their old allies. If Western Europe tries to muddle through the present crisis, the skeptics in Congress will inevitably put together a coalition, with the new liberal isolationists joining the old conservative isolationists, to cut back on U.S. forces—and this time they will have the votes to win.

The bottom line is that West Europeans cannot have their defense on the cheap anymore. Europe can no longer rely solely on the threat of a U.S. nuclear escalation to compensate for NATO's conventional inferiority, because that has lost credibilty in the era of U.S.–Soviet parity. And there is no way that the United States will assume the responsibility for matching the Soviet Union's conventional forces. West Europeans must recognize that they no longer face a question of whether they can save money, but whether they can save the alliance.

As a result, Europe must develop a European solution to the problem of the conventional defense of Europe. That must involve to some extent the integration of West European armies. This idea was rejected when France voted down the proposal for the European Defense Community in 1954. It was made impossible when France pulled out of the integrated command of NATO in 1965. But an integrated defense force is an idea whose time has come.

Over the last forty years, while some Europeans have fought abroad against unconventional guerrilla forces, no European country has fought a significant conventional conflict outside Europe, except for the Suez intervention in 1956 and the Falklands War in 1981. Apart from defending Europe, the conventional forces of our allies have had virtually no rationale for existing. It makes sense, therefore, to maximize the effectiveness of those forces for their principal purpose. That can best be achieved by reviving the idea of a true collective defense of Europe, beginning with the full integration of forces on the central front in Germany and extending the concept geographically on a pragmatic basis. France will need to alter its relationship to NATO, but its leaders already recognize the need to cooperate more closely with its allies, as evident from West Germany and France's plan to form a fully integrated brigade.

As West Europeans assume a greater responsibility for their own defense, a European should be designated as supreme allied commander, and Europeans should be put in charge of the negotiations for arms control in Europe. That does not mean the United States would abdicate its responsibility. As long as the United States risks the lives of its troops in Western Europe, it must have a major voice in shaping the East–West agreements affecting their security. Our role, however, should be simply to stipulate the kinds of accords we would prefer. Overall, since arms control in Europe will affect Europe's security more than ours, Europeans should take the lead in the negotiations.

Negotiations for further arms control in Europe should focus on the conventional balance. It is the imbalance in the instruments of conventional offensive warfare—artillery, tanks, and troops—that creates the threat of war and, in turn, the need for a nuclear deterrent. For fifteen years we have tried to address the issue in the Mutual and Balanced Force Reduction Talks. Moscow filibustered, and we acquiesced to negotiating on the Soviet nuclear agenda rather than forcing the Soviets to negotiate on their superiority in conventional forces, which is the reason we need nuclear weapons in the first place. As a result, our arms-control effort has sought to treat the symptoms, while the disease has run unchecked. That must not continue. When Europe takes charge of arms control, it must focus on the major threat to peace: Soviet superiority in conventional forces.

As it strengthens its forces, NATO should also expand its mission. When Soviet influence expands in key areas of the Third World, it affects not only American but also European interests. When Moscow succeeds in picking off one geopolitical target after another, it is an assault on the security of countries on both sides of the Atlantic. Since we share similar interests, we must fashion a joint response.

We must recognize that since 1949 the Soviet Union has changed its strategy. The principal Soviet offensive thrust no longer aims at the central front but rather at the exposed flanks. Kremlin leaders know that the industrial democracies are highly dependent on key sea-lanes and resources in the Third World. Even with a sustained program to substitute nuclear power for oil, Western Europe will still depend on imported oil for over two thirds of its energy in 1995. Moscow has focused on that Achilles' heel, fomenting revolutions and deploying proxy armies in resource-rich countries.

The West will fall just as surely if outflanked in the Third World as it will if overrun on the central front. European economies cannot survive without access to the resources and markets of the world. A Soviet advance in the Third World is as much an attack on the Western alliance as would be an assault on Europe itself. Western Europe should not expect the United States alone to play the role of policeman of the world. That idea is obsolete. Peace is everybody's business. We need a posse, not just a lone vigilante, to keep the peace. Real peace will not be built unless all countries contribute their share in building it and keeping it in good repair. It is particularly important for the Europeans to do so because ultimately the United States could survive alone but Western Europe could not.

NATO countries should take an active role and cooperate in defending Western interests around the world. They have centuries of experience in world affairs to draw upon, especially in areas in which they were colonial powers. France's actions in central and sub-Saharan Africa are an excellent model. Elite French forces have intervened over a dozen times over the last forty years to forestall Soviet gains in Africa.

Terrorism should be another target of NATO's expanded mission. A terrorist attack on the citizens of one country is an attack on all civilized countries. Terrorism is an international challenge to international order and it requires an international response. The NATO allies should develop a program of cooperation and joint action to deal with terrorist attacks.

Our cooperation should extend to our economic-aid programs. We should jointly target those strategically important countries which most need our assistance. The United States should be willing to take advice from the Europeans in choosing the means to implement our aid. They have a great deal of experience in working with their former colonies and can often play the lead role more effectively than the United States. Its ties with France have enabled the Ivory Coast, for example, to become one of the few prospering countries in Africa. Great Britain's vast experience with its former colonies is an invaluable asset for the West.

Acting together we can achieve more than acting alone. We should therefore expand the mission of NATO. Together, the United States and Western Europe can succeed in blunting the Soviet geopolitical offensive in the Third World and in devising economic-aid programs that encourage prosperity instead of larceny.

Our new Year of Europe must also create a consensus on how the countries of NATO should approach their relations with the Soviet Union. We need to present the Kremlin with a united front politically. We must not allow the Soviets to play one side of the Atlantic against the other, thereby exploiting the fissures in our alliance to increase their influence.

For Americans, a united front requires that we tone down our rhetoric. Bellicose anti-Soviet speeches may charge up conservative audiences in the United States, but they send chills through our allies in Europe. In the European mind, hot rhetoric about the Cold War does not sow doubts about Soviet intentions, but rather stimulates fears about American recklessness. With a firm but reasoned tone, we can communicate the same message to West Europeans, but without gratuitously straining the alliance.

For Europeans, a united front requires linking policies toward the Soviet Union with Soviet behavior in the world. Soviet intentions should be measured by actions, not atmospherics. Europeans, usually more realistic than Americans about how the real world works, should be the first to recognize that improving the atmospherics of East–West relations without resolving substantive East–West issues is a chimeral gain. We all should remember that the Soviets need better relations with the West more than the West needs better ties with the Soviets.

In addition, West Europeans should cooperate with us far more than they have done in developing a concerted effort to block illicit exports of strategic technologies to the Soviet Union. Some of their actions have been shockingly irresponsible. In the mid-1980s, the Soviets worked through Japan and a NATO country, Norway, to obtain the machinery necessary to make their submarines quieter. As a result, the United States will need to spend more than $50 billion to restore its previous superiority in antisubmarine-warfare capability. West Europeans should recognize the danger to the West posed by leaks of high technology to the Soviets. After all, while the United States operates submarines in the North Atlantic, West Europeans must live along its shores.

Most of all, an effective Western united front requires NATO to mobilize its economic power. It is both our greatest asset—NATO's economies outproduce the Soviet Union's by over three to one—and our least-exploited one. Since Moscow spares no weapon in its struggle against the West, we should lose no opportunity to use our best assets to constrain the Kremlin.

As Gorbachev seeks to revive the Soviet economy, our economic power will provide us with unprecedented leverage. Soviet economic growth depends in part on access to Western trade and technology. We can be certain that in the wake of a U.S.–Soviet arms-control agreement we will see Soviet trade delegations make the rounds of Western financial centers shopping around for investors. It is no accident that Gorbachev explicitly requested an opportunity to meet with U.S. businessmen during the summit in December 1987.

Neither the Reagan administration nor the West Europeans have placed adequate political conditions on an increased East–West trade. The United States not only ended the Carter grain embargo but also negotiated a new grain deal to appease American farmers. West European governments have sought to cut whatever deal the Soviet market would bear. Both have adopted the shortsighted policy of scurrying after economic deals without linking them to Soviet international behavior. Without an ironclad linkage to Soviet restraint in the world, an increase in trade will end up subsidizing our own destruction. It is a myth to proclaim that economic sanctions will not hurt the Soviet economy. This is like saying that a lifeboat will not float because it has leaks. Plug the leaks, and sanctions will work.

We should be willing to strike economic deals with Moscow—but for a price. We can set that price only if Western countries cooperate in formulating a strategy to capitalize on their economic power.

In the new Year of Europe, NATO must resolve to take sweeping actions. Its usual middle-mush solutions will not forestall a fundamental crisis. Our reevaluation of the alliance should not be driven by recriminations, with each side thinking up a menu of punitive steps for the other, culminating in a dissolution of the alliance. Instead, it should be a cooperative venture to forge a common approach to the world of the 1990s. The alliance has brilliantly served the purpose which brought it into being forty years ago. But the threat it was designed to meet has profoundly changed, and the alliance must be changed to meet it. The world in 1999 will be very different from the world in 1949. If the forty-year-old alliance is not radically overhauled now it will be obsolete by 1999.

We should not heed the counsel of those who believe Europe is washed up economically and politically. That view will be proved wrong. There are already visible signs of the coming European recovery. It is hard to believe that only six years ago Britain was written off as the sick man of Europe. Today Britain leads the industrial democracies in the growth of economic productivity and GNP—and Britain's progress is a harbinger of Europe's.

Western Europe has the potential for a second renaissance in the 1990s. Great nations that decline to make the sacrifices necessary to provide for their defense lose a sense of self-respect which is difficult to define but is painfully obvious to those who experience it. No one nation of Europe can become a superpower. But a united Europe can be a superpower. Rather than playing the role of honest broker between East and West or, worse still, of a pawn in that struggle, Western Europe can and should be an equal participant in its own right. A Europe dependent on the United States for its defense will, at best, be consulted before decisions are made which affect its security. Even more likely, it will be informed only after the fact. This is an intolerable situation for great nations.

The peoples of Europe have the strength, the education, the industrial capacity, and the technological expertise to step into the front rank of nations. A substantial but affordable increase in their conventional military power will qualify them fully to play a leading role in shaping their own and the world's future. But the Europeans will not tap their potential unless they mobilize themselves to take charge of their own destinies. For their own sake, they should take on more of the responsibility for their own military security, and we should work to help them realize their potential. In a new Year of Europe, we need to reshape the North Atlantic Treaty Organization, not only so that the alliance will meet the new challenge it faces, but also so that our allies will be able to play a political role worthy of their heritage.

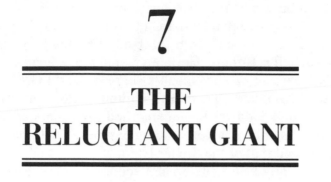

THE
RELUCTANT GIANT

Only one new economic superpower has emerged in the world since World War II. Only one Asian country in history has entered the first rank of modern industrial powers. That same country has the most stable democracy in Asia. It is Japan, an ancient storied land whose economic and political success stories in the last forty years can only be described as mind-boggling.

Tocqueville foresaw that the United States and the Soviet Union would be the most powerful nations in the world and also the world's most powerful adversaries. But in his time Japan still lay beyond the reach of the West's consciousness, shrouded in mystery within the closed society created by its rulers. Commodore Perry opened Japan in 1854, and around the same time its leaders realized the key to its future lay in making judicious use of Western influences.

Japan's development was steady, but the West was slow to sense it. In 1924, on one of the rare occasions when he made a mistake in predicting the future, Winston Churchill said, "Japan is at the other end of the world. She cannot menace our vital interests in any way." Seventeen years later the British Empire and its allies were overwhelmed by the Japanese Empire in the Pacific theater of the most destructive war of all time. And just as Churchill could not have predicted the war with Japan, he could not have predicted

221

that forty years after the war Japan would be a trusted member of the Western community of democratic nations and would be on the verge of becoming the strongest economic power in the world.

As late as 1929, Japan's share of world economic production was 4 percent, compared with the United States's 34 percent, 10 percent each for Britain, Germany, and the Soviet Union, and France's 5 percent. Today Japan's share of world GNP is 10 percent, second only to that of the United States. In 1945 it was defeated, and its industrial plant smashed, by American bombs. In 1987 it was America's largest trading partner after Canada, and its GNP surpassed that of the Soviet Union.

It is frequently said that Japan's economic miracle is the most significant development of the postwar era. But even if there had been no war Japan would still have become one of the world's mightiest industrial powers. If anything, the war accelerated the process. In the early 1950s Japan's legendary Prime Minister, Shigeru Yoshida, said, only half facetiously, "Fortunately, Japan was reduced to ashes by air raids. If Japan introduces new machinery and equipment now, it should be able to become a splendid country with productivity far higher than the countries that have won the war. It costs much to demolish machinery, but the demolition was done for us by the enemy." The fact that he was right is a reflection of why the conservative policies and principles enunciated by Yoshida are still in large part observed by Japan's leaders today.

It is fashionable to write and talk about the Japanese economic miracle. But the more impressive Japanese miracle was the birth of democracy in a society that had been ruled for centuries by warlords and emperors. Planted by the American occupation under the visionary leadership of General Douglas MacArthur and nurtured by Yoshida and his carefully groomed sucessors, democracy has taken hold and put in deep, lasting roots. In the twentieth century Japan's great achievement has been an economically powerful Japan. America's great achievement has been a democratic Japan. No nation in history has conducted a military occupation with such admirable intentions and such lasting, beneficial results as the United States. No nation has made as much of such opportunities as Japan. One of the greatest ironies of our time is that the average income of a citizen of the nation that lost the war is, at $16,000 a year, only $2,000 lower than that of a citizen of the nation that won. Just over twenty years ago Japan's average personal income was 25 percent of the United States's.

Japan's transformation into a pro-Western industrial democracy is one of the most fortuitous developments of the postwar era. While it is an Asian rather than a European nation, it is as critical to the Western alliance as any member of NATO. Strategically, it holds the Eastern ramparts. Economically, its might is indispensable if we are to have a unified Western economic policy. And practically, it has much to gain from an alliance with the West because it has just as much to lose as the United States and the Europeans from further Soviet advances.

Japan has become an indispensable member of the Western alliance. If it were to fall under Soviet domination the Pacific would become a red sea. In 1983 Prime Minister Nakasone pledged that his country would be an "unsinkable aircraft carrier" in the effort to deter Soviet aggression in the Far East. His dramatic metaphor did not even go far enough, because it implies a far-too-passive role for the Japanese. The United States, Japan, and Western Europe make up over two thirds of the world's total economic output. The day that all that economic might becomes part of a single geopolitical strategy—matching public and private development aid, military expenditures, and trade—is the day the West will win the Cold War. Against the combined and unified forces of freedom, totalitarianism can never prevail.

The Western alliance is immeasurably stronger with Japan than it would be without it. Both the United States and Japan should be proud of the partnership that produced a democratic Japan out of the bitterness and destruction of war. But the war and the American military occupation that followed it—and the period of Japan's dependency on the United States that followed the occupation and that continues today—have had negative results as well as positive ones.

Japan is now governed by a constitution written and translated into somewhat awkward Japanese by Americans. It contains an antiwar provision that at the time sparked little controversy in a country that was exhausted by war but that today, with a healthy sense of national pride on the rise, some Japanese find insulting. In the meantime Japan, like West Germany, remains dependent on the United States for critical elements of its national defense.

A relationship based on dependency can breed contempt on both sides. So can the harsh memories of war. Pearl Harbor was only forty-seven years ago, the Bataan death march only forty-six years ago, and Hiroshima and Nagasaki only forty-three years ago. A Japanese who is thirty-five years old today was born in a country that was under military occupation and ruled from Washington, D.C. Americans and Japanese have their own ways of remembering these events and judging whether they were right or wrong. On the surface Americans and Japanese, perhaps better than any other former antagonists in modern history, have overcome their differences and learned to work together to their mutual benefit. But it is an unfortunate fact that many Americans, who have no experience of foreign military occupation, still resent the Japanese for starting the war, and many Japanese, who have no experience of foreign military aggression, resent the occupation. And seared into the consciousness of every Japanese is the realization that Japan was the first and only nation to experience the horrors of nuclear war.

These resentments become significant, and dangerous, only when they are exacerbated by other factors—such as the bitter economic disagreements that have clouded U.S.–Japan relations in recent years. Unless the leaders of both Japan and the United States act with courage and foresight, today's temporary economic pressures could do permanent damage to one of the most important and fruitful bilateral relationships in the world.

While it is by no means the most important element of the relationship between the United States and Japan, the most neuralgic issue is the trade imbalance. In 1986 the Japanese sold $60 billion more worth of goods in the United States than we sold in Japan; this was the major factor in creating a worldwide U.S. trade deficit of $170 billion. Japan's critics say this imbalance costs American jobs and complain that the Japanese have closed their markets to American goods.

There are a number of actions Japanese policy-makers could take to increase the amount of money Japanese have to buy imported goods and services. It could buy American rice for $180 a ton; instead it forbids rice imports to protect Japanese farmers, whose rice costs $2,000 a ton. A change in property-tax and zoning policies could ease the astronomically high cost of land and thereby give consumers more money for other expenditures. For instance, the price of a parcel in downtown Tokyo is 900 percent higher than a comparable parcel in midtown Manhattan. In the suburbs some medium-sized houses that cost $70,000 in the mid-1970s now cost as much as $1 million. And while the Japanese have canceled so many import-blocking tariffs that they now have fewer in force than the European Economic Community, they could do more to lower the bureacratic, nontariff barriers that prevent American firms from participating to a significant degree in such projects as the massive new Kansai Airport in Osaka Harbor.

The perennial and politically popular complaints of American protectionists notwithstanding, however, the Japanese are not entirely, or even principally, responsible for the trade deficit. Changes in the value of the dollar and the yen have also had powerful effects. For fourteen of the years between 1955 and 1975, *Japan* had the trade deficit, importing more than it exported. But then the value of the dollar, and American demand for fuel-efficient Japanese cars, took off and Japanese imports began to flow into the United States. When the dollar plunged against the yen in 1987, the edge began to come off the trade deficit and Japan began to suffer from the high yen as American exporters had suffered from the low yen a year or two before. Finally, before we go too far in pointing out the beam in the Japanese eye we should examine the mote in our own eye. We cannot blame the Japanese for the huge U.S. federal budget deficit, nor can we blame them because they have outcompeted the United States in industries such as consumer electronics.

The critical question is whether the United States should punish Japan with protectionist legislation if it fails to take the actions we believe it should take to improve our trading posture. The answer is no. Since entering Congress over forty years ago I have been a free-trader, but I base my argument here not on the evils of protectionism but on the realities of the balance of power in the world. Japan, like all nations, pursues policies it believes are in its national interest. Among allies and friends there are always disagreements over such policies. But unless the short-term disagreements are more important than the long-term relationship, punitive measures must be avoided. This is a simple lesson that protectionist politicians in the United States should learn once and for all.

Instead the American attitude toward Japan vacillates between friendliness when times are good to thinly veiled, occasionally ugly hostility when times are bad. Last year one senator called the Japanese "leeches," while a congressman, angered at the Japanese for dumping low-price semiconductors on the American market, said, "God bless Harry Truman. He dropped two of them [atomic bombs]. He should have dropped four." Such comments, while reprehensible, are not surprising from American politicians anxious to hold on to their jobs during a time when protectionist sentiment is running high. But a coequal partner like Japan, in a strategic alliance such as the West's, cannot at the same time be a convenient political punching bag every time the trade issue flares up. The Japanese notice the vicious tone of the trade debate in the Congress and inevitably wonder whether they can count on our friendship in other areas. We should note that last summer a book reached the Japanese bestseller lists entitled *Japan Is Not Bad, America Is Bad.* Another popular book, *Japan in Danger,* argued that the United States was making Japan a scapegoat for its own economic problems.

The most important ingredients in the U.S.–Japan relationship, as it is between any two friendly nations, are trust and respect. Both sides must accept that while we have been and will continue to be tough economic competitors, we are partners in preserving peace and should act accordingly. Among the hundreds of government leaders I have met over the past forty years there were none whose personal friendship I cherished more than the Japanese prime ministers I was privileged to meet—Yoshida, Ikeda, Kishi, Fukuda, and Sato.

Secondary crises such as the trade imbalance or fluctuations in the values of currency should not be permitted to interfere fundamentally with the relationship between the two strongest economic powers in the free world. These occasional irritants are nothing compared to the turmoil that would result from a serious rupture in our relations.

The United States and Japan are mature nations that can withstand some heavy weather in their relations. But because of the special character of our postwar relationship and the differences between our two cultures, both sides must tread carefully. Smashing Toshiba radios on the steps of the Capitol—as a group of American congressmen did last year when a subsidiary of the Japanese company, apparently without the government's or the parent company's knowledge, sold key defense technology to the Soviets—is not the way one member of an alliance should behave during a dispute with another.

As they are about the trade issue, some of Japan's critics in the United States are too quick to jump on Japan for adhering to the forty-year-old American-imposed proscriptions on military activities. It is true that the balance of power in the world has changed profoundly since World War II. But we should not expect the Japanese to deal with the psychological scars left by the war as easily as the balance of power. Relations between nations can change with the grasp of a hand, the flourish of a pen, or the flash of a bomb. Relations between people take longer.

When I visited Tokyo as Vice President in 1953, Japanese newspapers gave eight-column headlines to my statement that the United States had "made a mistake" in imposing constitutional restrictions on defense spending on the Japanese after World War II. I believed then that Japan should do more to provide for its own defense. Because of Japan's enormously increased wealth and the fact that the Soviet Union is "reaching out its hand" in the Pacific, the case for what I urged thirty-five years ago is far stronger today. But there are understandable reasons why the Japanese have been slow to take such advice.

In the 1950s, with full American acquiescence, Japan adopted a policy that permitted it to devote virtually all of its resources to its domestic economy. Military expenditures were kept at a minimum, both because of Japan's made-in-America constitution, which strictly limits its military activities, and because of our protective nuclear umbrella. But as the growth of our economy slowed in the 1970s and the growth of our defense budget shrank after the Vietnam War, Japan's low defense spending became an issue in the United States. The key slogan of the argument was, "No more free ride."

What many fail to realize is that the Japanese are still not psychologically equipped for a major military buildup, for reasons Americans ought to be able to grasp. Recently, and especially during the tenure of Prime Minister Yasuhiro Nakasone, the Japanese have begun to emerge from the shadow of their shattering defeat in 1945. But to understand why for over three decades the Japanese were reluctant to extend themselves militarily and why to this day they remain profoundly ambivalent about defense spending, all we have to do is examine what happened in the United States in the wake of Vietnam.

For five years after our failure in Indochina the United States became increasingly isolationist as military budgets were slashed and every use of American forces abroad was examined with such a hypercritical eye that the U.S. was effectively rendered impotent as a world power. Today, thirteen years after the end of the war, even the smallest commitment of American military power to protect our interests in Central America or the Persian Gulf is bitterly criticized by the media and by isolationists in Congress. Such is the impact that defeat in war can have. Before we preach to the Japanese—who lost 1.2 million people in battle in World War II—about devoting more to defense, we should remember the paralyzing bout of indecision and isolationism that the United States suffered after losing 55,000 men, and for a time our national pride, in Vietnam.

To the extent that Japan's reluctance to rearm is a product of the traumas of defeat in war, we should sympathize with them. To the extent that it is a rationalization that enables them to enjoy the status of an economic superpower without the responsibilities of a military one, it is unacceptable. While the Japanese reluctance to rearm is to an extent understandable, it is also true that by depending on the United States for its security Japan has had the luxury of diverting more of its resources to building an economy that now competes with, and in some areas outcompetes, our own.

There are three purely practical reasons why the Japanese must eventually abandon the essentially passive role they have played on the world scene ever since it was imposed on them by defeat in war and by policies established by the victors. Each reason has to do not only with our national interest but with theirs.

First, the United States that took the responsibility for defending Japan controlled almost 50 percent of the world's economy. The United States that sustains that commitment today controls only 27 percent. As a result, Japan's free ride on defense is becoming far too tempting a target for American Japan-bashers. Eventually, if such resentment spreads, our critically important and mutually beneficial relationship with Japan could be harmed.

Second, Japan must realize that, for a great power, playing a role on the world stage is not a privilege; it is a responsibility. There is nothing pleasant about having to divert resources to defense spending and foreign aid that could be applied to problems at home. We do it because we have to, not because we want to. This is the burden that weighs on any prosperous and free society that wants to protect its interests in a world that is by and large inhospitable to freedom. The United States was an isolationist power before World War II; the war made it a world power in spite of its natural inclinations. Japan must also rise to do its duty as a world power.

The third and by far most important reason is that unless Japan does do its duty as a major power, it can never hope to have real national security.

Geographically Japan is an island. But if it continues to attempt to function as an island geopolitically, it cannot survive. A commentator has said that Japan strives to be "no man's enemy, and a salesman to all." This is a worthy but hopelessly impractical goal. The reason is brutally simple: the position Japan occupies on the globe makes it a de-facto target of the Soviet Union. Japan plays an integral part both in Soviet planning for a possible war in the Pacific and in the Western alliance's scheme for deterring and if necessary fighting such a war.

The Soviet conventional buildup in the Far East over the last decade has been ominous. Between a quarter and a third of Soviet military power is now aimed at the Pacific theater. In 1976 its Asia force was 31 tank divisions, 2,000 combat aircraft, and a 755-ship Navy. Today it has 41 divisions, 85 new Backfire bombers armed with nuclear missiles, 2,400 combat aircraft, and 840 ships. Even after its medium-range nuclear missiles are removed from Asia according to the terms of the proposed INF treaty, every key target in Japan will be covered by the Soviet Union's strategic nuclear weapons.

Even more troubling is that, Gorbachev's Asian "peace offensive" notwithstanding, the Russians have been flexing their substantial muscle. In 1986 Soviet aircraft intruded into Japanese airspace 350 times; estimates were even higher for 1987. In 1986 the Soviets also staged exercises in the Kurile Islands, which they seized from Japan in 1948, that simulated an invasion of Japan's northernmost island of Hokkaido.

Under Nakasone, Japan's response to the Soviet buildup was admirable. Caught between the Japanese people's desire for better relations with the Soviets and his own realistic assessment of the Soviet threat, the Prime Minister put national interest ahead of his political interest time and time again. For the first time Japan has participated with the United States in full-scale three-service military exercises. It has agreed to guarantee the security of sea-lanes up to 1,000 nautical miles from its coastline. It has purchased and deployed sophisticated American F-15 fighters. It has tacitly allowed into its ports U.S. warships that are presumably carrying nuclear weapons, in spite of its understandable discomfiture about such weapons. It has shared intelligence with the United States to an unprecedented extent, agreed to participate in SDI research, and—probably most important—finally exceeded the symbolic one-percent-of-GNP restriction on its defense budget.

Taken together, these policies comprised the biggest step forward in the area of national defense in Japan's postwar history. Some were toughed through by Nakasone in spite of brutal opposition from his political opponents. The measures were positive and encouraging, but they were not enough. Eventually, not necessarily today, but in the foreseeable future, the Japanese must do far more. They must do it not for our sake but for their own. They must do it because of the simple, overwhelming imperative of national survival.

In the short term a major military buildup by Japan would cause more problems than it would solve: it would relieve a relatively insignificant portion of the American burden for defending Japan while at the same time fostering regional unrest, especially among nations such as China and Korea that fear a militarily resurgent Japan. But in the long term it is both inevitable and proper that Japan take on a military role in Asia commensurate with its economic power. In view of Japan's actions during and before World War II, China's and Korea's misgivings are understandable, but each should ponder what it fears more: Japan's 180,000-man Self-Defense Force or the Soviets' 785,000-man Asian army, Japan's 270-plane air force or the 2,700 aircraft in the Soviets' Far Eastern department.

The new postwar world demands a reassessment of the balance of power in Asia. For the foreseeable future, the stronger Japan is, the safer Asia will be. Japan is the indispensable linchpin for any strategy for peace in Asia.

Today Japan's Self-Defense Forces could hold out as few as two days against a surprise Soviet conventional invasion. Some commentators who counsel against a major Japanese buildup say that the United States's security guarantee is sufficient to stop such a Soviet move. Regrettably, it would not be. Since the United States does not have enough ground forces in place to match the Soviets, stopping such an invasion would be difficult at best. The United States would quickly be faced with the necessity of considering the use of nuclear weapons based at sea or on the American mainland.

While these weapons are loaded and ready, the danger is that the Soviets would see the threat of their use as an empty cannon. The concern that the United States would not risk a nuclear World War III by using U.S.-based strategic nuclear weapons against a Soviet army marching on Western Europe was the principal reason the United States deployed intermediate-range nuclear weapons in Europe in 1979. The same holds true in the Far East, only more so. An American President who used nuclear weapons to halt a Soviet conventional attack on Japan would be risking a massive nuclear attack on the United States—a risk a President would be unlikely to take. The Soviets know this. As a result, Japan today is dangerously vulnerable to such an attack. Eventually Japan must develop the capacity to defend itself *by* itself against Soviet conventional forces. It does not have to match the Soviets man to man. It only has to do enough to make a Soviet invasion too costly to contemplate.

Japan cannot undertake a full-scale military buildup now. The memory of World War II is still too strong among its neighbors. But that will change—especially if Japan begins to play a greater role as a supplier of development aid and investment to Third World nations in Asia and elsewhere. When Japan shows the world that it is willing to invest in a peaceful, prosperous, and free Asia, its neighbors' misgivings about its military posture will slowly but surely fade. If it follows this course in the twenty-first century Japan will be a true superpower—willing and able to defend its own interests and those of its friends and allies in the Pacific region.

In the past the Japanese have been criticized for not spending more on aid to developing nations, since they spend substantially less than the United States on defense—just over one percent of their GNP compared with 7 percent for the U.S. To their great credit the Japanese in recent years have bolstered their foreign aid even as many other strapped industrial nations have cut back. In 1987 Japan announced new programs totaling $30 billion on top of its $8 billion a year in regular aid, most of which goes to Asian nations that in turn trade heavily with Japan. This is a welcome step, but it does not go far enough.

The basic question is how much each country in the alliance spends on national security, not just for the military portion of its national-security budget. The United States spends 8 percent of its GNP on national security, of which 6 percent is for military expenditures and 2 percent is for economic aid. Japan spends just 2 percent of its GNP on national security, which includes one percent for its military and one percent for its basic economic-aid program. Japan should match the U.S. total for national security by allocating enough for economic aid to make up for its shortfall in military expenditures.

As labor costs rise at home, Japan has begun to reach into the the developing world for cheaper labor markets, just as American multinational corporations have done. Depending on how these investments are made and managed, they can either help the developing world or hurt it. As American economic power spread over the world after World War II the myth of the "ugly American" arose. Above all Japan must avoid the "ugly Japanese" syndrome. In 1985, a government official in a Southeast Asian country which has good relations with Japan told me, "The trouble with the Japanese is that they are like semiconductors—they take everything in and give nothing in return." This is an unfair exaggeration, but it points up a potential danger for Japan. Our neighbors in Latin America have often made that same complaint about U.S. multinational corporations. Any rich foreign power, no matter how beneficial its activities in a Third World country, makes an attractive target for left-wing politicians and revolutionaries. Japanese businessmen abroad should not be expected to be philanthropists, but they must conduct their business in a way which does not add fuel to the smoldering ashes of anti-Japanese sentiment among peoples who were victims of Japanese aggression in World War II. If the Japanese play their Asian cards right, they will prove again that an economic superpower whose industrial plant becomes multinational can do immeasurable good both for itself and for the countries in which it operates.

To say Japanese businessmen are not philanthropists is not an insult. Like businessmen everywhere they want to maximize profit, and they do not necessarily want to build up other nations through developmental aid, investment, and technology transfer to the point where those nations will become Japan's future competitors.

In the long run, though, they inevitably will compete with Japan. Ironically, this is the way the relationship between the United States and Japan developed. After the war Japan's economy was shattered; now, in large part because of our help, Japan's economy competes with ours. American businessmen used to complain about the difficulty of competing with Japan's cheap labor. Now the Japanese are worried about competing with Korea's cheap labor. In the near future China's cheap labor will be an awesome challenge to both Japan and the United States.

Within the narrow, parochial framework of trade and profit, Japan's emergence as a rival of the United States may seem to some to be an unfortunate development. But in the broader context of the East–West struggle, it is a profoundly positive development, because in the community of free nations Japan's strength complements our own, just as the strong economies of Western Europe do.

Japan must take the same broad view of its own relationships with poorer nations. It does not want these nations to slip into the Soviet orbit; if that happens Japan will be compromised strategically and also weakened economically. Miserably poor communist nations are poor markets for the goods of Japan or any other producer nation. For this reason Japan's economic relations with communist Nicaragua, Cuba, and Vietnam, while perhaps profitable in the short run, will be counterproductive for Japan and the West in the long run. The Soviets use their far-flung outposts to spread tyranny and economic ruin throughout their regions. It would be better for Japan to put less stress on trade with these nations and more on trade with nations that need help to resist the siren song of communism.

Recently Japan has taken the first steps toward easing the debt problems of some Third World nations by refinancing their loans. These actions, together with its increased aid programs, show that Japan recognizes that investing in the future of the developing world is in large part the same as investing in the future of Japan.

It is desirable that Japan begin to play a more active role in world affairs. It is also inevitable. Far better for Japan to share the responsibility and the credit for building a new Pacific peace than to be burdened by the memories of a bloody past. In the United States today there are still thousands of men—some of them leading figures in Congress and elsewhere—who fought the Japanese in World War II. To these and to countless others the idea of a resurgent Japan is an uncomfortable one, just as it is to many in Asia. But in another fifty years, no one alive will remember World War II. In one hundred it will be as remote an event as the Civil War and the Mexican–American War are to Americans today. By then Japan will long since have recognized that as a major world power its destiny is to be answerable to or dependent upon no other nation.

If Japan is to become a full partner in the Western alliance it will need two ingredients besides economic and military power. It will need a more internationalist state of mind and the kind of leaders who are willing to assert Japan's interests on the world stage.

The leadership side of the equation is already taking shape.

At a meeting of Western leaders many years ago de Gaulle said of a postwar Japanese Prime Minister, "Who is this transistor salesman?" It was a brutally revealing characterization. In 1967 Lee Kwan Yew of Singapore struck a similar theme when he said to me, "The Japanese inevitably will again play a major role in the world. They are a great people. They cannot and should not be satisfied with a world role that limits them to making better transistor radios and sewing machines, and teaching other Asians how to grow rice."

De Gaulle and Lee, both giants among world leaders, had hit upon an important point. With the exception of Yoshida, whose high-handed style brought derision from his left-wing opponents but gave a lift to his war-weary people at a time they desperately needed it, most Japanese premiers have been decidedly low-key. The "low posture" that Japan took in the world called for a low-posture style of leadership. In the last three decades Japan has had many outstanding leaders, all of whom faithfully followed the policies Yoshida set in place: free enterprise, economic growth, stable government, and close security ties with the United States. They were the policies and the leaders Japan needed for its first step toward recovering from war.

During the five-year tenure of Yasuhiro Nakasone—the first former Foreign Minister to serve as Prime Minister in the postwar era —Japan took the second step. It began to take on more of the responsibility for its defenses. And for the first time a Japanese leader sought to be an active, outspoken member of the exclusive fraternity of leaders of major democratic powers. Nakasone served longer than any premier since the legendary Sato and Yoshida, and he moved his country forward just as decisively. He set a new standard for Japanese premiers. It is to be hoped that his highly skilled successor, Noboru Takeshita, will continue in the new Nakasone tradition.

Since the end of World War II Japanese prime ministers have held formal governmental authority, while the role of the previously all-powerful Emperor has been strictly ceremonial. Still, the role the Japanese monarchy plays as a unifying force should never be underestimated. One of General MacArthur's wisest decisions as he molded the new Japanese democracy was to permit the Emperor to remain. When Emperor Hirohito finally passes from the scene, Japan will have lost a spiritual leader who deserves great credit for the progress his country has made.

Many people outside Japan have considered the Emperor just a pleasant nonentity, puttering around in his garden or indulging in his hobby of oceanography. No one who knew him could possibly have shared that view. I met him twice, in 1953 when I was Vice President and again in 1971 when I was President. I was deeply impressed by his gentle, courteous demeanor. But while his manner was low-key he showed a keen interest in and understanding of international issues.

Hirohito was responsible for bringing the war to the earliest-possible end by urging his countrymen to lay down their arms after the bombings of Hiroshima and Nagasaki, thus preventing a lengthy guerrilla war of resistance. His consistency and equanimity helped his people rebuild their country from defeat in war to the status of an economic giant in peace. He had a ready grasp of the challenges Japan faced and also of his responsibility to inspire his people to meet them.

In the long run the health of any alliance depends not only upon the qualities of its leaders but upon the development of an alliance mentality. In the case of the Western alliance, what is needed is a more equitable relationship between its two most powerful members: Japan and the United States.

Japanese and Americans have yet to find what is known in politics as a level playing field on which each can deal with the other as equals confident of their equality. Too many cultural obstacles and bad memories remain. In Japan there is still a residue of the fear of Western influences that kept it in isolation for centuries before Commodore Perry forced the door open. Even as they perfect the game of baseball in the summer, belt out choruses of the "Ode to Joy" in the winter, and eat hundreds of thousands of Big Macs each year, the Japanese resist any Western influences that seep very far below the most superficial level. In fact, their enjoyment of Western pastimes and fads is magnified by the constant awareness of their foreignness.

For their part Americans have their own suspicions of the Japanese. Even if it were not for the memory of World War II, the vast cultural differences between East and West would remain. Fashionable young Americans know all about sushi but could not begin to fathom Shinto, the ancient faith still observed by millions of Japanese. American farmers are understandably resentful because the Japanese government restricts the importing of their $180-a-ton rice, but few Americans realize that the official doctrine of Japan's ruling party is to restrict the importing of rice at least in part because rice grown from Japan's own soil is "the core of our spiritual civilization." The folkways of Japan remain so obscure to most Westerners that many businessmen bound for Tokyo feel they need to take courses to brush up on which topics of conversation are safe and which are risky and what is expected of a guest in a Japanese home.

We often criticize the Japanese for keeping to themselves culturally and for pursuing their own economic interests too doggedly without regard to the rest of the world, but in many ways Americans are no different. Before the United States entered both world wars most Americans wanted nothing to do with Europe's conflicts even though the forebears of most Americans had come from Europe. Until the end of World War II Americans had far less in common with the Japanese than with the Europeans. Since 1945, however, the United States and Japan have had the common ground of democracy and free enterprise upon which to build. These must be the foundations of the friendship between our two nations.

Our European military and economic partners are our cultural partners as well. With the British we share language, while with the British and with the French and the Germans we have the common ground of ancestry, philosophy, literature, and music. But the finest element of our European heritage is political liberty. We did not invent it; we inherited it. And we have in turn shared it with Japan. One of the greatest challenges for the United States in the future is to recognize that because of our common commitment to liberty we have just as strong cultural ties with the Japanese as with the Europeans.

But it is not just a one-way street. The Japanese must open up to us, too—not just their markets, but themselves. They must learn not to fear "Western contamination"; they must realize that the cultural and racial homogeneity that has been one of their greatest strengths may be a hindrance in their effort to become an integral part of a heterogeneous worldwide alliance of freedom and prosperity.

We *are* different culturally, and those differences are not going to be removed—nor should they be. The cream does not come to the top in homogenized milk. In the long run, if each partner contributes his particular strengths in the common quest for peace and prosperity, both will emerge immeasurably stronger.

Japan's cautiousness toward America may be the result in part both of the residue of the war and of the regrettable fact that many American politicians find it far too easy to instruct the Japanese how to behave. As the most powerful member of our alliance we are apt to conclude mistakenly that we are also the most wise. Sometimes our military and economic power and our willingness to project it in the world have made us suspect among weaker nations, and often we project intellectual arrogance as well. From our commentators and congressmen and senators the advice to the Japanese comes fast and furious: "Spend more on defense. Inflate your economy to create more demand for our goods. Spend more on developmental aid in the Third World. Commit funds and moral support to our efforts in the Persian Gulf."

It would be good if the Japanese did all of these things. But they will not because we tell them to or because it is in our interest for them to take certain actions. Instead they may well have an agenda for us: "We will spend more money on your goods if you tackle your budget deficit. We will spend more on defense and venture into the Third World if you show that you too have a consistent foreign policy, a middle ground between 'in with both feet' as in Vietnam and 'head in the sand' as in the Vietnam syndrome.''

The Japanese are shrewd, polite diplomats who would never publicly state their case in such a crude, tit-for-tat fashion. By the same token they will not react positively to receiving their marching orders in an equally crude way from us, in the form of statements by government officials, speeches in Congress, or newspaper editorials. In dealing with the Japanese we often forget that international affairs are a subtle art that is fraught with the potential for misunderstanding. We would never treat our European allies so cavalierly unless we were willing to face dire consequences, such as the years-long Franco–American chill that followed President Johnson's public criticism of de Gaulle. And yet we are all too willing to lecture, cajole, even threaten the Japanese. What are they to conclude? That we take their friendship for granted? That we think we have the right to throw our weight around because we won the war? During the last forty years the United States has proved itself an enthusiastic friend of Japan, especially when U.S.–Japanese friendship has been in our interests. We have yet to prove ourselves a dependable friend in the long term—since forty years, to the Asian mind, is only a moment. To deserve and earn the trust not only of the Japanese but of all our friends and allies in the world, we must stop criticizing them solely for the sake of domestic political gain. And we must resist lecturing those whom we would not permit to lecture us.

In the final analysis the greatest impediment to the development of a healthy alliance mentality between the United States and Japan is that the two nations are not yet equal members of the alliance.

One observer in Japan said, "For Japan to be equal requires Japan to be separate. If Japan were not separate, it could only be inferior, and would soon be a colony of the West." The irony of this statement is that because Japan depends upon another nation for its security it to an extent is a colony of the West; it is equal only as an economic power. Thus the Japanese have the opposite dilemma to that of the Soviet Union, whose status as a superpower comes only from its military strength. Just as the Japanese are self-conscious about depending on the United States for their security, the Soviets are self-conscious about their economic backwardness. The problem with the Soviet economy is communism. The problem with Japanese national security is Japan's inability to protect itself as a result of both political and psychological constraints.

What will help banish Japan's fear of losing its individuality is a more activist role on the world stage—diplomatically, developmentally, and eventually militarily. The Japanese people have good reason to be repelled by the thought of war, and many do not want their nation to rearm. Americans are also repelled by war. The difference is that Americans support a level of national-security spending that is adequate to protect their country against any aggressor. The Japanese attitude will inevitably change, especially if Japan's neighbors become less concerned about its reemergence. With the change will come a new self-confidence among Japanese, born of the certain knowledge that Japan is once again a truly independent nation. A more active and confident Japan will mean that the prospects for freedom and peace in the Pacific in the next century will be infinitely greater.

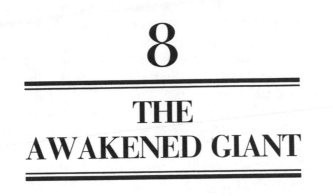

8

THE
AWAKENED GIANT

China's twentieth century has been a crucible of revolution and suffering, of poverty and promise, of political and ideological upheaval, of order fashioned out of chaos and chaos forcibly thrust into the midst of order. Within sixty years China has been wrenched from ancient kingdom to infant republic to communist dictatorship. It has swung between angry rejection of any hint of Western influence and cautious acceptance of the benefits of good relations with the West. It is one of the world's most homogeneous societies, but for most of this century it has been at war with itself.

During its years of hostile isolation after the 1949 revolution China was distrusted and feared by many in the West. It was the mysterious, smoldering red giant of the East, preoccupied with imposing a punishing, fanatical code of ideological purity on its people at the same time the peoples of the West were enjoying an explosive postwar economic boom. Few Western leaders took the time to study China or its torturous history. One who did was Charles de Gaulle. To the surprise of some of his anticommunist supporters he recognized the People's Republic of China in 1962. Asked why, de Gaulle answered, "Because China is so big, so old and has been so much abused."

When I was out of office during the 1960s, my own thinking about China had already begun to change as a result of the Sino–

Soviet split and the advice of such statesmen as de Gaulle and Konrad Adenauer, both of whom told me it was essential for the United States to develop a relationship with China. But I will never forget a conversation I had with Herbert Hoover in New York City in 1963, when I went to see him on his eighty-ninth birthday. He gave me the opposite advice. We should not deal with the Chinese, because they were "bloodthirsty," he said. He shuddered visibly as he described his experiences in China as a young engineer in 1900. It was the time of the Boxer Rebellion, a violent uprising by a small group of fanatics against Western exploitation. Both the Boxers and the government troops who smashed the rebellion committed horrible atrocities. Hoover and his wife recalled seeing thousands of bodies float past in the river that ran by their settlement.

They were witnesses at the dawn of a savage century. Civil war came two decades later, when the forces of Sun Yat-sen brought down an empire that had ruled for two millennia. In the 1930s China suffered under a brutal Japanese invasion and occupation in which the Chinese government says 22 million people died. After World War II, more than 5 million died in another civil war and in the consolidation of the new communist regime following the victory of Mao Tse-tung's forces over Chiang Kai-shek's in 1949. Twenty-seven million people starved to death during the industrialization drive and forced collectivization of the late 1950s and early 1960s, ironically dubbed the "Great Leap Forward" by China's leaders. A few years later Mao dragged his country through the ideological wringer of the Cultural Revolution, violently disrupting the lives of millions of his countrymen and leaving deep scars that still remain today among the educated classes. One of the casualties was Deng Pufang, the son of Deng Xiaoping. The fanatical Red Guards threw him out of a window, and he fell three stories to the ground. He is now confined to a wheelchair.

Yet one of the miracles of our time is that China, which has endured the worst scourges of the twentieth century, is destined to be one of the world's leading powers in the twenty-first century. One hundred and sixty years ago Napoleon said of China, "There lies a sleeping giant. Let him sleep! For when he wakes he will move the world.'' The giant is awake. His time has come, and he is ready to move the world.

After a half century of war with others and with itself, China is united. In just fifty years it has grown from 400 million people to over one billion. Under the leadership of Deng Xiaoping, one of the most remarkable statesmen of the twentieth century, it has moved away from doctrinaire Marxism. By lifting the deadening weight of total bureaucratic planning, Deng has freed the enormous potential of a fifth of the world's people. If China continues to follow Deng's path, our grandchildren will live in a world not of two superpowers, but of three: the United States, the Soviet Union, and the People's Republic of China.

The China I visited for the first time in 1972 was not even a major power. It was, and to a large extent remains, a developing country. Some experts concluded at the time that the Chinese had responded favorably to our initiative only because they wanted access to Western markets and Western investments. One predicted that the first question Mao would ask me was, ''What is the richest country in the world going to do for the most populous country in the world?'' He was wrong. During over twenty hours of meetings I had in 1972 with Mao and with Chou En-lai, the Chinese did not raise economic issues. What mattered to China's leaders was not American money but American muscle. China and the United States were brought together by the overriding imperatives of national security.

Our rapprochement may have been the the most dramatic geopolitical event of the postwar era. But the most significant such event was the Sino–Soviet split during the early 1960s, after which China's former ideological mentors and economic benefactors in Moscow became threatening adversaries. China's unease about Soviet troops massed along its northern border, Soviet missiles targeted on its cities, Soviet aid to its antagonist India, and Soviet territorial ambitions elsewhere in Asia gave it no choice but to reach out to the Soviet Union's most powerful adversary, the United States. China and the Soviet Union are communist nations;

as a free nation the United States is a natural ideological adversary of both. But the Chinese knew that the Soviet Union threatened them, while the United States did not. As I told then party head Hua Guofeng in Beijing in 1976, there are times when a great nation must choose between ideology and survival. Hua agreed. In 1972, China had chosen survival.

Just as a few hard-liners in Beijing were stubbornly opposed to relations with the capitalist United States, our decision to seek a new relationship with China was traumatic for some Americans who felt we would betray our democratic principles by dealing with communists. But like the Chinese we had no other practical choice. If we had not undertaken the initiative and China had been forced back into the Soviet orbit, the threat to the West of Soviet communist aggression would be infinitely greater than it is today. It was in the interests of both nations that we forge a link based not on common ideals, which bind us to our allies in Western Europe and around the world, but on common interests. Both sides recognized that despite our profound philosophical differences we had no reason to be enemies and a powerful reason to be friends: our mutual interest in deterring the Soviet threat.

That threat continues to concern us. In fact, it is greater today than it was sixteen years ago. The specter of encirclement haunts the Chinese. In 1972, the PRC had friendly relations with North Vietnam, Americans were in South Vietnam and Cambodia, and Afghanistan was neutral. Today Vietnam, Cambodia, Laos, and Afghanistan are pro-Soviet and anti-Chinese. In 1979 China clashed with the Soviet-backed Vietnamese, suffering 20,000 casualties.

But even if there had been no Soviet threat, it was imperative that we build a new relationship between the world's most powerful nation and the world's most populous nation. One reason was the obvious economic and cultural benefits that would grow from friendly relations. The other was the harsh realities of the atomic age. When I met with Charles de Gaulle in 1967, he said that while he had no illusions about China's ideology, the United States should not "leave them isolated in their rage." I responded, "In ten years, when China has made significant nuclear progress, we will have no choice. It is vital that we have more communications with them than we have today." The modern world cannot afford the risk of the misunderstandings and misjudgments that can occur when powerful nations fail to communicate in spite of their differences. Our estrangement from China, justified though it may have been on purely ideological grounds, was an ideological luxury neither we nor they could afford any longer. Nuclear weapons represent many things to many people; to responsible national leaders, they represent a compelling reason to search for common ground.

In the long run the Sino–U.S. relationship will endure not because of fear but because of hope. Nothing will come between us so long as neither side harbors territorial ambitions against the other or the other's friends and allies. We have nothing to lose from friendship with each other; we have everything to gain. In just over sixteen years the United States, whose trade with China had been virtually nil during the years 1949 to 1972, has become China's third largest trading partner. China is still a developing country, but it is developing at an extraordinary rate. Between 1978, when Deng's reforms began, and 1983 the personal income of China's 800 million peasants—the earliest beneficiaries of the reforms—increased by 70 percent. Some experts predict that at the beginning of the next century the GNP of China will be greater than that of West Germany.

To keep this in perspective, however, it is important to add that in the year 2000 the per-capita income of sixty million West Germans will be $20,000 a year, compared with $875 for China's one billion people. China's new Communist Party General Secretary, Zhao Ziyang, recently said matter-of-factly that it could take as long as one hundred years for the modernization drive begun by Deng to bring China to the level of advanced countries such as the United States. Some of Zhao's predecessors in the communist world—especially Mao in China and Stalin in the Soviet Union—thought such progress could be forced in a matter of years rather than decades. Tens of millions of Chinese and Russians died in the resulting upheavals. To some analysts Zhao's more realistic predictions sound like lowered expectations. To me, they simply sound Chinese. Unlike many leaders in both East and West, Zhao knows that instant solutions are no solutions at all. But he is also supremely confident that a superior people will inevitably produce superior results once their productive and creative energies are released.

When we again talked about China in 1969 de Gaulle said, "It would be better for you to recognize China before you are obligated to do so by the growth of China." He was right. The potential of a billion of the ablest people in the world will inevitably make China into an economic giant and also a military giant. Our goal now and in the remaining years of the twentieth century should be to make certain that the China of the twenty-first century will be an independent giant—not necessarily pro-Western, but definitely not pro-Soviet.

The two-decades-long freeze between Washington and Beijing was an unnatural estrangement between two peoples who, as events since 1972 have shown, have much to offer each other. So long as China was allied with the Soviet Union, we had no choice but to be adversaries. With that barrier removed, we have powerful reasons to be friends.

Today the people of the United States and China are partners in China's development. Assuming that both sides stay the course, in the twenty-first century the Sino–U.S. relationship will be one of the most important, and most mutually beneficial, bilateral relationships in the world.

China's economic revolution is a product of two dramatic changes of outlook by its leaders: their new attitude toward the West and Deng Xiaoping's economic reforms in 1978. The Sino–U.S. rapprochement in 1972 gave China access to Western markets and technology; Deng's reforms in 1978 enabled China to put its new access to use. The first change followed China's realization that it needed a way to balance the threat of Soviet military power. The second followed China's realization that it needed an alternative to the Soviet economic model that was threatening to doom the Chinese people to permanent poverty.

These two declarations of independence from Soviet domination and influence were the products of three strikingly different leaders.

Mao and Chou were the two immutable forces behind the 1949

revolution. Working in tandem they changed China forever; the few times they were at odds they nearly ripped it apart. When I met them in 1972, to the outside world they appeared in the studied guises of Mao the philosopher and Chou the administrator. During our first meeting Mao pointedly brushed aside discussion of specific foreign-policy and domestic issues; such matters, he said, were to be taken up with Premier Chou. "I discuss the philosophical questions," he said. Sunk into an easy chair in his cluttered, book-lined study, presenting his visitors with inscribed copies of his collected poems, Mao affected the posture of father of his country, a beloved and bemused figure who occupied a space just outside and above the course of everyday events. The reality was different. Until his death in 1976 Mao remained the pivotal force in China.

Both men had been dedicated revolutionaries. After the communists took power in 1949, Mao continued to be a revolutionary. Chou became a nation-builder, a consolidator of central national authority instead of a destroyer of it. He brought the same cold, calculating ruthlessness to bear on building a new China that he had previously brought to bear on driving the old China, in the form of Chiang Kai-shek's army, from the mainland.

Chou had turned from revolutionary politics to the challenge of how China was to be governed after the revolution. But Mao did not want the governing to get in the way of what he saw as a permanent revolution. He was quirky and unpredictable—"a man inhabited by a vision, possessed by it," as André Malraux described him to me before my 1972 trip. To China's masses he was poet, prophet, pedant, and frequently punisher. In the 1960s, believing that China was losing its revolutionary zeal, he unleashed the Cultural Revolution to gouge out all Western influence. Chou and the gradual policy of economic modernization he had set in motion were engulfed in the frenzy of Mao's Red Guards. In the end Chou, and his partnership with Mao, survived. Its most lasting consequence, besides the revolution itself, was China's split from the Soviet Union and its rapprochement with the United States.

China's second revolution, the sharp turn away from Marxist-Leninist economic doctrine, was engineered by a leader who had been with Mao and Chou on the Long March that preceded the first. Deng Xiaoping was, and remains, a dedicated communist whose presence at the creation of the new China in 1949 and contributions to the consolidation of the regime earned him a position as a trusted subordinate of Mao and Chou. But his anguish over the failure of Mao's Great Leap Forward caused him to rethink his faith in doctrinaire Marxism-Leninism, and his first tentative reform proposals in the 1960s caused the Maoist radicals to rethink Deng. In 1967 he was sent into internal exile, but by 1973 he had reappeared as a potential successor to Chou En-lai, whose own first cautious steps toward economic modernization had also been thwarted by Mao. In 1975 Deng and Chou, by now near death, had begun work on the "Four Modernizations"—the principles that govern China today—when the radicals lashed out again, returning Deng to exile and leaving Chou to spend the last few months of his life on the fringes of power. But soon the nation-builders won out over the fanatics, the "Gang of Four" was crushed, and Deng—twice down for the count—was China's "paramount leader."

I have met Deng four times—in Washington in 1979 and in Beijing in 1979, 1982, and 1985. Each time I left Beijing more impressed with his driven determination and his total self-confidence. And each time my impressions of the leader were strengthened by the changes under way in the nation he led. The people brim with confidence and with curiosity about things Western and American. When I met Mao and Chou in 1972, the young women who translated for us were dressed in baggy gray Mao suits and had short, severe haircuts. The Chinese communists had apparently taken too seriously Henry Higgins' admonition "Why can't a woman be like a man?" When I visited Canton in 1985, we were served by beautiful Chinese girls wearing high heels and stylish, multicolored gowns. My host observed, "You will note that we have more color in our clothes today. The same is true of our ideology."

It would be naive to read too much into either change. China's leaders are still communists, not capitalists. And despite their warm hospitality and their seemingly insatiable thirst for contact with the West, the goal of their broad economic reforms is not to *change* the essence of China but to make China stronger by importing those influences that can be put to work in China *without* changing it. This is in accordance with Chinese tradition. For centuries China has never been permanently conquered by foreign invaders or foreign ideas. It has absorbed them. In commenting on Mao's revolution, Singapore's Prime Minister Lee Kwan Yew told me in 1967, "Mao is painting on a mosaic. When the rains come they will wash away what he has painted, and China will remain."

Until Deng came to power in 1978, the effect of China's doctrinaire Marxism was to give every Chinese an equal share in poverty. Today, some are being given a chance to earn their way out of poverty. Deng recognized that his choice was between equality at the price of poverty and progress at the price of inequality. As he compared the plight of his desperately poor country with what the Chinese people have accomplished in Singapore and Hong Kong and on Taiwan, he made the choice of progress with some inequality over rigid equality and no progess.

My first glimpse of China in 1972 was during the dismal wake of the Cultural Revolution. The superficial changes since then are astonishing. China is still a poor Third World country. But a majority of China's people now have access to television. The streets of the big cities are crowded with people wearing Western-style trench coats and sweat suits. Teenagers go to American movies, hear concerts by Western rock groups, and eat Kentucky Fried Chicken. Women who once tucked their short hair under Mao caps today make appointments at Elizabeth Arden's salon in Beijing. Tourists from China's distant provinces flock to the capital, clutching their Japanese-made cameras, to see the Great Wall and the Forbidden City. In 1972 most of the people in Beijing were shuffling along on foot; today they ride bicycles, and some have automobiles.

More significantly, China's economy is booming. It grew at a rate of 11 percent in 1986, three times the average rate in the industrialized West. The most striking success story is in agriculture. In the first two years of Deng's reforms, farmers' incomes rose more than they had in the previous twenty years of Mao's era. Because of the new incentive system, under which farmers are permitted to keep and sell whatever they produce over and above their government quotas, China now produces enough to feed its one billion people and have enough left over to export. Han Xu, China's ambassador to the United States, recently pointed out to me that China, with only 6 percent of the world's arable land, now feeds 22 percent of the world's people. In contrast, Russian peasants still laboring on Stalin-style collective farms are unable to produce enough to feed the Soviet Union's 250 million people.

The West has been watching with breathless anticipation every move Gorbachev has made. Each minor concession to human rights, each hint of reform or Glasnost, has been met with enthusiastic applause from a Western audience that is all too eager to expect great things from each new Soviet leader. It is true that what happens in the Soviet Union is fraught with special significance because of its status as a military superpower. But so far Gorbachev has only shown himself willing to oil the faltering engine that Stalin built. Deng, through his methodical plan to modernize Chinese agriculture, industry, and science, has begun to completely rebuild China's engine. So at least for the moment the young, vigorous Gorbachev, well-cut suits and well-turned phrases notwithstanding, must take a backseat to his eighty-four-year-old, Mao-suited, chain-smoking Chinese counterpart with the guttural laugh and the spittoon at his feet. What Gorbachev so far only dreams, Deng does.

By acting boldly, Deng has run great risks. Reducing the authority of the central government over the economy threatens those in the Communist Party bureaucracy whose power resides in the exercise of such authority. Reorganizing China's armed forces threatens the defense establishment. And toying with Western notions of economic freedom risks activating the severely xenophobic strain in the Chinese character that fueled the Boxer Rebellion, the Cultural Revolution, and the brief reign of the Gang of Four.

The conventional wisdom says that China's reformers cannot continue to permit economic freedom without significantly altering its totalitarian political system. Many experts say that if farmers and factory managers are given the freedom to act in the marketplace, they will demand freedom to act in the political realm as well. If the party's authority to control the economy is limited, its authority to control the people will be weakened, too.

As is often the case with great leaders, however, Deng has looked over the heads of the experts into a future he can see but they cannot imagine. It is true that what he is doing has never been done in a communist nation. But it is by no means clear that it cannot be done. In the end, if the conventional wisdom about Deng's reforms is proved wrong, it will be for one simple reason: they work. Deng is gambling that, power and ideology aside, China will not turn its back on a good thing.

Some in the West feared that China had done exactly that in 1987 when Deng was forced to remove his chosen successor, Hu Yaobang, as head of the Communist Party. Hard-liners blamed Hu for demonstrations in China's big cities by students who wanted more political and academic freedom to match the new economic freedoms. Hu was faulted for failing to maintain rigorous ideological discipline, and Deng himself responded to the demonstrations by promising to strike back ruthlessly against those who encouraged any more like them.

Deng's actions drew sharp criticism from Western editorial writers who expressed their disappointment that he had apparently reversed what they had believed was a promising march toward a new, democratic China. These critics showed a total lack of understanding of Deng's goals and predicament. The source of his authority is the Communist Party. He needs that authority to govern China. Deng realizes that his reforms must not strain the party's authority to the point where it strikes back again and deals him a mortal blow—or, even worse, loses its capacity to maintain order. And while some Western superhawks would like nothing better than to see China convulsed by another revolution, such a development would cause untold deaths and plunge China, and Asia, into turmoil.

By the end of 1987 the reformers were again firmly in control, and it was clear many had underestimated Deng. His reforms may not be popular with the aging hard-line conservatives in the government, but they are popular with the people, many of whom for the first time since the revolution are finding they have enough income to afford luxuries, such as televisions and refrigerators, that were unimaginable in Mao's China. More money in circulation has caused some corruption and inflation. Tensions may develop between the countryside and the cities as a result of the industrial sector's inability to produce enough to satisfy increased consumer demand. All these problems can be dealt with without reversing the overall course of the reforms. But what can never be reversed are the Chinese people's new expectations for the future. One of the unhappy lessons of history is that those who have never tasted prosperity and freedom can live indefinitely without them. But once people have them, they will not give them up without a fight. The political turmoil Deng has unleashed through his reforms is nothing compared to what will happen if they are quashed by Beijing's hard-liners.

When Deng relinquished operational control over China's government to Zhao at last year's party congress, many Western observers commented condescendingly about how extraordinary it was for a communist leader to step aside gracefully and voluntarily, leaving younger, carefully groomed successors behind to carry on his policies. They failed to recognize that this is extraordinary under any form of government, including democracies. De Gaulle put down his apparent successor Georges Pompidou; Churchill put down Eden; Adenauer put down his own able Finance Minister, Ludwig Erhard, so cruelly that Erhard once broke into tears when he described to me one of Adenauer's slights. Japan's Shigeru Yoshida was a rare exception. He carefully prepared men such as Ikeda, Fukuda, and Sato to serve after he had left the scene. As a result Japan has been ruled for nearly a quarter century according to Yoshida's conservative, pro-Western principles.

In such situations it is not only the system that matters. It is also the leader. The West is known for orderly, solemn transfers of power that can nonetheless leave policies in complete shambles. In authoritarian and totalitarian governments there can be forcible ousters of leaders, such as the removal of Habib Bourguiba as President of Tunisia last year, that leave basic national policy unchanged. In stepping aside as he did, leaving behind him both the men and the policies he wanted to leave, Deng performed a deft political miracle.

Like Japan's Yoshida, Deng did not feel threatened by able men under him in government. Instead he considered it the ultimate triumph for a leader's policies to be carried on after his death by well-prepared successors. He is still in good health today. But as an awareness of his own mortality looms larger, Deng has come to the paradoxical realization that the key to a leader's immortality is to be humble enough to recognize that other men can, and must, fill his shoes. Deng will be remembered for many remarkable achievements during his career. But history has few examples of strong leaders who face up to their mortality instead of being forced to do so by others. His simple statement "I am stepping down before my mind becomes confused" is an eloquent demonstration of his greatness.

The ouster of Hu Yaobang, his lifelong friend, must have caused Deng great anguish. Zhao was his second choice, but he is an extraordinarily good one. He is a tough, intelligent economist and technocrat, but he is also colorful, even charismatic. At a cocktail reception during last year's party congress he was assuring Western journalists that the impeccably tailored Western-style suits he and his colleagues were wearing were not imported. To prove his point he grabbed the lapel of a top official standing nearby and turned it over so that everyone could see the label that said "Made in China."

Zhao has enthusiastically embraced Deng's reforms and has even taken some promising new steps forward, giving small factories more freedom, permitting peasants to buy and sell their government land leases, and, probably most important, adopting new guidelines for keeping the Communist Party out of day-to-day government. Many antireform hard-liners have been put out to pasture. But others who believe that Deng's pace of reform was too quick remain. Until Zhao fully consolidates his power he will continue to look to Deng to mediate disputes with conservatives. The unanswered question is who is the one among many who has the strength and vision to replace Deng when he finally leaves the scene. In a communist country only one can be the leader. Whether that leader is Zhao will depend upon how successfully his skills as a political tactician match those he has already exhibited as an economic one.

But it remains highly doubtful that China, having come this far along Deng's promising new road, will ever turn back. Like people, nations can learn from their mistakes. China embarked on its experiment in partial economic freedom only after its experiment in total economic planning exploded, or rather sputtered out, in its face. During Deng's years as a disciple of Chou and Mao, China was dead in the international water, humiliatingly dependent on Soviet largesse. After the failure of the Great Leap Forward, Deng realized that the people of China were being kept from reaching their potential at home and China was being kept from reaching its potential on the world stage. One of Mao's and Chou's greatest legacies is that they finally brought China into the twentieth century by turning it toward the West. The legacy of their successor will be that he unbound China from the ideological strictures of the past and prepared it for international leadership in the future.

Deng came to power as an old man with young ideas. His principal rivals were not the younger men below him but the other octogenarians around him. They feared the end of the China they knew; he welcomed and encouraged it. They cherished the ideals of the revolution in which they and he had fought; he knew that those ideals would turn to ashes in a billion hungry mouths unless fundamental changes were made in the Chinese system. In the sixteenth century a French scholar nearing the end of his life wrote despairingly, "If youth but knew, and old age only could." At eighty-four, Deng knew, and Deng could. The combination was explosive, and it has sent a fifth of the world's people hurtling toward new prosperity and world leadership.

Too many naive observers in the West persist in looking at Deng and seeing a Chinese Thomas Paine, a democratic revolutionary whose long-range plan is to bring an end to communist rule. Deng's actions have indeed been dramatic, even inspiring. But Deng is a reformer, not a revolutionary. As a communist he does not want a capitalist China or a democratic China, but he is not a prisoner of his ideology. Above all he is a nationalist who wants a strong China that has the economic and military power it needs to pursue foreign and trade policies that will make it a superpower in the twenty-first century.

While Deng's explicit goal was not more political freedom, if the economic reforms work political change could follow. The change must be gradual and sure—fast enough to keep up with the people's expectations, but not so fast that the existing political structure cannot cope. Deng himself said it best: "If I could enable people to improve their lives gradually, then I think the policy itself is a sure guarantee of its continuity." The key to success is time. Given enough time, what today seems so new to the Chinese will take on the appearance of normalcy; younger leaders who have been exposed to the reforms, and who benefit from them, will become advocates of continuing and expanding them. The success of Deng's vision will give freedom a good name. China will realize that it has nothing to fear from freedom and everything to gain.

For Deng's reforms to survive, the United States and the West must play a central role. China's economic development depends upon a stable world economy and consistent, friendly relationships with its trading partners in the industrialized world. If the West lets China down—by slowing the pace of its investments in China, by lashing out at China in the form of protectionism, or by failing to pursue enlightened foreign policies in the Pacific region— China's economy will be harmed, and antireform elements within China will be helped.

The concern over the Soviet threat which brought us together in 1972 may not be enough to keep us together in 1999. If that is our only motive for friendly relations we leave our fate in the hands of the Soviets. Our common security interests brought us together. If the threat recedes, our common economic interests can keep us together. If we want China to sustain its orientation toward the West we must give the Chinese a sustained economic stake in good relations with the West. Beijing's pro-reformers must be able to show their skeptical colleagues that China will profit from Deng's new policies more than it would from a return to the Soviet model and the Soviet fold.

The Sino–U.S. relationship will last into the twenty-first century, and strengthen with each passing year, if the United States proves to be a dependable friend. Our relationship is healthy and strong, but we must work to keep it that way. It cannot withstand being neglected or taken for granted. But in surveying all we have accomplished in the first sixteen years, we can be justifiably hopeful about what remains to be done.

Before 1972, there was no trade between the United States and China, no tourism, no academic exchanges, no technological and cultural exchanges, no military relations. Today, bilateral trade is about $10 billion a year. Over 250 U.S. companies have offices in China, and Americans have invested $1.5 billion there. Of the thirty thousand Chinese students now studying abroad, fifteen thousand are in the United States. A quarter of a million American tourists visit China each year. A modest program of military relations, including some sales of defensive arms to China, is under way. Young American diplomats now covet postings in Beijing, Shanghai, and Canton, and young Chinese diplomats cherish assignments in Washington, New York, and Los Angeles.

Through these and other developments, China is coming to know America and America to know China. Between two societies that once seemed so different, so threatening, so unbridgeably alien to each other, a web of understanding and interdependence is being formed that will help cushion the inevitable jolts that occur from time to time in the relations among all friendly nations.

The foundation of a lasting Sino–U.S. relationship has been laid. We must now build upon it.

Our first priority must be to redouble our efforts to increase bilateral trade. The current levels are more than we dreamed possible when we first opened the door to China. But it is still far too little. Our trade with Taiwan's fifteen million people is ten times as great as with the PRC's one billion.

Because a large percentage of its exports consist of textiles, China is all too vulnerable to protectionist sentiment in the United States. In spite of our trade deficit with our Asian trading partners, including China, President Reagan deserves great credit for resisting demands that he raise trade barriers. He must continue to do so, as must his successor. Protectionism is a viscerally satisfying quick fix, but it is always counterproductive in the long run. Japan, which is the primary target of the protectionists, has an economy which is so strong that it could probably absorb new U.S. trade restrictions. But they would have a devastating impact on China's developing economy and conceivably on the strategic balance in Asia and the world. If the open door to the West closes, China would again be forced to knock on the gates of the Kremlin.

The West must also increase China's access to the technology it needs for industrial development. We should not sell highly sensitive technologies that could be used against us militarily to any potentially hostile nation. But neither should we be overly rigorous about technologies that have no military application but that would be indispensable to modernizing the Chinese economy. Many of these will also be available to China from other trading partners in the industrialized West. Better the Chinese get them from us so that we will be in a position to reap the benefits.

The future of the Sino–U.S. relationship is as much in the hands of American businessmen as in those of its statesmen. As Khrushchev once said to a group of Western business leaders, "You stay in power, while the politicians change all the time." But as befits their long-range role American businessmen must learn the Eastern art of taking the long view. The Chinese think in terms of decades and centuries, while hard-driving Westerners often think no further ahead than the bottom line at the end of the current fiscal year. Many businessmen returning from China complain about the maddeningly slow pace of the Chinese foreign-trade bureaucracy. Americans are used to pitching a deal in the morning, smoothing the rough edges over a three-martini lunch, and tying up the loose ends that afternoon with a few phone calls and telexes. But the hard-and-fast sell will not work in China. The Chinese remember when the Western powers exploited their country unmercifully, and the memory has made them tough bargainers.

Nonetheless Americans who stick it out now, when the Chinese economy is just beginning to expand, will be glad they did. Over 8,300 joint ventures between Chinese and Western firms have been approved, and over 150 foreign companies have been permitted to set up wholly owned subsidiaries—in stark contrast to many other developing countries such as Mexico, which is so paranoid about outside investment that it puts heavy restrictions on foreign ownership. Those investors who have their foot in the door in 1988 and keep it there will reap unimaginable rewards as China grows and prospers. For those doing business in China, patience will lead to great rewards.

The worst mistake we could make in our China policy is to

indulge in the uniquely American practice of piously instructing other countries about how to conduct their political business. The Chinese are a fiercely independent people who have always chafed at attempts by others to influence or dominate their affairs. Statements of concern from Americans, in government or in the media, about apparent antireform or antidemocratic trends in China will serve no purpose other than to offend and alienate the Chinese leadership and possibly produce an effect that is exactly opposite to what the naive critics intend. Americans on both the left and the right must resist their bighearted urge to lecture the Chinese on human rights. And it is ludicrous for us to attempt, as some in the Reagan administration have urged, to impose our views about abortion on China, an overcrowded country where the choice is between population control and starvation.

Most important, we must avoid any misstep on the difficult issue of Taiwan. The position we took in 1972 in the Shanghai Communiqué, which has been reinforced in subsequent Sino–U.S. understandings, is the one that should govern our policy in the future. The Chinese on both Taiwan and the mainland maintain that there is only one China and that Taiwan is part of China. Our only interest is that in deciding the issue among themselves, the Chinese should decide it peacefully. We cannot and should not broker a deal. The most sensitive issue is arms. We must strictly adhere to our commitment to provide only defensive arms to Taiwan, lessening the pace of our military aid only as tensions between Taiwan and Beijing lessen.

But we must make it clear that in building our friendship with the Chinese on the mainland we will not sacrifice our Chinese friends on Taiwan. Julian Amery put the issue eloquently: "It is often necessary and legitimate to abandon causes long supported and to dissolve pledged bonds of alliance. But it is always wrong to abandon men who have been friends to their fate. We may have to jettison their interests but we should leave no stone unturned to save at least their lives." Two of the blackest pages in the history of American diplomacy were our complicity in the murder of Diem and our insensitivity to the fate of the Shah after we greased the skids for his downfall and thus helped bring Khomeini to power. We must not commit a similar atrocity against the Taiwanese.

Many Americans who are preoccupied with the Taiwan issue fail to realize that Deng is under as much pressure, if not more, to act on Taiwan from conservatives in his own government as American Presidents have been from the pro-Taiwan lobby in the United States. It is in neither our interests nor those of our friends on Taiwan to provoke a confrontation with Beijing. Deng hopes that the agreement he made with the British on Hong Kong, by which the crown colony will revert to Chinese control in 1997 under the principle of "one country, two systems," will serve as a starting point for a comparable arrangement on Taiwan. In any case, the more sensitive we can be to Chinese concerns on this issue, the better, both for Deng and for Taiwan. The issue is enormously complex and has no simple solution. But the Chinese are a very clever people. I am confident they will eventually resolve it peacefully.

The Chinese will watch what the United States does elsewhere in the world just as carefully as they watch what we do in China. Recent developments have given them good reason to be concerned about our consistency and dependability. Our loss in Vietnam, followed by the spread of Soviet power throughout Indochina, was a devastating strategic blow to China, which suffered twenty thousand casualties in a 1979 war with Soviet-backed Vietnam that would not have occurred if South Vietnam had not been defeated by the communist North.

The Chinese were deeply troubled by our geopolitical hibernation during the late 1970s. When I saw Mao in 1976 six months before his death, he asked me rather ruefully, "Is peace America's only goal?" I answered that we wanted a peace that was more than the absence of war—a "peace with justice." At that time, regrettably, my words were empty. America was in the throes of the Vietnam syndrome and in no mood to fulfill its international responsibilities. Twelve years later our resolve has stiffened considerably as the rancor and bitterness of our Vietnamese experience have faded, but it has not yet been put to a real test, and the Chinese know it. Still, the national-security imperatives that brought us together remain a critical element in our relationship.

The Chinese will continue to count on us to bring pressure to bear on the Soviets to withdraw from Afghanistan; to maintain a military presence in the Pacific to balance Soviet strength; to pursue hardheaded arms-control agreements with the Soviets that will not leave them with a strategic advantage they could use to blackmail us and our friends; and to continue to resist the spread of Soviet influence in the developing world. We should do all these things in our own interests as well as in theirs.

In these and other areas, our interests and those of the Chinese are similar. Aggressively pursuing our foreign-policy interests will automatically bolster our relationship with China; failing to act when we should will hurt the relationship. Until China's defense establishment becomes stronger than it is today, the essence of its military deterrent is ours. But we must never forget that we act for our sake, not China's. Pandering to the Chinese will only earn their contempt. We can expect that in spite of our cordial relations Beijing will continue to indulge in its traditional anti-capitalist, occasionally anti-American public rhetoric. We should not object to this any more than the Chinese should object to our speaking out against communism.

But our convergent interests will diverge suddenly and sharply in the event China moves beyond rhetoric and embarks on a newly expansionist, aggressive phase in its foreign policy. For example, in part to make money and in part to offset Soviet overtures to Khomeini, the Chinese in 1986 sold $1 billion in weapons to Iran. Such a policy has its understandable motivations, but it also has its inescapable consequences. The Reagan administration reacted properly when it took measures to deprive China of high-technology equipment it wanted and needed.

As they have become more sophisticated in economic policy, so too have the Chinese become more shrewd in foreign policy. They pursue an independent, carefully calibrated range of initiatives: taking tentative steps toward relations with South Korea without endangering their long-standing ties with the communist north; gradually improving relations with their former enemy Japan without permitting an uncontrolled flood of Japanese imports and influence; keeping a line open to Iraq at the same time they sell weapons to Iran; and, most significant, pursuing talks and exchanges aimed at warming the chill between Beijing and Moscow.

Signs of a Sino–Soviet thaw have caused considerable confusion and even some consternation in the United States. Some superhawks had hoped that the two communist giants would go to war —in spite of the fact that even a conventional clash between China and the Soviet Union would probably escalate into a nuclear World War III. Others, pointing to such factors as a nearly sevenfold increase in bilateral trade between 1982 and 1986, fear that a Sino–Soviet rapprochement will create a newly united communist monolith that will threaten us.

Neither of these dire outcomes is likely. Deng wants better relations with the Soviet Union because they will permit him to focus more of his resources on economic development and less on defense. And he wants to reduce tensions that might escalate into war. For China the twentieth century has been a century of war. Above all China now needs a century of peace. But Deng does not want to return to the pre-1961 relationship, when China was economically dependent on the Soviet Union. He knows that China's greatest need is for economic progress. Here it is no contest between the West and the Soviet Union. The West offers everything; the Soviet Union offers very little. Only if China gives up on the West will it turn back to its ominous neighbor in the north.

Another reason China will be reluctant to return to its old relationship with the Soviet Union is that it never again wants to be a junior partner in the communist bloc. China's days of dependency are over. It is a major player in a world filled with nations that realize the force it is destined to become and that are eager to play a role in helping it develop its potential. In recent years one leader after another, Western and communist alike, has found it in his and in his country's interests to ride what one journalist called the "milk train to China" and stand with its leaders on the Great Wall. China's leaders are wise to receive every supplicant. Deng summed up China's independent foreign policy succinctly when he told me in 1985, "We are not going to tie ourselves to one chariot."

For the same reason, at least for the moment there is a limit beyond which the relationship between the United States and the People's Republic of China cannot grow. We are not allies. Just thirty-five years ago we were enemies. Thousands of Chinese and Americans fought each other in Korea. One of Mao's sons was among the casualties. Today we are new friends who have been brought together after years of hostility, even hatred and war, by coldly calculated common interests. These interests could change, and the friendship would change with them. We have no shared experiences, struggles, or ideals to hold us together in the face of shifting international realities; absent a major political reform movement in China, our philosophies of government will remain diametrically opposed to each other. Therefore to a large extent this promising new relationship is hostage to events over which neither side has complete control.

We must avoid romanticizing the relationship or putting too much stock in superficial curiosities about each other. Neither student exchanges nor tourism nor blue jeans nor American rock music nor cloisonné jewelry will hold us together if either China or the United States behaves in a way that the other finds unacceptable. Relations between great nations are not a tea party or a love fest; they are complicated, intricately structured devices that have to be watched and tended constantly. Unless we take care, anything that can go wrong probably will.

For the sake of our grandchildren in the next century, however, we must ensure that our relationship survives and grows. Today we are dealing with a nation that is just beginning to feel its way in the modern world; tomorrow they will be dealing with what could be the dominant power in the world. Between now and then the new friends could become new allies, and the shared experiences and values that are missing today could come to be as a result of now-unimagined events in a changing, violent, unpredictable world.

At our meeting in Hangzhou in 1972, Chou En-lai and I completed the negotiations for the Shanghai Communiqué, which marked the beginning of a new, peaceful relationship between the United States and China. To commemorate the event, we planted a three-foot-high sequoia that I had brought with me from California. It was a sapling from the oldest and tallest tree in the world, in California's Sequoia National Park. At the time neither of us was sure the tree would grow in Chinese soil.

The soil and the climate proved to be friendly. In October 1987 Governor Thomas Kean of New Jersey visited Hangzhou. His hosts showed him the tree, now ninety feet tall. Even more significant, they said that forty thousand saplings from the tree were thriving in seven Chinese provinces.

The Chinese people and the American people are among the ablest in the world. They are both endowed with enormous potential. As we look into the twenty-first century, the soil and the climate are right for a productive Chinese–American relationship that could move the world to unprecedented heights of peace and freedom.

9

THIRD WORLD BATTLEGROUNDS

The countries outside the industrialized West and the Soviet bloc are commonly lumped together and called "the Third World." It is a virtually meaningless term—just about as useful as "none of the above" in describing over 150 countries spread north and south of the equator over four continents and containing people of all races and religions. What most have in common is that they are grindingly, desperately poor. The average per-capita income of the over three billion people of the Third World is less than $800 a year, compared with $18,000 in the United States. They are poor for many reasons, but the single largest is that they have not yet found the way to productively harness their own vast human and natural resources.

We cannot solve all their problems. But in the years ahead we must do everything we can to help *them* solve them. If we do not we will be abrogating our moral responsibilities. We will also be permitting an endless cycle of poverty, despair, and conflict that will inevitably prevent us from building a structure of real peace in the world.

The most insidious aspect of the term "Third World" is the suggestion that we need a single, all-encompassing "Third World policy." Most of those who think, speak, and act in such simplistic terms are playing variations on the same theme. We are rich, they chant, and the Third World is poor. That much is true. But then they go on to say that the solution is "a transfer of resources from north to south"—in other words, the developed world should give the undeveloped world more money. They reduce the world with all its diversity and complexity to the simplistic dimensions of a Dickens novel: the selfish tycoon ignoring the starving beggar with the outstretched hand.

Western liberals spend far too much time on this kind of guilty hand-wringing over the Third World and far too little time rendering the kind of practical assistance the developing world can actually put to use. Recently a book critic writing for a major American newspaper condemned Kipling's *Gunga Din* for its racist overtones, but, over two centuries after the British arrived in India and a generation after the European powers abandoned their colonies, many Western intellectuals and politicians still have a superior, "white man's burden" mentality toward the poorer nations.

There is one simple reason why share-the-wealth schemes have never worked and never will. The developed world did not cause the Third World's problems by itself, and it cannot solve them by itself. It is the height of arrogance, even racism, to suggest otherwise. We can show these struggling nations the way because we have traveled the road from poverty to prosperity ourselves. But we do them no favors by simply carrying them along on our backs. We would only be creating a permanent underclass of pauper nations seeking handouts. Each step forward we take for them is really two steps backward as they become more dependent on our help and less able to cope on their own when our ability or willingness to help is exhausted.

But in shedding our counterproductive sense of guilt about the developing world, we do not shed our responsibilities. Poverty, malnutrition, disease, and war in these nations may not be our fault, but they are definitely our problems as well as theirs. If we stay on the sidelines, we will witness a competition for the future of the developing world that the West is certain to lose.

The Third World is important for four reasons:

First, the Third World has enormous natural and human resources. It produces most of the world's oil and other raw materials. Without them the industrial economies would collapse. By 1999, four out of five people on earth will be residents of the Third World. In 1899, the ten largest cities in the world were in Europe, the United States, and Japan. By 1999, eight out of ten will be in the Third World.

Second, the Third World is where the real Third World war is already being fought. In Asia, Africa, Latin America, and the Mideast, the Soviet Union is waging unconventional war to gain domination over the nations that have the oil and other resources vital to the survival of the West. Poverty, malnutrition, and disease are the ideal breeding grounds for political turmoil. Despair, despotism, and cynical Soviet opportunism all combine in the Third World to create a festering climate of economic stagnation and political instability.

Third, the Third World is the worldwide epicenter of war and revolution. Since the end of World War II, eighteen million people have lost their lives in Third World wars. This is more than were killed in action in World War I. Over forty wars rage in the Third World today. Most have nothing to do with the Soviet Union, but they have everything to do with the U.S.–Soviet rivalry. The greatest danger of war between the superpowers is the possibility of the escalation of a small war where superpower interests collide. A small war always has the potential of igniting a world war.

Fourth, we cannot in good conscience tolerate the status quo where the West is an island of wealth in a vast sea of poverty. We should not tolerate it, and the billions who live in the Third World *will* not. I have been to most of the Third World countries. The cold statistic of a low per capita income does not capture the picture of abject poverty and misery that one sees if he can break away from the restraints of protocol and guided tours. One quarter of the Third World's people live below the threshold of absolute poverty. Forty-five percent of urban dwellers and 85 percent of rural dwellers lack adequate sanitation facilities. Thirty thousand people die *every day* from dirty water and inadequate sanitation. Average life expectancy in much of the Third World is less than fifty years; it is over seventy in the United States. At the end of this century, the Third World's infant-mortality rate will be four times that of the United States. Because the average population growth in the Third World is three times as great as the West's, the Third World's average per-capita income could decrease by the year 1999.

If the next century is to be a century of peace, the causes of misery and war in the Third World must be addressed. Its security needs must be met, its economic potential fulfilled, and its political aspirations satisfied if the suffering that has plagued so much of the globe in the twentieth century is to be eradicated in the twenty-first.

The causes of unrest and poverty in the Third World are different in every direction we look.

In the Far East we see the stark contrast between the vitality produced by economic freedom and the depressing dullness of totalitarian communism. The color of communism is gray, not red. In Latin America we see a similar contrast as the security of many promising but sometimes unstable young democracies is threatened by aggressive Soviet satellites. In the feuds between India and Pakistan we see the unforgivable waste of resources that both nations need for the good of their people being spent instead on an ongoing religious and political rivalry. In poverty-stricken Africa we see living, and dying, proof of the fallacy of throwing good money at bad governments in nations that are poorer today than they were before the West pumped in hundreds of billions in aid. And in the Mideast we see the traditional rivalry of Arab versus Jew evolving into a conflict between Islamic fundamentalists on the one hand and Israel and the moderate Arab states on the other. Unless these nations overcome their differences and recognize that they face a far more dangerous threat emanating from Tehran, the Mideast will remain the most potentially explosive area of the world—the cradle of civilization that could become its grave.

In Asia we see incontrovertible proof of which social, economic, and political policies permit nations and people to live and grow and which cause them to decay and die. The world has never before had such an effective contrast in the same region between the misery produced by communism and the rich blessings of political and economic systems that permit a large measure of freedom.

Singapore, Hong Kong, and Taiwan give the lie to the commonplace notion that developing nations without natural resources are doomed to poverty. Singapore's economy has grown an astounding 7.5 percent a year over the past quarter of a century. If this trend continues, in 1999 it will have a higher per-capita income than the United States. The population of the 404-square-mile British protectorate of Hong Kong has a life expectancy of seventy-six years and a per-capita income of almost $7,000; its economy has no external debt. At the end of the 1940s, the average income in Taiwan was $50, roughly equal to that of mainland China. Today its per-capita income is $3,500, ten times that of the People's Republic 120 miles away.

South Korea has replaced Japan as the Asian economic miracle most talked about by the West, the Soviets, and the Chinese. A 6.5 percent average annual growth rate over the past generation has allowed a war-devastated nation with a per-capita income of $50 in 1953 to develop into a potential economic giant with a per-capita income of $2,200 and a literacy rate higher than that of the United States.

Some explain away the economic success stories of Asia as the products of some mystical characteristics of the "inscrutable East." But while Orientals are well known for their hard work and high productivity, these countries' successes are the results of well-considered and practical economic strategies that need not be unique to Asia. They all followed free-market policies designed to spur growth and increase their peoples' wealth. They responded to the opportunities offered by the world economy, interacting with it and profiting from it rather than stubbornly denying its existence as Marxist-Leninists do.

Political freedom in these countries does not meet American or European standards. But they do provide basic economic, social, and religious rights, and in absolute terms they look like Disneyland compared to their drab communist neighbors. In South Korea students have been arrested for holding demonstrations to urge that free elections be held earlier; in North Korea there are no demonstrations, no free elections, and no freedom at all. In Lee Kwan Yew's Singapore young people are sometimes lectured by their stern Prime Minister for letting their hair grow too long; in Pol Pot's Cambodia they were machine-gunned for holding hands.

Progress toward democracy around the world may never proceed at the speedy pace we would prefer. In view of the poor record of the twentieth century's various revolutions and "national-liberation movements," we should be thankful it is proceeding at all. In fact, throughout noncommunist Asia today we see nations moving toward representative democracy. In one of the most significant political achievements of the twentieth century, 90 percent of South Korea's eligible voters went to the polls in December 1987 to end an era of authoritarianism and begin an era of democracy. Taiwan has also taken irrevocable steps toward free, multiparty elections. Hong Kong may soon have representational self-government. Thailand has strengthened its democracy. In all these nations, material progress may well be matched by political progress by 1999.

South Korea is a classic example of how national security and economic growth have prepared the ground for the seeds of sturdy representative government. Some critics contend that it took too long to achieve democracy. But those who take the historical perspective, especially in the context of the rest of the Third World, must conclude that South Korea's accomplishments in providing political stability, producing economic progress, and moving toward democracy are spectacular.

Across the 38th parallel from South Korea the people incarcerated in communist dictator Kim Il-Sung's closed society know neither the challenges and benefits of democracy nor the satisfactions of economic success. This is not because North Koreans are any less hard-working than South Koreans. It is because they live under a system that demands servility rather than encourages initiative. Totalitarian communism such as North Korea's is the cause of Asia's worst failures and greatest suffering.

Those who opposed United States participation in the Vietnam War because they thought communism would bring prosperity to

Asia must now face the hard facts of the hard life tens of millions now lead in today's Indochina. As Lenin said, "Facts are stubborn things."

Vietnam is one of the world's poorest nations, with a per capita income of less than $160. In South Vietnam before the fall of Saigon in 1975 it was $500. For the 600,000 South Vietnamese who drowned in the South China Sea trying to escape the savageries of their Soviet-backed conquerors from the north, the communist peace was the peace of the grave. Even thirteen years after the end of the war, at a time when Americans are understandably eager to put the Vietnam experience behind them, 1,500 boat people are still putting Vietnam behind them every month.

Communism also killed the once-independent, prosperous nation of Cambodia. In a matter of days the brutal Khmer Rouge, acting according to a grim master plan prepared years before when their leaders lived in Paris, emptied the city of Phnom Penh so that they could create an agrarian communist society. Families, those with educations, monks and priests, racial minorities, and all suspected and imagined resisters were slaughtered. Children were encouraged to turn their parents in to the executioners. During the next three years over two million out of seven million starved or were liquidated. Today, after being occupied by 140,000 Vietnamese troops, Cambodia is one of the most malnourished nations in the world. Twenty-one percent of its children die before reaching age five, the average life expectancy is forty-six years, and the per-capita income is $80 a year. For all intents and purposes, the nation of Cambodia has ceased to exist.

Today's Cambodia will be tomorrow's Philippines if the ruthless, brutal communist New People's Army succeeds at its avowed goal of overthrowing the elected government. The NPA has used negotiations with Manila as all communists do: to consolidate military gains and to sap the will of the enemy to win. Neither the government of Mrs. Aquino nor a democratic Philippines will survive unless she accepts the fact that the NPA must be defeated militarily.

Neither the administration nor the Congress has paid sufficient attention to this critical situation. If the Philippines becomes another Third World battleground, American interests, those of

Japan and our Western allies, and those of the Philippines' neighbors throughout the South Pacific, including Australia, all will suffer.

Mrs. Aquino's election as President rejuvenated the spirit of the Filipino people. A majority still support her. But political legitimacy without economic growth and military security is fragile. And in the Philippines personal legitimacy is rare among government officials. No one questions President Aquino's own integrity. But in view of the fact that her family is one of the two richest in the country, it is particularly important for her to make sure that the "Philippine disease," a deadly combination of nepotism and corruption, does not infect her government.

We should not make the mistake of treating the Filipinos as our little brown brothers. We do them no favors when we subsidize policies we know will fail. We should substantially increase our economic aid, but only if it is used to implement sound economic policies. Otherwise we waste money on building false hopes. As tens of thousands have shown after they emigrated to the United States, the Filipinos are a talented and hard-working people. All they need is government that will tap their enormous potential. If President Aquino vigorously implements a market-oriented economic policy she will be able to harness the energy and enthusiasm of her people and attract the foreign investment she needs to spur greater growth.

The Philippines' neighbor to the south, Indonesia, is one of the least known, most underrated nations in the world. It was the first Asian country I visited as Vice President in 1953. I saw it through the eyes of President Sukarno, one of the most charismatic leaders I have ever met. He had elaborate dreams for the future of his newly independent country. But his irresponsible policies and personal corruption turned into a nightmare for Indonesia. His successor, President Suharto, has slowly brought the nation back from the chaos of Sukarno's last years. Indonesia could well become a giant in the twenty-first century. It is rich in natural resources. It has enormous strategic importance. It is the fifth most populous nation in the world. The Indonesians, blood brothers of the Filipinos, are a capable people with great potential. All they need is continued strong leadership to provide political stability and new economic policies that reward initiative and attract foreign investment.

Two of Indonesia's neighbors, New Zealand and Australia, are among the most important and promising nations of non-communist Asia and also the most frequently overlooked. One does not have to agree with its foreign policy to agree that New Zealand's Labor government is providing a vivid example of how economic policies that rely on private enterprise are far more effective in providing progress than policies that put excessive faith in government planning. If Australia's Labor government, whose foreign policy is much more to our liking, were to follow New Zealand's example, this geographical giant would without question become an economic giant in the next century.

If the malignant cancer of Vietnam can be prevented from spreading, the future of noncommunist Southeast Asia is bright. One reason is the dramatic change in China's attitude toward its neighbors. In 1953, all the leaders I met in Indonesia, the Philippines, Thailand, and Malaysia feared the communist giant to the north for its support of revolutionaries in their countries. Today China has good relations with all its neighbors except Taiwan. It is still feared, but for different reasons. As China modernizes its economy it could swamp the smaller economies, particularly in labor-intensive, mass-production industries such as textiles. That is why farsighted leaders in Malaysia and Thailand are planning moves into high-technology industries.

Violent change drags a nation down, while peaceful change can take it to infinite heights. The legacies of both are written on the face of the Far East. Its stark contrast between freedom and tyranny should help other developing nations that face this choice make the right one.

On the Asian subcontinent, the struggle between India and Pakistan is a tragic example of a Third World conflict that would exist even if there were no Soviet Union. India is the world's largest democracy with close ties to the Soviets. Pakistan is a United States ally that is gradually evolving toward democracy. Since they were granted independence from Great Britain in 1947 over five

million people have been killed in the slaughter that followed partition and in two wars between the two new countries. With
250,000 belligerent, heavily armed troops still facing off across the
border, this conflict can only be compared with the Mideast as the
major source of instability in the Third World.

India is a country of great hope and great misery. In 1999 it will
have over a billion people. One third of the world's poor live there.
In one area India has had remarkable economic progress. In the
1960s it combined wise use of technological and financial aid with
free-market incentives, and the agricultural sector responded with
an explosive boom. India now produces enough food to feed its
800 million people and still have some left over for export. This is
one of the world's most exciting examples of how wise government
policies can unleash the energies of an able people and solve a
problem many thought could not be solved.

The rest of the Third World should learn lessons from India's
successes in the 1960s. It should also learn from India's failures in
the 1970s and 1980s. A promising industrial base grew in the 1960s,
but government bureaucracy, the poison that saps the vitality of
most Third World economies, grew faster. Like Chinese and Filipinos, Indians who leave home prosper in nations such as the
United States that do not frustrate initiative and hard work. The
average Indian emigrant to the United States has a higher income
than an average American. But in India the remarkable industry of
individual Indians is wasted in an economy stifled by excessive
government regulation and protectionism.

Yet to its great credit and despite incredible odds, India still has
one of the Third World's few working democracies. In 1947, when
India received its independence, it had a population of over 400
million: 250 million Hindus, 90 million Muslims, 6 million Sikhs,
and millions of Buddhists and Christians; 500 independent princes
and maharajahs; 23 main languages with 200 dialects; and 3,000
castes with 60 million "untouchables" at the bottom of the heap.
Whatever differences we may have with Jawaharlal Nehru and his
successors, governing such a country with a democracy, except
for a brief period of martial law under Mrs. Gandhi, is one of the
most remarkable political achievements of the twentieth century.
One is reminded of Dr. Johnson's famous comment on a woman

preaching, "It is like a dog walking on its hind legs. It is not done well, but you are surprised that it is done at all." Those who believe India is not governed well should remember how miraculous it is that it is governed at all.

Pakistan has also suffered from political and economic strife throughout its thirty years of independence. Since 1977 it has been led by President Zia ul-Haq, an enlightened military leader who has provided the political stability essential for economic growth. But he recognizes his people's democratic aspirations and has implemented a process of gradual democratization that, if not frustrated by political violence or Soviet pressure from Afghanistan, will lead to another round of free elections in 1990.

Traditionally Pakistan has been an ally of the United States, while India's foreign policy has tilted toward the Soviet Union. Pakistan today holds the front line against Soviet expansion into South Asia. It supports the Afghan freedom fighters and plays host to over three million refugees. These courageous policies have been deadly dangerous. In retribution Soviet aircraft attacked Pakistan over 600 times in 1986 alone, and the number of attacks increased in 1987. Soviet agents are attempting to destabilize Pakistan with terrorist bombings and by fueling ethnic strife.

That a democratic nation such as India can have a pro-communist foreign policy is one of the geopolitical paradoxes of this century. It is the only major noncommunist country that has not condemned the Soviet invasion of Afghanistan and is one of the few nations to have full diplomatic relations with Kabul. It is the only noncommunist country to have an embassy in Phnom Penh. It has extensive military and economic relations with the Soviet Union. The Soviets deal directly with almost all levels of the Indian public and private economy and even contribute to Indian politicians. In 1985 India supported the United States at the UN 8.9 percent of the time—less than communist Mongolia.

It is hard to understand why India fears Pakistan as an aggressor. India has a population of 800 million; Pakistan has a little over 100 million. India has twice as many combat aircraft as Pakistan and the fourth largest conventional army in the world; Pakistan has the thirteenth. India is concerned about American military assistance to its foe, yet during the past three years the Soviets have supplied

India with twice as many weapons as Pakistan has received from us. India detonated a nuclear device in 1974 and is now vociferously objecting to the Pakistani nuclear program. President Zia has repeatedly proposed signing a nonproliferation treaty; India has refused to do so.

The greatest external threat to South Asia is Soviet expansionism. The Pakistanis know this, and some Indian officials, businessmen, and correspondents have begun to express concern that India's policy of looking to the West but leaning to the north may prove fatal. The Indians can sleep with the bear only so much longer without being mauled.

The greatest internal threat to these two countries is economic stagnation that could undermine their political stability. Poverty feeds the ethnic discord that weakens the Indian nation. Poverty can frustrate Pakistan's transition to democracy. For two of the poorest nations in the world to be spending $8 billion a year for arms to be used against each other is obscene. The time is long past for strong statesmen in both countries to declare peace with each other and declare war on the poverty that plagues both their countries.

The Arab–Israeli conflict is another example of a forty-year war that wastes enormous resources desperately needed for economic development. The conflict would exist even if the Soviet Union played no role in the Mideast, but Kremlin leaders have exploited it at the expense of our interests in the region. At the same time, the Middle East is a part of the Third World in which active U.S. involvement has been indispensable to advancing the cause of stability and peace.

None of the countries directly involved in the Arab–Israeli conflict has achieved a high standard of living for its people, and many are saddled with the twin crises of massive indebtedness and huge population growth. Yet since the partition of Palestine after World War II, the Israelis and the Arabs have fought five full-scale wars —in 1948, 1956, 1967, 1973, and 1982—and have been engaged in endless skirmishes and military incidents. Most countries in the world measure their military expenditures in terms of percentage of GNP; in the Arab–Israeli wars, military spending of the countries involved could be measured in terms of multiples of their GNPs.

The United States can and should play a constructive role in helping to resolve the conflict in the Mideast. As Henry Kissinger has said, the Soviet Union can help the nations of the Mideast to wage war, while the United States is the only nation that can help them make peace. We have achieved a great deal in the last forty years in the region. Since 1948, we have guaranteed the survival of the state of Israel. We have also been the only force consistently pressing for a just resolution of the conflict. One of the greatest American diplomatic achievements of the postwar period was President Carter's negotiation of the Camp David Accords that established peace between Israel and Egypt in 1978. But we must not rest on our record. If we fail to promote the cause of peace, we will encourage those who want to advance their causes through war.

In the 1973 war, I ordered the massive airlift of equipment and materiel that enabled Israel to stop the two-front advance of Syria and Egypt. In her memoirs, Golda Meir, Israel's Prime Minister during the Yom Kippur War, wrote, "The airlift was invaluable. It not only lifted our spirits, but also served to make America's position clear to the Soviet Union, and it undoubtedly served to make our victory possible." Our commitment to the survival of Israel runs deep. We are not formal allies, but we are bound together by something much stronger than any piece of paper: a moral commitment. It is a commitment which no President in the past has ever broken and which every future President will faithfully honor. America will never allow the sworn enemies of Israel to achieve their goal of destroying it.

There are strong reasons, other than the moral one, for the United States's support of Israel. It is the only democracy in the Mideast. It is the only nation whose population challenges Japan's as the world's best educated. With virtually no natural resources it has built an industrial economy that competes successfully in the world economy. Its armed forces are among the best in the world. Israel has impressed the world with all it has accomplished during forty years of war. It will astonish the world with what it can accomplish in forty years of peace.

But our interests and Israel's require more than our unquestioning political support. America needs to renew the active diplomatic role played in the Carter administration. Some observers disagree with this view. They argue that if the United States simply continues its foreign aid to Israel and gives unswerving support to Israel's refusal to negotiate on the question of the West Bank and the Golan Heights, Israeli security will be ensured for the indefinite future.

Their view is misguided for two reasons. First, we cannot afford the present distortion of our foreign-aid budget. Three billion people in the Third World are eligible for U.S. foreign aid. Israel, a country with a population of only two million, receives over one quarter of the entire budget. Our aid to Israel and Egypt totals over half our foreign aid. That policy cannot continue. There are many countries in which the United States has a major strategic stake and which desperately need our aid. We cannot help the Philippines or the struggling democracies of Central America build for peace if we are too strapped from subsidizing war in the Mideast.

Second, a policy of complacency puts American and Israeli interests at risk. Many Israelis are content with a diplomatic stalemate. While it might serve their interests in the short run, it will lead to disaster in the long run. Israel has won the last five wars and will win the next one. But with each round of violence it loses more men, and the prospect of a stable peace recedes still further. Moreover, just as the Koreans and the Vietnamese learned to fight, so will the Arabs. Israel's interests lie in negotiating peace now, when it is stronger than its adversaries, rather than waiting until their growing strength forces Israel to do so. Despite our friendship, Israel cannot survive forever as an island in a sea of hatred.

A continued stalemate also undermines moderate Arab governments that are willing to negotiate with Israel. Many supporters of Israel believe that the peace process should stop now that Egypt has opted out of the conflict. In their view, the United States should conclude a strategic alliance with Israel and keep all other

Arab states at arm's length. That serves the interests of neither the United States nor Israel.

We should ask ourselves some fundamental questions. How long can the moderate governments of Jordan and of Egypt, which was once described by Napoleon as the most important country in the world, survive against the twin threats of radicalism and fundamentalism in the absence of progress in the peace process? How long will these governments be willing to pursue their present pro-Western policies if pressure from pro-Israeli groups prevents the United States from using its leverage to advance the peace process and even from selling arms to a deserving state like Jordan? Israel must accept that its own interests require the United States to establish close ties with the moderate Arab states—and that those states will remain stable partners in peace only if the diplomatic process advances toward a wider peace instead of miring down in a stalemate.

Time has never been on the side of peace in the Middle East. An Arab–Israeli war has broken out every decade in the postwar period because a political stalemate was permitted to form in peacetime. The United States should therefore adopt a more realistic policy in the Middle East. It should seek good relations with moderate Arab states, particularly Jordan, Eygpt, and Saudi Arabia. It should also actively press forward with the peace process. Sending the Secretary of State on semiannual tours to consult with the leaders of the region will never succeed in advancing productive negotiations. Just as Kissinger did in his shuttle diplomacy in 1973–74 and President Carter did at Camp David in 1978, America must use its leverage to bring the parties together and to create incentives for settlement.

The next step in the peace process must focus on the future of the West Bank and the riot-torn Gaza Strip. An observation made by David Ben-Gurion should guide our policy. He said that the "extremists," who advocated the absorption of Arab lands, would deprive Israel of its mission: "If they succeed, Israel will be neither Jewish nor democratic. The Arabs will outnumber us, and undemocratic, repressive measures will be needed to keep them under control." Israel's interests require a peace settlement for the land occupied in 1967. If Israel annexes these lands, it will become a binational garrison state, with disenfranchised Arabs composing about half its population. Moreover, given the high birth rates of the Palestinian people, Jewish people will soon be a minority in the Jewish state. If it continues its military occupation and gradual colonization of these territories, it will eventually bring about a united Arab world hostile to Israel, with greater opportunities for Moscow to enter the region than ever before.

President Eisenhower kept the Soviet Union out of the Mideast in 1956 and 1958. I did so in 1973. But now that the United States no longer has nuclear superiority it will be virtually impossible to keep the Soviets out if there is another Mideast war.

It is time for honest, open debate on the future of the peace process. All sides must cool their rhetoric. Those who deviate from the hard line of some of Israel's more extreme supporters should not automatically be labeled anti-Israel. That happened to me and other friends of Israel when we supported the Reagan administration's sale of AWACS planes to Saudi Arabia in 1981 and its plan to provide fighter aircraft to Jordan in 1986. Everyone must understand that being a friend of Israel's neighbors does not make one an enemy of Israel. American and Israeli interests require that the United States have friendly relations with the moderate Arab states. Improving those relations will be impossible if America fails to use its leverage and influence to press forward with the peace process.

Independence was always proclaimed as the first step toward healthier and more secure Third World societies. But the sad historical fact is that independence did not guarantee prosperity. Most of Latin America fell into an abyss following its independence more than 150 years ago. Most of Africa was dragged into a black hole of negative growth since its independence in the last two generations.

The hearts of the West go out to Africa. So does its money. In 1985 and 1986 tens of thousands of generous Americans and Europeans reached into their pockets for famine relief for Ethiopia. They were pouring food into a political sinkhole, not into hungry mouths. Western governments have been doing the same for decades. Between 1965 and 1984 the United States and other industrial countries provided over $200 billion in aid and investment for Africa. But the people still starve, and Africa's gross domestic product in 1983 was 4 percent lower than thirteen years before. The stark fact is that despite aid, despite all the kind thoughts and good intentions the world has to offer, the average African is poorer than he was in 1960.

The reason is terrible governments. Most of them practice some form of socialism. Most are corrupt. Most are dictatorships. In communist Ethiopia, Mozambique, and Angola, human misery is caused by coldly calculated national policy. But except for countries such as Egypt, Morocco, and Tunisia in North Africa and a few sub-Saharan nations such as Botswana, Senegal, Cameroon, Malawi, Mauritius, the Ivory Coast, and Kenya, Africa has abysmal leadership. Africa's lesson for the twenty-first century is that all the foreign aid on earth will not improve the lives of the people of the Third World if it is spent by governments that have bad policies.

The examples are discouraging and virtually endless.

Ethiopia levies an import fee on famine aid which at its peak raised more money for its Soviet-backed Stalinist government than the export of its top commodity, coffee. While thousands of tons of food rotted on the docks and hundreds of thousands of people starved in the desert, Ethiopia spent $100 million on a lavish celebration of the tenth anniversary of its communist revolution. Of the one million killed by famine in 1984–85, three quarters died as a result of President Mengistu's policy of forced farm collectivization.

President Mobutu of Zaire is so rich that he could use his personal fortune of $5 billion to erase his country's staggering national debt and still have $500 million to live on. Meanwhile real wages have fallen since 1960, and half of the children born in his country die before reaching age five. The Mobutu Suspension Bridge, the longest in Africa, opened in 1984 with one deck for cars and one for trains. There is no railroad anywhere nearby, and during its first six months of operation an average of fifty-three cars a day passed over.

In the Sudan, a multimillion-dollar sugar plant was built on a swamp and sank, while a twenty-year-old milk-bottling plant has never been used to bottle milk because there was no means to refrigerate the milk and ship it to market.

Because of price controls in Zambia farmers pay over a dollar for fertilizer for every dollar's worth of food they grow, thus making it more profitable to grow no food.

Between 1979, when it opened, and 1984 Togo's $42 million steel mill operated at 22 percent efficiency in part because Togo did not have enough of the materials it needed to make steel.

Liberia, which is a special responsibility of the United States, is an economic and political disaster area.

I visited Ghana in 1957 and saw the British turn the colony over to its new American-educated President, Kwame Nkrumah. This was the first time I had the privilege of meeting Dr. Martin Luther King. We spent over an hour together talking about our hope that this first black colony to receive its independence would be an example for the rest of postcolonial Africa. We were both optimistic, because Ghana was one of the richest countries in the Third World, with twice the per-capita income of Korea. When it celebrated the thirtieth anniversary of its independence last year Ghana was an utter shambles, a bleak landscape of unfinished monuments to Nkrumah's ego and factories that operate at a fifth of their capacity.

Africa proves that a government does not have to be communist to enact economic policies that stymie foreign investment, penalize personal initiative and savings, and build bloated, parasitic economic-planning bureaucracies. Its governments are notoriously unstable. Between 1957, when Ghana became the first European colony to be granted independence, and 1985 Africa had seventy-two coups, thirteen assassinations of heads of state, and dozens of wars. Civil wars and genocide in Nigeria, Rwanda, Burundi, and Uganda have killed over three million people.

The picture is not unremittingly bleak. When President Felix Houphouet-Boigny of the Ivory Coast took power in the former French colony in 1960, he did not expel the Europeans as many other Africa leaders did. He permitted French investments and technicians to remain and allowed profits to flow back to France. Today there are 35,000 French nationals in his country, three times as many as before independence. This cuts against the grain of the policy adopted by black Africa as a whole, which considers European influences to be a barrier to progress and an affront to their national pride. Black Africa as a whole has a per-capita income of only $216; the Ivory Coast's is $1,000.

Four years ago Togo's struggling steel plant was leased to an American entrepreneur. Before 1984 its 380 workers had never made more than 4,000 tons of steel in a year. Last year, 150 employees made 9,000 tons. Other governments are also making halting steps toward privatization, a small but encouraging sign that the rest of Africa is learning Houphouet-Boigny's lesson: that a nation can have pride and progress at the same time.

But a human being cannot have pride without some political freedom, and politically Africa is still in the Dark Ages. Forty out of forty-four sub-Saharan countries, containing 85 percent of the population of black Africa, have unelected governments not accountable to their people in any way: Angola, Benin, Burkina Faso, Burundi, Cameroon, Cape Verde, the Central African Republic, Chad, Comoros, Congo, Djibouti, Equatorial Guinea, Ethiopia, Gabon, Ghana, Guinea, Guinea-Bissau, the Ivory Coast, Kenya, Lesotho, Liberia, Madagascar, Malawi, Mali, Mauritania, Mozambique, Niger, Nigeria, Rwanda, São Tomé and Principe, Seychelles, Sierra Leone, Somalia, Sudan, Swaziland, Tanzania, Togo, Uganda, Zaire, and Zambia. In Zimbabwe the democracy established at the end of white-minority rule in 1979 is on the ropes. Prime Minister Robert Mugabe has called for a one-party state and is cracking down on the two main opposition parties.

Another country with no democracy for its black citizens is South Africa. These oppressed blacks make up 5.5 percent of the population of Africa's 412 million oppressed blacks, but they command the lion's share of the attention of Western officials and journalists. South Africa's blacks want political equality, and we want them to have it. But being for it is one thing, while doing something effective about it is another. Demagoguery does not produce democracy.

Many Americans who are indifferent toward misery in the communist world and the rest of Africa become apoplectic over racial injustice in South Africa. One reason is that the cause of the dilemma is so easy to understand. As two Western analysts recently put it, "People in the West . . . have used South Africa as a ventilation valve for their own moral and political frustrations, finding in it a convenient surrogate or an easy analogy for issues at home whose complexity has rendered them intractable." Satisfying though their outrage may be to many Western leaders and intellectuals, it is no substitute for policy. Blood should not have to run in the streets of South Africa so that American college students and professors and newspaper editors can feel morally vindicated.

Our policy should be to encourage vigorously a transition to power-sharing that does not disrupt the South African economy, which has enabled South African blacks to enjoy a much better life than African blacks in general. South Africa has the continent's largest black middle class. It has more professional black women than the rest of the continent put together. More blacks own cars in South Africa than Russians own cars in the Soviet Union. If we encourage a violent solution in South Africa and the country descends into bloodshed and economic chaos and ruin, both blacks and whites will be the losers, and the Soviet Union will be the only winner.

The Soviets have invested heavily in the African National Congress, and they have not done so because they are good democrats. Last year a young ANC member told a prominent U.S. television journalist that he had been taken to a training camp in the Soviet Union and taught techniques of guerrilla warfare, sabotage, disinformation, and terrorism, all to be used against South African whites. He was asked what he would owe the Soviets if he and his fellow revolutionaries ever came to power. "Gratitude," he said with a smile. "Only gratitude." But the Soviets are not in the market for gratitude. They are in the market for South Africa. The richest country on the continent in natural resources and economic development and the most important in strategic location, it is one of the most tantalizing prizes in the Third World. Moscow covets both the treasure trove of minerals, many of which the U.S. relies upon for its defense industry, and also the shipping routes around the Cape of Good Hope, through which 90 percent of Western Europe's oil passes.

If the ANC revolutionaries succeed, African blacks will simply trade their white African rulers for white Russians. If the United States can assist in the evolution of South Africa into a pluralistic, economically prosperous nation, it will serve as an inspiring role model for other struggling African nations. If the ANC and its Soviet sponsors succeed in South Africa, it will provide just another model for totalitarian dictators.

A race war against South Africa is not the way to end racism in South Africa. It *is* the way to end the lives of millions of people, the prosperity of both blacks and whites, and also the country's orientation toward the West. A race war is precisely what will happen if the West continues to assault the South African economy through counterproductive economic sanctions and the ANC continues to gain in its campaign for influence inside South Africa and legitimacy outside it.

After a year and a half of U.S. trade sanctions and forced divestment by U.S. firms, their failure is glaringly apparent. As a result of these measures South African blacks have no more political freedom than they did before. All that has changed is that their economic position is weaker. Now that we have turned to punitive measures our diplomatic leverage over Pretoria is vastly diminished, and the government has cracked down hard on dissent. The eighty American corporations forced to pull out of South Africa can no longer enforce the fair-employment practices that had made life significantly better for blacks. Thousands of jobs are threatened, and some moderate black leaders, realizing that sanctions hurt black workers far more than Apartheid, are questioning the policy they once championed.

The ANC encourages economic sanctions and other policies they hope will bring about mass unemployment among blacks and thus increase their "revolutionary consciousness." So far, fortunately, the U.S. Congress's sanctions have not had that effect. When Congress reviews these measures, it can decide either to toughen them—and thus make the ANC's policy America's policy —or abandon them and adopt a new strategy of prodding Pretoria down the road to reform through a combination of relentless diplomatic pressure and positive economic incentives. Since it will not provide instant democracy for blacks a gradual policy may not suit liberal American intellectuals, but it will serve the best interests of the people of South Africa, black as well as white.

Those who contend that the reason for bad government in Africa is that most of its people are black miss the mark. Except for Ethiopia and Liberia none of the forty-two governments in black Africa was in existence thirty-one years ago. Fifteen of the twenty countries in Latin America had independence for over 120 years before they became democracies.

In 1815, even as he was helping bring about this new era of Latin American independence, Simón Bolívar asked, "Is it conceivable that a people recently freed from its chains can ascend into the sphere of liberty without falling into the abyss?"

If he were here today, he would be depressed as he read about the chaos in Haiti, the communist dictatorships in Cuba and Nicaragua, the authoritarian regimes in Chile and Paraguay, and the economic crisis in Mexico. But Bolívar, one of the Western Hemisphere's most farsighted statesmen, would look beyond these immediate problems and point out that Latin America is still in a promising historical position. It has great problems, but unlike some other parts of the world Latin America has the human and natural resources to solve its problems and to move into an era of unprecedented progress with freedom in the twenty-first century.

When I returned from my riot-marred trip to South America in 1958, I said that the only time that Latin America made the front pages in the United States was when there was a revolution or a riot at a soccer match. My comment was only partly facetious. We pay far more attention to what happens on the other side of the world than to our next-door neighbors in the Americas. Our attention now is justifiably focused on preventing the spread of communism in Central America, but we should also develop policies to encourage economic growth and political stability throughout all of Latin America before other countries become vulnerable to communist subversion. If the giant political forest of South America ever catches fire, any success we may have in extinguishing the brushfire in our Central American backyard will appear empty indeed.

Latin America's greatest promise, and one of its biggest problems, is its huge population. At the beginning of World War II it had 130 million people, about the same as the United States. Today, 300 million live in Latin America and 230 million in the United States. By the middle of the next century, Latin America will have three times as many people as North America. By 1999 the two most populous cities in the world will be Mexico City and São Paulo, Brazil. During this century it has been customary for people in Latin America to refer to the United States as the giant of the North. In the next century we will be referring to Latin America, and two great nations in particular, as the giants of the South.

Brazil and Mexico illustrate the challenges facing Latin America and also its virtually unlimited potential.

Brazil today has been compared to the United States at the end of the last century. It is a vast, largely unexplored land with a multiracial and -ethnic population of 135 million. It is the fifth-largest country in the world, with the sixth-largest population and the eighth-largest economy. Unfortunately, economic growth has far outpaced political and social development. Brazil has some of the Third World's most magnificent cities surrounded by some of the most notorious slums; a friend once described Rio de Janeiro to me as a beautiful lady with dirty underclothes. Brazil also has the unenviable distinction as being the Third World's largest debtor nation.

If Brazil's current economic crisis can be resolved, its democracy will be strengthened and a brilliant future will be assured. The solutions are free trade, more private enterprise, and a reasonable compromise on the debt issue.

Brazil's economic planners should open their markets and integrate their country further into a world economy where they already compete strongly. But we cannot expect them to do so if we maintain our restrictions on Brazilian imports. The giant of the North and this giant of the South, military allies in World War II, must now become economic allies through reciprocal trade policies that will serve the interests of both countries.

So that Brazil can compete more vigorously in the world economy, the government, which controls almost two thirds of the nation's industry, should reduce its role in the domestic economy by embracing the privatization movement. Brazilians are born entrepreneurs. In 1986 a million people left salaried jobs to create over 200,000 new businesses. The government should leave economic growth to the people and concentrate instead on improving social conditions. Half of all Brazilians are under twenty years old, and half of these get no education. Millions still live in poverty.

The Brazilian debt problem is as much political as economic. The government must not succumb to the populist urge to repudiate its debts or to increase anti–free-market policies. On the other hand, the lending governments and bankers must not dictate such unreasonable terms to Brazil and other debtors that their governments will feel impelled to consider repudiation. This tragic development would undermine stability in the lending nations and the Third World alike.

Today Brazil is going through one of the greatest political and economic crises in recent history. There is a hard road ahead, but also great rewards. Its leaders and people are learning one of freedom's harshest lessons: A system which places no artificial ceiling on success sometimes provides no floor for failure.

I am confident that Brazil will overcome its difficulties, because I have great respect for the political skill of its leadership. Our ambassador to the United Nations, General Vernon A. Walters, probably knows Brazil better than any other American. I vividly remember his telling me thirty years ago, after a communist-led mob attacked our motorcade in Caracas, Venezuela, that the Brazilians' Portuguese background gave them a different outlook from that of their neighbors, whose heritage is predominantly Spanish. "You see the difference when you go to a bullfight," he said. "The Spanish kill the bull. The Portuguese only tease it." With equally subtle, discerning leadership that avoids violence and guarantees security without destroying liberty, Brazil will inevitably be an economic superpower in the twenty-first century.

Long before the conflicts in El Salvador and Nicaragua erupted like a Central American volcano, Charles de Gaulle observed, "Central America is but an incident on the road to Mexico." Our immediate neighbor to the south, with a population of 80 million, is one of the Third World's largest countries. Because of its great human and natural resources, its potential is huge. Its problems are equally as great.

Over ten million American citizens are of Mexican descent, and probably as many Mexicans live here illegally. Our history also overlaps, sometimes in painful ways. Many Mexicans who know that history have not forgiven us. The Mexican–American War in the nineteenth century and the exploitation of Mexico's resources by some American corporations in the early twentieth century were glaring examples of indefensible American imperialism. But it is time for responsible leaders in both countries to recognize that we cannot continue to visit the sins of Latin America's past on its future.

Mexico and the United States have a stake in a cooperative, friendly relationship that would serve the interests of both countries. Above all, Americans must learn to treat Mexicans with the respect that they deserve. When I visited the University of Mexico in 1955, I asked its director, Nabor Carillo Flores, about his academic background. He said that he had a bachelor's degree from the University of Mexico and that for his doctorate he had gone to a younger institution—Harvard! It was a quiet but effective reminder that the United States, in the Mexican's eye, was the new kid on the block. We may not agree with Mexico's neutralist foreign policy nor with its one-party politics, but we should respect its right to chart its own independent course, provided the course is not antagonistic to our interests.

The severe economic crisis in Mexico today obscures the fact that its growth rate of 6 percent a year from 1945 to 1970 was one of the best in the Third World. The oil that was discovered in the 1970s proved to be a blessing and a curse. Mexico's leadership saw the oil boom as the opportunity to borrow and spend profligately; it missed the opportunity to wisely use oil profits to diversify and develop a private-sector economy. Instead, Mexico became overly dependent on oil. By borrowing against anticipated oil revenues, it increased its international debt from $4 billion to over a $100 billion in just over a decade. When the bottom fell out of oil prices, Mexico was left with one of the largest debts in the Third World and an economy paralyzed by bureaucracy. The government today controls over two thirds of the economy, and government spending is 53 percent of GNP with the usual fallouts of inflation, inefficiency, and corruption. Without further reductions in its harsh import controls and further stimulus for its private secter, Mexico will continue to founder.

Mexico's next President, Carlos Salinas de Gortiari, could provide the kind of leadership Mexico needs in its hour of crisis. He is a topflight economist who thinks and acts pragmatically. If he is to lead the nation rather than merely preside over it and steal from it as have many of his predecessors, he must decide whether Mexico will have a state-dominated economy or a diversified free-enterprise economy.

A leader can be only as great as the problems he must overcome. Salinas de Gortiari could go down as Mexico's greatest President if he breaks Mexico's shackles to the past so that it can reach for the rewards the future holds in store.

After my trip to South America in 1958, I had a fascinating conversation with Luis Muñoz Marín, the gifted governor of Puerto Rico. He expressed his deep regret about the violent demonstrations during several of my stops. He said, "I am very proud of my Latin heritage. We Latins are devoted to our families. We have demonstrated great talents in music, literature, and the arts. We are deeply religious. But I must admit we have never been very good at government." He went on to say that Latin American nations either had too much government or had too little—either dictatorship or chaos. He concluded, "Too often we simply have not been able to maintain that all-important balance between order and freedom."

Although most of Latin America gained independence from Spain and Portugal 150 years ago, the spread of democratic government is a far more recent development. Just ten years ago, only a few had democratic governments: Colombia, Costa Rica, the Dominican Republic, Jamaica, Suriname, and Venezuela. Since then ten more—Argentina, Bolivia, Brazil, Ecuador, El Salvador, Grenada, Guatemala, Honduras, Peru, and Uruguay—have joined their ranks.

While this is reason for great hope, we cannot ignore the dark historical background against which these events are shedding welcome new light. With few exceptions Latin America has suffered four centuries of authoritarianism and chaos. In this century alone there have been over 190 coups and interventions in Latin America and the Caribbean. Over 140 million of the people live in poverty, barely able to feed and house themselves.

Latin America's new democracies have found it difficult to produce greater prosperity or responsible economic policies. The region's total external debt is $400 billion. Inflation in Brazil, Argentina, and Peru is over 100 percent. While many Latin Americans are disenchanted by some of their elected leaders, they do not yet reject their newfound democracy. But if moderate elected leaders do not produce a way out of poverty, voters may choose radical, antidemocratic leaders who promise to do so.

It is fashionable, particularly in intellectual circles, to blame Latin America's poverty on the United States. Some claim that the United States keeps Latin America poor by importing cheap Latin American raw materials and exporting more expensive manufactured goods. These "dependency theorists" blame external factors for Latin America's plight and overlook the internal historical and cultural roots of the problem. The Catholic liberation theologists append to this condescending theory a typically flawed Marxist class analysis of society. These mutually reinforcing myths could create a self-fulfilling prophecy. In suggesting that Latin Americans are too weak to control their own fate and too passive to solve their own problems they perpetuate the directionlessness and stagnation in which the lethal bacillus of communism thrives.

Those who blame the United States for Latin America's problems should consider what happens when a nation turns to communism instead. For years, Castro's Cuba was hailed as a viable alternative development model for Latin America. That farce is now completely exposed. During most of Castro's dictatorship, the Cuban GNP has actually declined. If the trend continues, the Cuban model of development will land Cuba among the poorest and most backward nations in Latin America by 1999.

Latin America's poverty is not caused by dependency on the United States, and it will not be solved by communist revolution. It will have sustained economic growth that benefits all of society only by abandoning the legacy of government economic control. Statist economies and their ugly progeny—mismanagement, bureaucracy, and corruption—are stultifying the energies of the people. Nationalized industry, state subsidies, and price and import controls have created inflation, deficits, and uncompetitive, inefficient businesses that squander the region's resources and its future.

There are signs that Latin America is finally responding to the intolerable conditions bred by economic authoritarianism. The cry for economic liberty and reform is loudest from Peru, an exceptionally poor nation trying to preserve its young democracy while grappling with a deadening government bureaucracy and fighting "The Shining Path," the most brutal communist terrorists in the hemisphere. From the midst of this highly uncertain environment sounds the clarion voice of economist Hernando de Soto, whose book *The Other Path* is a pivotal study of the extraordinary entrepreneurial dynamism of Peru's underground economy. It shows that government has been frustrating the energies of the people instead of liberating them, which it could do by protecting legal property rights and eliminating the tyranny of bureaucracy. De Soto reminds us of the link between political and economic freedom. One reinforces the other. Whenever possible we must support Latin American solutions to Latin American problems, which is why *The Other Path* should be required reading for all American policy-makers dealing with the region and the Third World in general.

To prosper, Latin America needs more trade. The Soviets have recognized the potential for Latin American trade, and this has been a major topic of discussion in their recent diplomatic forays into the region. For political as well as diplomatic reasons Latin America would find it much more preferable to trade with us than with the Soviets. If we seize this opportunity by opening our markets to Latin goods while encouraging them to open theirs to ours, we stand a chance of seeing the Western Hemisphere develop into one of the most booming free-trade zones in history.

No American administration since the end of World War II, including my own, has had an adequate Latin American policy. The next President must end this pattern of neglect. In doing so he should avoid continuing to smother Latin America with slogans. Our "Alliance for Progress" and "Good Neighbor Policy" brought little progress and left too much of the neighborhood on the wrong side of the tracks. We can best aid Latin America by implementing and expanding to South America the Kissinger Commission's recommendations for economic aid to Central America. Our goal should be to encourage the development of free-market economies.

The United States must continue to demonstrate that we want democracy and economic prosperity for all of Latin America. If it can harness the energies of its peoples and resources, the region will unquestionably be a free world economic giant in the next century.

The only constant in the Third World is change. We do not have to accept Engels' philosophy to recognize the profound appeal of his words "It is necessary to change the world." Change will and should come in the problem-plagued Third World. The only question is whether it will come by peaceful means or violence, whether it destroys or builds, whether it leaves dictatorship or freedom in its wake.

Two kinds of revolutionary change are threatening the Third World today. The first is communist revolution. Even though the twentieth century has left no doubt about the brutality and failure of communism, there are still those who carry on a romance with violent revolution. They encourage the destructive fires of communism by traveling to Nicaragua to pick coffee for the Sandinistas, supporting the terrorism of the communist-dominated African National Congress, and referring to the ruthless New People's Army of the Philippines as "Nice People Around." From their comfortable distances they rarely get their own fingers burned, or lose their homes, or see their families taken away in the middle of the night. Ignorant of history and self-deluding about current events, they are strangely silent when the charred remains of revolutions become apparent.

In the 1930s they were fans of Stalin, until he turned the Soviet Union into a slaughterhouse. In the 1950s and 1960s their hero was Mao, the "agrarian reformer" who unleashed an ideological firestorm in which tens of millions of Chinese perished. Before communism engulfed Indochina in 1975, they triumphantly celebrated the virtues of the Vietcong and the Khmer Rouge. When the new regimes in Vietnam and Cambodia laid waste to their people and countries, they were momentarily tongue-tied—until there were new communist revolutionaries to talk about in Nicaragua and El Salvador. Children should not play with fire, and these naive proponents of communist revolution are ideological children who are using the Third World as their playground.

The communist idea which had so much appeal in the Third World as little as fifteen years ago has been discredited by communism in action. It has failed to produce prosperity and peace in every Third World country where it is practiced. In Asia, the dead economies of the communist prison states stagnate next to the robust economies of the rimland states. In Latin America, where debt and growth are so completely intertwined, Cuba and Nicaragua have the highest per-capita debts and the lowest overall growth rates. In Africa, where plummeting living standards are the norm, the communist states of Mozambique and Ethiopia rank as the poorest and most destitute.

In the Moslem world from Morocco to Indonesia, Islamic fundamentalism has replaced communism as the principal instrument of violent change. As we discuss this recent phenomenon it is vitally important that we not allow the extremes of Moslem fundamentalism to blind us to the greatness of the Moslem heritage. The same religion that produced Qaddafi and Khomeini produced Avicenna and Averroës, two of the greatest philosophers in history. But the revolutionary vision offered by radicals on the fringes of the Moslem world is just as enticing as communism, and just as destructive. The communist revolution appeals to man's material needs. The Moslem revolution appeals to his spiritual needs. Communist ideology promises rapid modernization. Islamic revolutionary ideology is a reaction against modernization. Communism promises to turn the clock of history forward. Moslem fundamentalism turns it back.

Islamic revolutionaries denounce the atheism of the communist East and the materialistic secularism of the capitalist West. The Iranian demonstrators who stampeded four hundred pilgrims to death in Mecca in August 1987 were chanting "Death to the Soviet Union" as well as "Death to America." They threaten Western interests in the Persian Gulf and elsewhere and also the stability of the Soviet Union, whose population includes 55 million restive, spiritually oppressed Moslems.

Communist and Islamic revolutionaries are ideological enemies who share a common goal: the desire to attain power by whatever means necessary in order to establish dictatorial control based on their intolerant ideals. Neither revolution would bring a better life to people in the Third World. Instead they would make things worse. But one or the other will prevail unless the West develops a unified policy for addressing both the economic and the spiritual dimensions of the struggle now under way in the Third World.

The winds of change in the Third World are reaching tornado force. We cannot stop them, but we can help to change their direction. When people need and want change it is not enough to be against revolutionary change that would make things worse. The only answer to a bad idea is a better idea. Moslem fundamentalism is a faith. Communism is also a faith. As Whittaker Chambers observed in *Witness* thirty years ago, "The success of communism is never greater than the failure of all other faiths."

In many parts of the Third World and particularly in the Moslem world, prosperity alone is not enough. Iran is an example. The myth of the Iranian Revolution is that it was caused by the Shah's corruption, police repression, and the poverty of the masses. This is simply wrong. During the Shah's reign Iran was better off than any other country in the region except Israel. Its people were by far the best educated. I recall the Shah telling me in 1979, when I saw him in Mexico shortly before he went to Egypt to die, that he had sent tens of thousands of students to colleges in the United

States only to have them return and join the revolution against him. He liberated the women; many joined the revolution that put them back into the *chador*.

Khomeini's revolution was ostensibly against repression. It was actually against modern, Western values. As far as repression is concerned, he set the cause of women back a thousand years. He hated communism as much as he hated capitalism, seeing them as two sides of the same materialistic coin. Young people supported his revolution not because they wanted more freedom and better jobs, housing, and clothing, but because they wanted something to believe in more than materialism. Since the revolution the Iranian people have received exactly the treatment Khomeini promised. Whether it is exactly what they thought they would get is unknown, since the Ayatollah holds no free elections. But there is no denying that he offered a true revolution of ideas and that they embraced it with passion and conviction.

Western economic ideals produce growth and prosperity. Western political ideals produce liberty. The Third World yearns for both, but because the West has been better at sending money than at promoting its values the communists and now the Moslem fundamentalists rush to fill the void. In the years between now and 1999 the United States must lead the way in a campaign to seize the moral high ground from those who promise prosperity and fulfillment in the developing world and deliver poverty for the body and chains for the soul.

If the people of the Third World think we are interested only in winning the Cold War with the Soviet Union, we will lose the war for their hearts and minds. These people have tremendous problems. At least the communists talk about the problems. Too often we talk only about the communists.

We should launch a peaceful revolution for progress. To do so we need a coherent and consistent policy that addresses the security, economic, and political needs of the developing nations. We should understand that the Third World will not be a peaceful region of growth in the next century unless all three of these needs are met. Security without growth is an empty promise, growth without security is an imperiled promise, and growth and security without political development are an unfullfilled promise.

Security aid. While military aid to our friends and allies in the Third World is not the only answer to their problems, it is in some cases indispensable if they are to provide the security without which there can be no progress. Such aid should come with training assistance, not just in the use of these arms but in the proper conduct of the armed forces that receive them.

Economic aid. In 1986 we spent under $13 billion on foreign aid, approximately two tenths of one percent of our GNP. Considering that we spent over 6 percent of our GNP on national defense, we spent over thirty times as much money preparing for a war that we probably will never fight than for a war—the peaceful revolution for prosperity in the Third World—that we risk losing. Congress is now cutting the administration's foreign-aid requests. This is tragically shortsighted. But we do need some major changes in our foreign-aid programs. Too much of our aid has been poorly distributed. Too much aid has fed Third World bureaucracies, maintained the status quo, fueled corruption, and supported repression. Too much aid was spent on north-to-south wealth distribution and too little on wealth creation.

We should distribute our aid according to three principles:

1. There should be no aid without strings. All aid should have clearly defined and measurable goals.

2. Wherever possible, aid should be bilateral, not multilateral. There is a powerful political reason for this. Congress will not approve aid unless it clearly serves our interests. The World Bank's willingness to make discounted loans to communist governments does not serve our interests. Current commitments to multilateral agencies should be reviewed and tested for cost effectiveness and whether they are consistent with American foreign-policy interests.

3. We should insist on monitoring the economic performance of all governments we help. We should make sure that they are moving toward more private enterprise and that they are attracting capital rather than scaring it off. Aid should be used as seed money to promote the right conditions for building growth-oriented free-

market economies. Aid should encourage success, not guarantee failure; it should promote progress and not the status quo.

Trade. Even more than aid, the Third World needs trade. These nations stand a better chance of growing out of economic stagnation if we open our own markets to them. Instead, we are making a bad situation in the Third World far worse by continuing our self-serving agricultural subsidies.

A classic case is sugar. The U.S. government subsidizes our inefficient but politically powerful sugar growers by setting a price of twenty-two cents a pound. The world market price is ten cents less. Not only does this inflate the food bill of the average American family by $100 a year, but it has devastating effects on Third World sugar producers. Sugar production and refining have been many poor nations' key source of income and also frequently the first step in the evolution from an agricultural economy to an industrial one. Guatemala, Jamaica, the Dominican Republic, Colombia, Thailand and the Philippines depend for a large portion of their incomes on sugar exports. In 1985 alone, the Caribbean Basin countries lost $250 million in revenues because of our sugar barrier.

As a world military power we cannot act like a provincial power in the international economy. This is not an argument for altruism. It is an argument for the wisdom of farsighted self-interest and the idea that long-term growth for all is better than short-term expediency for a very few.

The debt crisis. The $850 billion in Third World debt is a hangover from the West's lending binge of the late 1970s. Like the Allied debt to the United States after World War I, it is a deadly drag on the world economy. Some say the debtors should not have borrowed the money. Others say the creditors should not have lent it. These arguments are no longer relevant. We are confronted with a condition, not a theory. There can be no substantial progress for the world economy unless debtor nations can attract investment and earn enough to afford to buy imports from the developed world. If the creditors insist on the austerity required to finance the debt in its entirety, responsible Third World leaders will be driven out of office and radical, irresponsible leaders pledged to repudiate the debt will take their places.

The December 1987 agreement between the United States and Mexico deals with only a small part of the Mexican debt, let alone the entire Third World debt problem. But it points the way to deal with the whole problem. Western governments and banks should share the burdens of refinancing debts on a basis within the capacity of Third World governments to pay. To reduce the burden makes sense for creditors as well as debtors. An agreement guaranteeing some repayment is better than insisting on everything and ending up with nothing.

Political growth. Throughout the Third World we see countries that have moved toward democracy once they have met their basic security and economic needs. We should not passively wait for this evolution to occur. Now is the time to support vigorously the cause of democracy in the Third World. To do so, we must first put aside two myths.

The first is that our relations with the Third World should be rigidly conditioned on the issue of human rights. However well intentioned, this approach is myopic and dangerous. The Mexican poet and commentator Octavio Paz has said, "Morality is no substitute for historical understanding." Evolution to complete political freedom is always slow and arduous. Not until seventy years ago did the United States allow half of its adult population, the women, to vote. Blacks were denied full voting rights until the passage of the Voting Rights Act of 1957. But we cannot help a government move toward democracy if we refuse to deal with it because its political human rights do not match our own. If an authoritarian government fails at economic growth, its people may turn to the siren song of the communists. If the nation becomes communist, the issue of human rights will be closed.

The second myth is that the Third World should take its political direction from the United Nations. While the record of the past three centuries attests to the economics of wealth creation, the UN has focused consistently, obstinately, and blindly on wealth redistribution. While the record of this century attests to the bloody abuses and abject failures of state socialism, the UN has been a propaganda mouthpiece for state socialism while regularly condemning democratic capitalism.

We should not force our political values on anyone, but we

should never hesitate to proclaim them. This means articulating the principles of civilian government, the rights and responsibilities of the individual, the limits of the state in a democracy, the rule of law, and the proper role of police as apolitical professionals.

This is a task not just for government but for private organizations as well. The AFL-CIO has a Free Trade Union Institute that helps develop trade unions throughout the world. By showing the role the trade union plays in a free society—in contrast to the role it plays under communism as a means of extending the oppressive iron fist of the state—the FTUI is preparing workers of the Third World for democratic government. The U.S. Chamber of Commerce has a Center for International Private Enterprise that promotes another essential sector of a democratic society: private business. Colleges and business schools should offer more scholarships to promising students from Third World countries so that they can learn about free enterprise.

In 1982, President Reagan founded the National Endowment for Democracy to help spread democracy throughout the world. It monitors elections and funds pro-West think tanks, civic organizations, business conferences, newspapers, women's groups, unions, and political parties in the democratic and nondemocratic world. It is in the straightforward business of promoting Western and American ideals as alternatives to systems abroad that do not work. It is not popular with many post-Vietnam politicians who are ashamed to promote our ideals. As a result the NED must battle Congress for the pitiful $15 million it receives each year. If we are serious about bringing prosperity, stability, and democracy to the Third World, we should increase that amount every year between now and 1999.

Democratic government is an art that requires vision. It is not accumulating buildings and airlines and dams to feed immature national pride. We should exemplify not the buildings of democracy but the building of it, by promoting the spirit of democratic government based on human dignity, the rule of law, and freedom for all. We should offer the Third World national security and economic prosperity, but ultimately we also must find ways to emphasize those essentially spiritual values of political life that have enabled us to create security and prosperity for ourselves.

Those who doubt our true role in the Third World should consider the words of its most eloquent leader, Singapore's Lee Kwan Yew. In 1985 he asked the U.S. Congress, "Does America wish to abandon the contest between democracy and the free market on the one hand versus communism and the controlled economy on the other, and this at the time when she has very nearly won this contest for the hearts and the minds of people in the Third World?''

10

A NEW
AMERICA

Like most great historical figures, Charles de Gaulle had the gift of prescience. Long before others, he saw the danger posed by the rise of Hitler, the awesome potential of motorized armed forces, and the possibility that France, defeated and humiliated in 1940, could recover and emerge from the war on the side of the victors. During his state visit to Washington in 1959, he turned his powers of insight to American politics. With the 1960 campaign only months away he told me, "I do not want to interfere in American politics, but my advice to a candidate for President would be to campaign for 'a new America.' " He was right. As Vice President, I could not take advantage of that advice, for it would appear I was repudiating President Eisenhower. But John Kennedy did run on that theme, and he won.

I would give that same advice to a candidate for President in 1988. Like Eisenhower, Ronald Reagan has been a very popular President. The American people have supported his leadership. They are glad America now stands tall abroad and has experienced a long period of growth and prosperity at home. They admire the way he has restored respect for America and the respectability of patriotism in America. But Americans are never satisfied with success. A candidate who tries to be a carbon copy of President Reagan and promises only to continue his policies will be left at the starting gate.

A call for a new America strikes a deep chord in the American temperament. Complacency is not an American characteristic. American history alternates between periods of quiet and periods of energetic change. But the quiet is always more apparent than real. A restless energy seethes beneath the surface. The status quo is at best a temporary rest stop on the road to greater endeavors— a pause to recharge our batteries before taking on new challenges. It is only a question of time before the other side of the cycle of American history bursts forth. For a great nation as well as a great man, true fulfillment comes not from savoring past achievements but only from embarking on new adventures.

With the beginning of the twenty-first century only twelve years away, there will be added appeal to call for a new America. A growing sense will develop that we need to gear up for new times, to prepare America for leadership in the next century. What we choose to do will profoundly affect what will become of the world. How we choose to lead and who is chosen to lead us are vitally important questions. What is at stake is nothing less than the future of civilization. Our actions will determine in large part whether the next century will be the best or the last one for mankind.

We have to ask ourselves what role the United States should play in the twenty-first century. Will the baton of world leadership pass to another nation after 1999? Is the United States—the oldest democracy in history—over the hill after two hundred years? To paraphrase Churchill, are we witnessing the beginning of the end or the end of the beginning of the great American experiment? All individuals go through the same experiences—birth, life, and death. Most individuals die when they no longer have a reason to live. Nations also experience birth and life. But for a nation, death is inevitable only when it ceases to have a reason to live. America has powerful reasons to live—for the sake of our posterity and for the sake of others.

To understand what is special about America, we should study our history. Without a shared vision of our past, we will find ourselves without a true vision of our future. As we celebrated the two-hundredth anniversary of our Constitution, some superficial observers propagated the myth that the American concept of government sprang almost by magic out of the minds of the remarkable men who assembled at Philadelphia. Even some of the Founders spoke of creating a "new order for the ages." But while the Constitution initiated a new order for the future, it was firmly grounded on old principles from the past. The ideas of English philosopher John Locke are reflected in both the Declaration of Independence and the Constitution. But as Paul Edward Gottfried has observed, "While Locke's teachings influenced both the American and French revolutions, other principles, Judeo-Christian, classical, even medieval, also contributed to the American government's founding and growth."

The Founders had the advantage of painting on a new canvas. But while they were not inhibited by the dead hand of the past, they borrowed liberally from the great thinkers of the past. Putting together those great old ideas, they produced a new idea, superior to any one or to the sum of the parts.

They were idealists, but they were very practical men. They had no illusions about building a new utopia, where human beings would cease acting like human beings. They knew that while people should strive for perfectibility, they could never hope to achieve it—that they lived in an imperfect world, inhabited by imperfect people. They knew that idealism without pragmatism is impotent, and that pragmatism without idealism is meaningless. They wanted to build a solid structure that would survive after they were gone. Never in history have any men built so well.

While they had been revolutionaries, they knew that a violent revolution would destroy what they had built. They therefore provided a process whereby the goals of revolution could be accomplished by peaceful change.

One principle motivated them above all others. They might not have read the works of Baruch Spinoza, but their handiwork represented the practical application of his words: "The last end of the state is not to dominate men, nor to restrain them by fear; rather it is to set free each man from fear, that he may live and act with full security and without injury to himself or his neighbor.

. . . The end of the state is really liberty." While praising the concept of equality, they rejected any system that would impose equality at the cost of stifling individual liberty, which is essential for the flowering of human creativity.

After experiencing the chaotic years under the Articles of Confederation, during which government was too weak, they wanted a strong government—one strong enough to protect the rights of people but not so strong as to threaten those rights. They had the genius to set up a system in which each of three strong branches of government, the executive, the legislative, and the judicial, would be a check on the strength of the others. In their wildest dreams they could not have imagined the megapower today of giant corporations, big labor unions, and media monopolies. But they would have been wary of any concentration of power that might threaten the rights of people because they believed that a free, strong people is indispensable to progress.

These practical men were motivated by what can only be described as a mystical faith in what they had created. It cannot be found in the words of the document, but they believed they were building not just for themselves but for others, not just for their nation but for other nations, not just for their time but for all time. They were not so presumptuous as to think of America as a world power, but they believed they were participating in a cause far greater than themselves.

They were not soft-headed do-gooders, but they believed in moral and spiritual values. They would have been appalled by the philosophy that seems so dominant in the capitalist world today— when so many seem motivated only by selfish, secular, materialist values and for whom the only god is money. They were conservatives, but their conservatism was leavened with compassion.

They wanted America to be not just a great country, but a good country. They were passionately patriotic, but they knew that patriotism, literally interpreted, means love of country. They wanted their country to be worthy of love.

To understand America's role in the future, we must first understand what America has meant to the world in the past. We have not been just another country on the world scene. We have been at the center of the revolutionary progress in man's material condition and have often been a decisive influence in the great political and military struggles of recent times. But we have been more than that. We have also been an ideological beacon—the physical embodiment of a unique philosophy of the relationship between the individual, society, and the state.

At the beginning of the twentieth century, America was not a world power. Economically, we were behind Britain and Germany in relative terms. Militarily, we were not even in the picture. While the great fleets of the imperial powers ruled the seas, we had only recently succeeded in sending a small flotilla around the world— and our land forces were even weaker than our navy. Politically, we were following a policy of deliberately avoiding involvement in the snits and quarrels of the Old World.

At the same time, the ideals that animated the American system carried a profound effect. They gave us boundless optimism about the promise we held out to the world. From the time of our national independence, Americans have believed that we represent ideals that are bigger than ourselves. Thomas Jefferson said, "We act not just for ourselves but for all mankind." Abraham Lincoln spoke of America as the "last, best hope of earth." Albert Beveridge spoke lyrically of America's "manifest destiny." Woodrow Wilson said, "A patriotic American is never so proud of his flag as when it comes to mean to others as to himself a symbol of liberty."

All these statements were made *before* the United States became an authentic world power. We believed deeply in the principles for which we stood. Our influence stemmed not from our military or economic power but from the enormous appeal that our ideals and their success had in the rest of the world. We were the only great power in history to make its entrance on the world stage not by the force of arms but by the force of its ideas.

In the course of this century, we have stayed true to our ideals. We have been a force for good in the world. We sought to temper the vindictive peace of the Treaty of Versailles. We were a decisive factor in preventing Hitler from making good on his promise of a thousand-year Reich. We have tried to hold the line on Soviet expansionism in Europe and Asia. We have certainly made mistakes in trying to uphold our ideals. But American idealism—sometimes naive, sometimes misguided, sometimes overzealous—has always been at the center of our foreign policy. One of our greatest strengths and greatest weaknesses as a world power has been the fact that we have never learned to act with the cold cynicism of Old World *Realpolitik.*

After his Kitchen Debate with me in Moscow in 1959, Khrushchev tried to demonstrate his flexibility as compared with his doctrinaire colleagues. Pointing to his Vice Premier, he said contemptuously, "Comrade Koslov is a hopeless communist." Khrushchev was ribbing Koslov for his dedicated idealism. In a sense, Americans have always been Koslovs. They have been dedicated idealists in their approach to the world but, unlike Koslov, not dedicated to foisting their ideals on the world. This has been to our credit. For Americans, a foreign policy must not be justified only on the ground that it serves our interests. It must also be consistent with our ideals. In a deeper sense, our interests are served only when we believe that what we do is right.

We stayed our course despite the sweeping changes that transformed the world in this century. In 1899 no one could have predicted this century's unprecedented material progress which has improved living conditions everywhere, with even the poor now enjoying better food, better housing, better health care, and a longer life span. No one could have predicted that man would smash the atom, explore space, and invent the computer. No one could have predicted that over one hundred million people would lose their lives in two world wars and more than a hundred smaller wars. No one could have predicted that the United States and the Soviet Union would replace Britain, France, and Germany as the principal world powers, that the European empires would collapse, or that totalitarian communism would rule 35 percent of the world's population.

As great as these changes have been, they will seem insignificant by comparison to those coming in the twenty-first century. It is therefore imperative that we decide today what role America should play in the future.

———

Our potential seems unlimited. We are the strongest and the richest country in the world. We can project our military power around the world, and we can influence all the great political issues of our time. Our culture, our ideas, and our economic and political systems have greater international appeal than ever before. It is no exaggeration to state that if allowed, hundreds of millions of people from around the world would emigrate to the United States.

But ironically, a new negativism afflicts America today. A growing chorus of pundits, professors, and politicians speak of the decline of American economic power and political leadership. They say that we have seen the end of the American century. They argue that American civilization has peaked and now faces an irreversible decline. They point out all around us the symptoms of decline —the problem of drug addiction among our young people, the crisis in education, the call for protectionism, and the appeal of isolationism. Brazil even beat us in basketball!

Are the new negativists correct? Does all this prove America's greatest days are behind us? Those who propound the new negativism will prove correct only if we permit their pessimism to become a self-fulfilling prophecy. Unlike the Marxists, we do not subscribe to a determinist view of history. We know we have a choice to make. We have the resources, the power, and the capacity to continue to act as a world leader. We can be a force for good in the twenty-first century. But there is still one unanswered question: Do we have the national will to play that role?

The new negativists argue that American national will power has collapsed. After his famous seance with his advisers at Camp David, President Carter declared that the United States was suffering from a deep-seated malaise. He was right in identifying a problem. But he was wrong in arguing that the malaise afflicted the American people. In fact it was a deadly virus which had infected the American leadership class. The same is true of the new negativism. The American people are not defeatist. They will respond to strong, responsible leadership. The problem has been that our leader class has failed to provide it.

If Moscow ever wins the U.S.–Soviet rivalry, the reason will be the failure of the American leadership class. As Robert Nisbet wrote, "We appear to be living in yet another age in which 'failure of nerve' is conspicuous; not in the minds of America's majority but in the minds of those who are gatekeepers for ideas and intellectuals.'' In the last forty years, the upper crust of America in terms of education, money, and power has lost its sense of direction in the world. It has become enamored of every intellectual fad that has caught its attention. Disarmament and pacifism are today's rage, and that could have a disastrous impact on the fate of the West. If our society's decision-makers and those who influence them lose the will to lead, there is a great danger that America's majority might not be able to reverse the slide to defeat.

President Reagan has proved how potent strong leadership can be. Despite the almost universal opposition of those who call themselves the brightest and the best, he won overwhelming victories in 1980 and 1984. He did so because he called on Americans to turn away from the negativism and isolationism of the 1970s and to move forward into a new era of opportunity at home and leadership abroad. The merits of the Reagan administration's domestic and foreign policies are fair subjects for debate. But no one can deny that President Reagan's buoyant and confident style has restored Americans' can-do spirit. While the Iran-contra affair tarnished the Reagan presidency, one of his major legacies will be that the spirit of the American people will be far better when he leaves office than it was when he entered it.

Yet there are those both on the right and on the left who ask why the United States should play a role on the world stage when we have so many urgent problems at home. Many were disillusioned by our failure in Vietnam. Others have despaired at the sight of corrupt leaders in developing countries wasting billions of dollars in American aid on graft and government boondoggles. And they have been outraged to hear those same leaders berate us at the United Nations. Critics on the right think the United States is too good to sully itself with the grimy politics of the world; critics on the left think the United States is not good enough to be able to contribute anything to the world. These old and new isolationists seek to shift to the Europeans and the Japanese, whose economies have long since recovered from the devastation of World War II, the primary burden of world leadership.

In addressing the future world role of the United States, we need historical perspective. At the beginning of this century, it did not matter whether America played a world role or not. Others who shared our values could do so. As we approach the beginning of the next century, that is no longer true. It is absolutely vital for America to play a major role. If the United States withdraws into a new isolationism, there is no other power that shares our values and possesses the resources and the will to take our place. At the same time, we can be sure that another power hostile to our values and interests, the Soviet Union, will do so.

If we pull back, we will turn over to Moscow the role of undisputed leadership; we will have made the world safe for Soviet domination and expansionism; we will see the rapid demise of peace and freedom, and the dawn of the twenty-first century will open a new age of barbarism on a global scale. If we pull back, we will eventually find that we have become an island in a red sea. We will have peace. But it will be the peace of retreat and defeat.

We must therefore reject the new isolationist agenda of withdrawing from Europe, curtailing our nuclear guarantee to our allies, erecting a wall of protectionist tariffs, cutting off support to freedom fighters, and retreating from the battle of ideas. In the superpower rivalry, to the extent that the United States prevails, the world will be safe for free nations. To the extent that the Soviet Union prevails, the world will be unsafe for free nations. Soviet-style tyranny survives by expanding. Liberty will expand by surviving. But to expand, it must first survive.

We must continue to assume the burden of leadership not just for the sake of others but also for our own sake. De Gaulle wrote, "France is never her true self except when she is engaged in a great enterprise." This is true for all nations. It is true for individuals. But it is particularly true for America. Only if we commit ourselves to be an active force for good in the world can America keep faith with its founding principles. Only if we commit ourselves to take part in the great enterprise of shaping the future of human civilization can we be true to ourselves.

In the twenty-first century, man will remake the world. We must play a central role in this great enterprise. We will remake the world materially through an explosion of technological innovation. We must try to remake the world politically through a strategy to achieve real peace. At the same time, we must not fail to address ourselves to the spiritual dimension of man.

Advances in science will transform the material world in the twenty-first century. It is estimated that 90 percent of all scientific knowledge has been developed in the last three decades. That knowledge will double by the turn of the century. In the years beyond, science will advance at an exponential rate. We are on the verge of an explosion of knowledge so tremendous that in its wake literally nothing in the world will remain the same.

In the years beyond 1999, we will see whole new industries develop and revolutionize our lives. Chemical fuel cells will enable us to build electric cars that can travel over a thousand miles without recharging. Superconductors will transform the transmission and production of electricity. Synthetic-fuel technology will create a permanent oil glut. We will conquer the problems of the fusion nuclear reactor and thereby develop an inexhaustible form of clean energy. Our descendants in the twenty-first century will look back and wonder what the energy crisis was all about.

We will see great advances in medical technology. In biotechnology, we will develop reliable artificial human organs for transplants. We will invent ways to regenerate damaged brain and nerve tissue. We will devise substances to lubricate arthritic joints. We will build machines that can scan inside the human body to diagnose problems and illnesses. Through DNA research, we will eradicate scores of diseases, perhaps even cancer and AIDS. For our descendants, life spans of 100 years will no longer be unusual.

We will be able finally to solve the problems of world hunger and poverty. We will see DNA researchers create new strains of crops that produce greater yields, that make more efficient use of sunlight, that resist disease and insects, and that thrive in poor soil. Famine will exist only in the history books. Futurist Herman Kahn predicted that the per-capita income of the world, which was

$200 when our country was founded and which is about $2,000 today, will grow to $20,000 in the twenty-first century.

We will see a continuing revolution in computers. We will perfect the voice-operated word processor. We will increase the speed of computers by whole orders of magnitude at a time. We will create artificial intelligence—computers that can not only execute complex calculations but also think creatively. We will see robot technology take over traditional manufacturing industries. In just twenty years, a computer as small as a cigar box will be able to store the equivalent of ten Libraries of Congress. And that will be child's play compared with the technology that we will develop later in the century.

These are just a few of the changes we can anticipate—and they will be dwarfed by those that cannot yet be foreseen. America needs to stay at the cutting edge of the technological revolution. To do so, we must enhance our competitiveness in the global economic system. Our business leaders must start to think about the next century rather than being obsessed only with the profit figures of the next quarter. Our educators must become serious about creating a first-rate school system at every level. Our political leaders must resist the protectionist impulse, for building tariff walls is the refuge of weak and declining powers.

We must also overcome the antitechnology syndrome of the 1960s. This is particularly true in the area of nuclear power. Antinuclear lobbyists have made building a nuclear power plant impossible. They claim to be concerned for the danger to the environment. But the fact is that nuclear power is the cleanest form of energy. Moreover, unlike the Soviet power plant at Chernobyl, Western nuclear plants have multiple safety systems. In addition, we will see advances in technology create nuclear power plants that are inherently safe, that will shut down the nuclear chain reaction automatically if the reactor temperature becomes too hot. In nuclear power, we have seen the future—and it works.

If America is to capitalize on the tremendous promise of the next century, we must reject the call of the antitechnologists. If we accept the advice of these modern-day Luddites, with their mindless opposition to scientific progress, we will condemn America to the status of a technological backwater.

We must also rededicate ourselves to the exploration of space. We will exploit space for practical purposes, such as communications satellites and space stations with laboratories for creating medical vaccines and flawless industrial crystals in perfect weightlessness. But we must do more than that. We must renew our spirit of exploration. Shortly after the Russians launched Sputnik in 1957, one of America's premier scientists was briefing the National Security Council on what we could gain from the exploration of space. He pointed to a chart which listed ten possibilities, including such items as weather, communications, and medical research. Then he turned to President Eisenhower and said, "Mr. President, probably the most important discovery we will make is not on this chart." No better case could be made for space exploration. After all, those who discovered America thought they were going to find the East Indies.

In the twentieth century, man landed on the moon; in the twenty-first, he will walk on Mars and then reach beyond our solar system, to the stars. We must be involved if only to take part in the thrill of the adventure and the challenge of the enterprise. In these great endeavors, we can ennoble the American spirit, we can unite ourselves in the pursuit of a common goal, and we can take pride in achieving together what none of us could have achieved alone.

As we transform the material world, we must try to remake the world politically. In the twentieth century, our technological progress outstripped our political progress. We must not let this happen in the next century, because our material progress has reached the point where failure to match it with political progress can lead to our total destruction. In the twenty-first century, if we are to maximize material progress not only for ourselves but for all mankind, we must find ways to match our scientific advances with greater political progress in reducing the chances of war and sharing the benefits of peace.

Compared with creating new and better inventions, our political tasks will be infinitely more difficult. We can expect massive changes in the political and economic balance of power in the twenty-first century. While the United States and the Soviet Union will remain the dominant powers at the turn of the century, all bets are off thereafter. At present growth rates, Japan will surpass the United States in GNP, and it will be as strong militarily as it chooses to be politically. China will become an economic and military superpower. If Western Europe matches its economic prowess with political unity, it too will join the ranks of the superpowers. We will no longer be able to lead by virtue of our superior economic and military power. Instead, we will have to lead by virtue of superior political vision.

For the balance of this century and the beginning of the next, the dominant players on the world stage will be the United States and the Soviet Union. We will see this great rivalry—so insightfully foreseen by Tocqueville—reach its climax. We will face two key questions: Can we avoid nuclear war? Can we avoid defeat without war? We must work to find ways to avoid seeing the scientific capacities that can produce unlimited progress used to produce unlimited destruction. We must at the same time defend our system and our values, not only for ourselves, but also for our posterity.

One of the most promising developments has been Gorbachev's recognition of the need to deal with the desperate internal problems of the Soviet Union. He is admitting that in important respects the Soviet system has failed. He knows that his superior military power—which was created at tremendous expense—cannot be used against his main adversaries without courting catastrophe. He knows that his internal economic problems constrain his capacity to compete for influence around the world. He knows that Moscow's steady expansionism into contiguous territories has now run up against formidable opponents on all fronts. He knows that the problems he faces will require at least a generation to solve. He needs a generation of peace—or to put it more precisely, a generation without war.

Our task is to formulate an agenda to exploit those twenty years for the cause of freedom and real peace. We must first of all reject the counsel of the new negativists in our great universities, in the news media, in big business, and in politics. One of the most disturbing aspects of their approach is the new isolationism. Unlike the old isolationists, those afflicted with the new strain of this deadly virus oppose not only American involvement abroad but also defense programs at home. They are obsessed with the twin fears of another Vietnam and of nuclear war and are incapable of facing up to the threat posed by the Soviet Union. Whenever Western interests are at risk, they can only tell you how not to do it. Their knee-jerk response to a crisis is to turn it over to the United Nations—which means, in effect, to do nothing.

If we have only twenty years before a reinvigorated Soviet Union turns its sights to renewed expansion, we have no time to lose. We must think boldly and act boldly. We must seek to shape the world; but we should not seek to remake the world in our image. We must recognize that a system which works for us may not work for others with different backgrounds. We must reject the fashionable but intellectually sterile doctrine of moral relativism. We deeply believe in our values. But one of the fundamental tenets of those values is that we will not try to impose them on others. Only by example and never by force will our values be extended to others.

We must restore the credibility of the U.S. strategic deterrent by reducing its vulnerability to a Soviet first strike. We must bolster our conventional forces for key theaters—like Europe, Korea, and the Persian Gulf—so that Soviet leaders will never believe they could win a war with conventional forces alone.

We must take advantage of Moscow's flagging economic strength to improve our competitive position around the world, fortifying our friends and improving ties with those we wish to be our friends. We must continue to build our cooperative relations with the other major power centers in the world: Western Europe, Japan, and China. We should help those who are fighting to prevent a communist victory and those who are trying to overturn a communist victory. We should also work to improve living conditions in other countries in order to undercut the political appeal of communist slogans. We should make it clear that even if there were no communist threat we would devote our efforts to reducing the poverty, misery, disease, and injustice that plague most of the people in the world. By investing in progress abroad, we are ensuring progress at home.

We should use our negotiations with Moscow to demonstrate our resolve in areas of irreconcilable conflict, to work toward mutually beneficial accords in areas of possible agreement, to increase contact between Soviet society and the West, and to structure as constructive a relationship with the Soviets as their international behavior permits.

Most of all, we must not fall into the trap of thinking that a reduction in U.S.–Soviet tensions means the end of the conflict. If Gorbachev stresses the need to solve his internal problems, we should not be conned into thinking that the system has changed or that the threat to the West has ended. Those in the West who believe he has abandoned the Soviet goal of a communist world should note the conclusion of his speech on the seventieth anniversary of the Bolshevik revolution: "In October 1917, we parted with the old world, rejecting it once and for all. We are moving toward a new world, the world of communism. We shall never turn off that road." Even as he pushes forward with reforms, Gorbachev will still press for Soviet interests and challenge ours—and he will be back in full force in twenty years. If we take the needed actions in the years before 1999, we will be ready for him.

We must avoid the danger of complacency. As Paul Johnson wrote, "One of the lessons of history is that no civilization can be taken for granted. Its permanency can never be assured; there is always a dark age waiting for you around the corner, if you play your cards badly and you make sufficient mistakes." We cannot allow Western civilization to meet with that fate. We have the needed physical and moral reserves, but we still have to demonstrate that we have the skill and the will to prevail.

As we attend to material needs and political problems, we must not ignore the need to address the spiritual dimension of mankind.

America stands for certain philosophical ideas. When the new negativists carp about America's demise, they are arguing not only that the United States has lost the will to lead but also that it has lost its faith in itself. They are right to point out the problem. Great civilizations in the past have declined not only because they have tired of the sacrifices necessary for leadership but also because they lost their sense of purpose and direction. A nation that has lost faith in its ideals cannot expect its ideals to have appeal to others.

To restore our faith we must look to our roots. Two centuries ago, the United States was weak militarily and poor economically. But the country created in the American Revolution caught the imagination of the world. Our appeal stemmed not from our wealth or our power but from our ideas. Too often today we emphasize only our military and economic power. While we pay homage to our founding principles on special days, our day-to-day dialogue is dominated by the message of materialism.

But there is more to this world than per-capita GNP statistics. When historians write about our times several hundred years from now, they will tell the story of a titanic struggle between two clashing conceptions of man and his place in the world. The American–Soviet contest is a struggle between the opposite poles of human experience—between those represented by the sword and by the spirit, by fear and by hope. The Soviets' system is ruled by the sword; ours is ruled by the spirit. Their influence is spread through conquest; ours is spread by example. We know freedom, liberty, hope, and self-fulfillment; they know tyranny, butchery, starvation, war, and repression. Those qualities that make the prospect of Soviet victory so frightful are the same ones that make it possible.

We believe in the primacy of the individual; the Soviets believe in the primacy of the state. We believe in a government with limited powers; they believe in a totalitarian system with all power in the hands of the party and the state. Our system was designed to give the individual the greatest scope for action consistent with public order and the rights of others. We have unlocked the creative energies of individuals, while the Soviets have locked up their most creative individuals. We have created a dynamic system—which is most admired not for its products but for its freedom—while the Soviets have built a stagnant society suffocated by bureaucracy.

The power of Moscow's sword cannot defeat the power of the West's spirit. In deriding the ability of the Church to affect world events, Stalin once wryly asked how many divisions the Pope commanded. That comment bespoke a failure to understand what moves the world. Ideas, not arms, ultimately determine history. That is especially true when statesmen who understand the way the world works are armed with powerful ideas.

Pope John Paul II is a perfect example. He is the most influential religious leader of the twentieth century. What is the secret of his enormous appeal to men and women of all faiths, all nations, all races? It is not just his exalted office with its magnificent pageantry and vestments. It is not that he is one of the world's most gifted linguists, has a warm personality, and knows how to use television. People listen to the Pope because they want to hear what he has to say—not just about religion but about the mysteries of life and the intricacies of statecraft. He lifts people out of the drudgery, drabness, and boredom that plague life for both rich and poor. He gives them a vision of what man can be if he will listen to what Lincoln called the better angels of his nature. Against such a faith as this, communism, the antifaith, cannot prevail.

When the new Soviet leader eventually travels to other parts of the United States, far more important than having him see our swimming pools, our shopping centers, our millions of automobiles is for him to see and to sense the spirit and the ideas that made these things possible. If we compete with the Soviets materially, we will win because our system works and theirs does not. But our greatest strength—from the time of our national independence—has been our ideas. Moscow cannot even compete on that level. Marxism-Leninism has nothing left to say to the world. Our freedoms enable us to search for new meaning in changing times.

America was founded by individuals who sought religious freedom, who wanted the right to worship God in their own way and to look for meaning in life on their own terms. We must not lose sight of this animating principle of our country. We should not allow our competition with Moscow to degenerate into a contest over which side can create the most bombs, the tallest buildings, and the highest per-capita GNP. If material wealth is our only goal, we are no different from the communists. We should heed Max Weber's warning against the destructive, selfish materialism—the bureaucratization of the human spirit, an "iron cage" for the West. We should channel the U.S.–Soviet competition into a debate over whose ideas will result in not only the strongest or the richest economy but also the most just society.

The communists deny there is a God, but no one can deny that communism is a faith. We believe it is a false faith, but the answer to a false faith can never be no faith. When America was weak and poor two hundred years ago we were sustained by our faith. As we enter our third century and the next millennium, we must rediscover and reinvigorate our faith.

Our greatest challenge in this respect is to enable all our citizens to share fully America's success. In creating a system based on equality and liberty, our Founding Fathers threw down a challenge to those who would follow. They knew that their society did not measure up to their ideals, particularly because of slavery. But they hoped that over time our system would evolve and someday match their vision. We must continue that pursuit. We must solve the problems of the urban underclass, the homeless, the poor, the disadvantaged. We must rectify the inequalities from which blacks and other minorities suffer. The fact that much of the black community in America is no better off today than it was twenty-four years ago when the Civil Rights Act was passed is a blot on our past and a challenge for our future. We must recapture the sense of compassion that was so eloquently demonstrated by millions in America and others throughout the world a few months ago when the plight of an eighteen-month-old baby girl trapped in an abandoned well touched our hearts.

We should not return to the failed government programs of the past. But we must not use those failures as an excuse to quit trying. We need new approaches to these problems. There will have to be profound changes in the attitudes of the poor and in society's attitudes toward the poor. We have learned that solving poverty is more complicated than simply giving poor people money. Before we can have constructive action against poverty, we need creative thought about the problem.

We will make no progress if the creativity of our young people is consumed in the purely selfish pursuit of financial gain and social status. Nietzsche wrote that he foresaw the day when such secular, rationalistic values would triumph and in doing so bring about the demise of civilization. He warned against what he called the "last man," a creature totally obsessed with security and comfort and incapable of throwing himself into a higher cause. Nietzsche rightly saw the last man as a repellent creature. We do not have to accept Nietzsche's nihilism to agree with his assessment. The West will become impotent as a moral force if its guiding philosophy degenerates into what Russell Kirk has called a kind of cosmic selfishness.

In the 1960s, we accepted the mistaken belief that we could create a great society simply by ensuring that its people were well fed, well housed, well clothed, well educated, and well cared for. All these are important, but a life limited to the realm of material possessions is an achingly empty one. We should remember the biblical admonition, "Man does not live by bread alone."

The search for meaning in life has gone on since the beginning of civilization. It will never end, because the final answer will always elude us. But it is vitally important that we engage in the search, because we will thereby develop a fuller, better life for ourselves. Some believe the answer will be found in the classics; others seek it in religion. Of this we can be sure: Meaning cannot be found in sheer materialism, whether communist or capitalist. The Supreme Court has ruled that our Constitution requires that we not teach religion in our schools. But removing religion from our schools should not mean rejection of religion in life. It is because they addressed spiritual values and fulfillment that the world's great religions—Judaism, Christianity, Islam, and Buddhism—have inspired people for centuries.

We need to restore faith in our ideals, in our destiny, in ourselves. We are here for more than hedonistic self-satisfaction. We are here to make history—not to ignore the past, not to destroy the past, not to turn back to the past, but to move onward and upward in a way that opens up new vistas for the future.

In addition to the great foreign-policy issues before us, we need to direct ourselves to a very basic question: How do we want America to be remembered? Do we want to be remembered as a people who built the biggest houses, drove the fastest cars, wore the finest clothes, produced the best athletes? Do we want to be remembered as a society in which rock stars were more admired than great teachers? In which beautiful people were more admired than interesting people? In which telegenic quality was more important than brains, bad manners more than decency, sensationalism more than truth, scandal more than good deeds? Or do we wish to be remembered as a people who created great music, art, literature, and philosophy, who acted as a force for good in the world, and who devoted themselves to the search for meaning and a larger purpose?

We need to realign our philosophical bearings—to return to the animating principles of our country and rededicate ourselves to perfecting our society according to those ideas. It is a tragic fact that war traditionally calls forth our greatest talents. War produces unity in a common purpose and stretches man to his ultimate. That is more difficult to achieve in peacetime—but we should make it our goal to do so. The total effort required to fight a war must be mobilized to build a better peace. Our best answer to Gorbachev's "new thinking" is a new America.

Saint Thomas Aquinas observed, "If the highest aim of a captain were to preserve his ship he would keep it in port forever." The sea may be stormy, but conflict is the mother of creativity. Without risks, there will be no failures. But without risks there will be no successes. We must never be satisfied with success, and we should never be discouraged by failure. In the end, the key is the call, the commitment, the power of a great cause, a driving dream bigger than ourselves, as big as the whole world itself.

In war, the Medal of Honor is awarded for conduct beyond the call of duty. In peacetime we must not be satisfied with doing only what duty requires—doing what is right only in the sense of avoiding what is wrong. A morality of duty is not an adequate standard for a great people. We should set a higher standard, what Lon Fuller described as the morality of aspiration—dedicating ourselves to the fullest realization of our potential, in a manner worthy of a people functioning at their best.

Let us be remembered not just as a good people who took care of themselves without doing harm to others. Let us be remembered as a great people whose conduct went beyond the call of duty as we met the supreme challenge of this century—winning victory for freedom without war.

Are we witnessing the twilight of the American revolution? Are we seeing the first stages of the retreat of Western civilization into a new dark age of Soviet totalitarianism? Or will a new America lead the way to a new dawn for all those who cherish freedom in the world?

In his Iron Curtain speech at Westminster College in 1946, Winston Churchill said, "The United States stands at this time at the pinnacle of world power. It is a solemn moment for the American democracy. For with primacy in power is also joined an awe-inspiring accountability for the future." Those words are as true today as when he spoke them forty-two years ago. We hold the future in our hands.

AUTHOR'S NOTE

This book is the product of a lifetime of study and on-the-job training in foreign policy. In essence I began it forty years ago, when as a Congressman from California and a member of the Herter Committee I made a fact-finding trip through Western Europe, which was only beginning to recover from the devastation of World War II. I finished it on my seventy-fifth birthday, nine days into the year that will see the election of the President who will have it in his power to make a far more devastating World War III less likely, or more so.

If the world of the twenty-first century is to be a safer, more free, and more prosperous place than the world of the twentieth, it is imperative that the United States play an even more prominent role on the world stage than it does today—imperative, but by no means inevitable. The challenge we face is great, as befits a great nation. The first nine chapters of *1999* are about what America must do to meet the challenge. The tenth chapter is about what our leaders must do to inspire the American people to *want* to meet it.

In preparing this volume I received wise counsel from Michael Korda and Bob Asahina at Simon and Schuster. Loie Gaunt and Carlos Narváez provided vital research support, while Carmen Ballard, Kathy O'Connor, and Rose Mary Woods contributed outstanding stenographic support. Four undergraduate and graduate-level students of international affairs—Dale Baker, Tom Casey, Nadia Schadlow, and Jim Van de Velde—submitted very useful background research. And for their immensely dedicated and astute assistance, I am particularly indebted to Paul Matulić, John H. Taylor, and Marin Strmecki, who once again served as my principal research and editorial consultant.

—RN
Saddle River, New Jersey
January 9, 1988

INDEX